BOB BULLOCK

NUMBER TWELVE
Clifton and Shirley Caldwell Texas Heritage Series

BOB BULLOCK
God Bless Texas

Dave McNeely *and* Jim Henderson

University of Texas Press | Austin

Publication of this work was made possible in part by support from Clifton and Shirley Caldwell and a challenge grant from the National Endowment for the Humanities.

Frontispiece: Bullock stands alone, hand on forehead, in front of a portrait of Jefferson Davis. It is Jan. 12, 1999, and Bullock has left the dais after swearing in Sen. Teel Bivins as president pro-tempore of the Senate, while Bivins conducts the morning call. Bullock has one week left as lieutenant governor. *Austin American-Statesman*/Ralph Barrera.

Requests for permission to reproduce material from this work should be sent to:
  Permissions
  University of Texas Press
  P.O. Box 7819
  Austin, TX 78713-7819

  www.utexas.edu/utpress/about/bpermission.html

♾ The paper used in this book meets the minimum requirements of ANSI/NISO Z39.48-1992 (R1997) (Permanence of Paper).

Library of Congress Cataloging-in-Publication Data

McNeely, Dave.
  Bob Bullock : God bless Texas / Dave McNeely and Jim Henderson. — 1st ed.
    p.   cm. — (Clifton and Shirley Caldwell Texas heritage series ; no. 12)
  Includes index.
  ISBN 978-0-292-71454-0 (alk. paper)
1. Bullock, Bob.   2. Bullock, Bob—Influence.   3. Politicians—Texas—Biography.
4. Lieutenant governors—Texas—Biography.   5. Texas. Comptroller's Office—Officials and employees—Biography.   6. Texas—Politics and government—1951–   7. Bush, George W. (George Walker), 1946—Friends and associates.   8. Power (Social sciences)—Texas—History—20th century.   I. Henderson, Jim, 1942–   II. Title.
  F391.4.B85M35 2008
  976.4'063092—dc22
  [B]

                                                    2007027903

For Katie, Carl, and Jenny Mueller,
and Stella McGriffy,
McNeely grandchildren

who will inherit the Texas this history shaped

AND

For Alexis and Garrett Henderson,

the reasons God made Texas.

The reasonable man adapts himself to the world; the unreasonable one persists in trying to adapt the world to himself. Therefore, all progress depends on the unreasonable man.

—GEORGE BERNARD SHAW

CONTENTS

PERSONAL PRIVILEGE

B ob Bullock lived his life on the edge. Personally and professionally, he did what he thought was right at the time. Some thought his behavior—like a hand grenade with the pin out—was contrived, that his legendary blow-ups and temper tantrums were strategically planned. Perhaps sometimes they were, and he indeed could use his huge temper to frighten people into doing what he wanted, or just to keep them off balance. But Matthew Dowd, a political strategist involved in Bullock's races in 1990 and 1994 for lieutenant governor, thought he lived life "intuitively." And indeed, his former son-in-law Steve Robinson, father of Bullock's only grandson, Grant, said Bullock lived his public and private life with abandon: "No borders, no fear."

He was a fan of the late President Lyndon B. Johnson and became the legislative mentor for George W. Bush, a presidential son and Texas governor who would go on to also occupy the White House. Bullock didn't make Bush president, but he could have prevented it had he chosen to.

One of my earliest memories of Bullock, though I'm sure I must have met him sooner, since I started reporting on Texas politics in the mid-1960s, was at one of the early Willie Nelson Fourth of July Picnics, in a field near Dripping Springs, west of Austin. The year was 1974. I had stopped off on my way from Dallas, where I was a political reporter for the *Dallas Morning News*, to South Texas, to work on some stories. I took a break with friends, and since I covered politics, some of them were involved in it. I had been invited to the gathering by Garry Mauro, an up-and-coming young campaign operative, who had driven Bullock around Texas the previous year when he was running for state comptroller. By early July, when the picnic was held, Bullock had already easily won the Democratic nomination, which at that time virtually assured election in historically Democratic Texas. Between us, Bullock and Mauro and I and a couple other folks lugged a large cooler full of beer into the picnic grounds.

The next memory was 1975, after Bullock had become comptroller. His office was conducting a series of raids against businesses that had failed to pass on to the state the sales taxes they had collected on its behalf. One was a restaurant in Dallas, and Bullock's troops tipped off the press that the raid was going to occur. I was eating a chicken-fried steak when the brigade arrived.

Back in those days when the press and politicians were somewhat more fraternal, I had drinks with Bullock and top staffers—some of whom were former reporters—in bars, but often in Bullock's refurbished office, where he had installed a wet bar. I left Dallas and moved to Austin in August 1978, to work as a general-assignments reporter for the *Austin American-Statesman*. In January 1979, I became chief of the newspaper's Capitol Bureau and began writing a column on Texas politics and government. Bullock had just been reelected comptroller, without opposition from either Democrats or Republicans.

Over the next quarter-century, Bullock was a continuing story. His explosive temper, combative behavior, and huge mood swings were as well known as the fact that the bluebonnet was the Texas state flower. If Bullock wasn't doing something to generate a story, just wait a few days.

I always found him fascinating. Many if not most politicians are cautious; Bullock was anything but. But he made things happen, gave women and minorities more opportunities than ever before in state government, and promoted young, smart people to jobs of huge responsibility. Some describe him as the smartest person and most adroit user of power they've ever known. And some can be reduced to tears simply remembering his abusive treatment.

In December 1988, Bullock was more than a year into a race to be elected in 1990 as lieutenant governor and thus presiding officer of the Texas Senate—the most powerful lieutenant governor in the country. I warned in my newspaper column that if he were elected, Texans should hope they get the good Bob Bullock, because there were two:

> The good Bob Bullock is a caring, decent, loyal human being, with
> a strong sense of democracy. He thinks government should serve

the people and search for new and innovative ways to deliver the most services to taxpayers for the least amount of money.

He will be up at all hours of the night, dictating memos and otherwise trying to figure out ways to make things run better. He will be a stern taskmaster to make sure that government efficiently helps those who can't help themselves and doesn't hurt those who can.

The bad Bob Bullock is mean, arrogant, sometimes petty, impetuous, mercurial, bullying. He sometimes carries loyalty to the point of keeping people around who shouldn't be, while making life so miserable for people who should be that they figure they'd rather work somewhere else.

I thought enough of that warning that when my friend Jack Martin, a political consultant who'd managed the last two races for U.S. Sen. Lloyd Bentsen, signed up to run Bullock's campaign, I blew those three paragraphs up on a copying machine until they occupied a full page. I sent it to Martin with a suggestion that he tape it to his bathroom wall, as a daily reminder.

Their relationship was tempestuous at first. Later, they developed such a close bond that Martin became Bullock's go-to person when he had something on his mind. Some of Bullock's chiefs of staff while he was lieutenant governor—and even his wife, Jan—would sometimes call Martin to calm Bullock down when he was on a tirade.

Bullock and I had an up-and-down relationship. While in some ways he appreciated those who gather and report the news, he was incredibly sensitive to what he took to be even the slightest criticism. While Bullock chewed me out only once in person, he did so several times in letters. Yet when my late wife, Carole Kneeland, was dying of breast cancer in 1997, Bullock stopped me in the Capitol to offer his airplane to fly her to Houston for treatment.

In the late 1990s, before Bullock died, I talked to my friend Jim Henderson about co-writing a book on Bullock. Henderson was a veteran reporter and writer whom I first met when we were on a Nieman Fellowship for journalists at Harvard University in 1975–1976. He had worked for more than a decade for the *Dallas Times Herald*, and had been runner-up for a Pulitzer Prize more than once. His newspaper folded in 1991, and he was making a living as a freelance author of books and magazine articles. We thought about basing a book on the fortunes and foibles of Texas government around this tempestuous figure.

Several things happened to postpone the project. One was that Jim took a job as the Dallas correspondent for the *Houston Chronicle*. So I began discussions with Bill Bishel, a senior editor at the University of Texas Press, about doing the book myself. He was interested. One evening at my friends Sandy and Ray Strother's house on the Big Hole River in Montana, I sketched out several pages of notes about what should be in the book.

When I woke up the next morning—September 11, 2001—Ray was glued to the radio. Terrorists had flown airplanes into the World Trade Center in New York. Everything went on hold.

It was two years later, in the fall of 2003, that the book idea began to reheat. I had concluded that I was unlikely to get it written by myself; I was still writing political columns for the *American-Statesman*. But Jim said he was planning to retire. We sketched out a rough outline and started to work.

That this book is only now coming out is testimony to how hard it was. Although it was exciting to restudy Texas political developments from the 1950s through the early 21st century, it was time consuming. In 16 years as comptroller and eight as lieutenant governor, Bullock affected an enormous number of lives. While we have interviewed dozens of people about their experiences with him, and have read of many more, we anticipate hundreds of telephone calls and other communications after this book comes out, saying "You should have talked to me." And probably just about every one of them will be correct.

And there are several people who knew him well who simply refused to talk about him—including former Gov. Ann Richards, right up until her death in 2006, seven years after Bullock's—either for reasons of loyalty, fear that his family or memory would somehow be hurt, a realization that if they told the truth they'd be in a no-win situation, or perhaps fear of retaliation by Bullock, even from the grave.

Jim and I would like to thank all those who took the time and trouble to talk to us, and apologize in advance to those we missed. Our special thanks go to Joy Anderson, Ken Armbrister, Bob Armstrong, Chuck Bailey, Ben Barnes, Reggie Bashur, Frasier Blount, Harry Bradley, Tom Bullock, Kent Caperton, Carlton Carl, Willie Chapman, Bill Collier, George Christian, Robert and Betty Dohoney, Matthew Dowd, Tom Duffy, John Fainter, Bruce Gibson, Bill Haley, Jerry Hall, Billy Hamilton, Greg Hartman, Paul and Bill Hobby, Molly Ivins, Cliff Johnson, Gordon Johnson, Karen Johnson, Rob Johnson, Sam

Kinch, Nick Kralj, Jack Loftis, Garry Mauro, Mark McKinnon, John Montford, Bill Ratliff, Steve Robinson, Mary Beth Rogers, Kim Ross, Andy Sansom, Babe Schwartz, John Sharp, Max Sherman, George Shipley, Cecil Stubblefield, Dan Van Cleve, Buck Wood, and dozens of others who shared their Bob Bullock memories with Baylor University's Bob Bullock Oral History Project, or with us, or both.

Even though they might have written an entirely different book in tone and content because there are so many varying views of Bob Bullock, we are also grateful to Jan Bullock, Glen Castlebury, John Keel, Jack Roberts, and Buck Wood for looking at parts or all of this manuscript and making helpful suggestions and corrections; and to Tom Dunning, Sam Coats, Mona Fults, Willie Chapman, Dennis Fagan, Patrick Beach, Debbie Cartwright, and others for reading the manuscript or providing valuable help in other ways.

Thanks to the great folks at the *Austin American-Statesman* for providing a front-row seat on the Texas political scene to Dave McNeely for more than a quarter century, and for the gracious use of pictures by the *American-Statesman's* fine photographers; and to Pulitzer Prize–winning cartoonist Ben Sargent of the *American-Statesman* for use of his cartoons. Thanks also to Texas Senate Media for use of their photographs.

We particularly thank all of our newspaper colleagues, who wrote the first draft of much of this history. And thanks particularly to the wonderful folks in the Texas Legislative Reference Library, whose careful collection and cross-referencing of all of these newspaper accounts made this possible. And we'd like to thank Bill Bishel, Megan Giller, and the wonderful folks at UT Press for their thoughtful work and enormous patience.

Finally, thanks to our families—my new wife, Kathryn Terwey Longley McNeely; daughters Michelle Mueller and Candace McGriffy and their families; my stepkids Adam, Bill, and Grace Ann Longley; and Jim's sons Rick and Greg. Their patience and support sustained us through literally thousands of hours of researching and writing this book. We hope you find it an accurate picture of a man who affected Texas history, of the political evolution of the last half of the 20th century in Texas, and of the workings of a government run by and for human beings.

Dave McNeely
Austin, Texas
April 2007

BOB BULLOCK

"THE LARGEST TEXAN"

O f all the Bob Bullock stories told and retold during the last four decades of the 20th century, one seems the most adequate abstract of his long and improbable career in Texas politics. It was not a tale of the profane tirades that became the essential body of Bullock lore; not of the drunken fistfights or illegal gun-toting or grand-jury investigations that would have ended the public service of less audacious and complex men; not of the bizarre, impulsive, and occasionally irrational behavior that caused many of his political cohorts, while acknowledging his genius, to speculate that he was, in fact, locked up in his own madness.

Unlike those treasured gems, this was a story not about what Bullock did, but what he was. And it was told by a future president of the United States who owed his political prosperity, in no small part, to the man he eulogized in the summer of 1999 as having a tongue "that should have been registered as a concealed weapon" but a man, nonetheless, who was "the largest Texan of our time."

"Everybody has a favorite Bullock story," said Gov. George W. Bush to the hundreds packed inside Austin's Central Christian Church that warm, drizzly Sunday. "The problem is, you can't tell most of them in polite company."

But there was one worthy of a G rating and, Bush was confident, appropriate for funereal company. It concerned one of his earliest encounters with the mythology that had grown up around the man who lay before him in a casket at the altar—an encounter that surely guided his conduct as governor and lent him immeasurable upward mobility.

Bush arrived in Austin in January 1995, an experienced campaigner—he had worked in his father's two presidential races, his own failed congressional bid in 1978, and his recent gubernatorial victory—but with no experience in governing and, by his own account, possessing an incomplete understanding of the curious and often inscrutable political chemistry of the State Capitol.

Since reconstruction, Texas had been essentially a one-party state divided into two camps: conservative and liberal Democrats. In the 1980s, however, what had been a barely perceptible Republican trot to power became a full gallop, and Democratic fortunes were turning as arid as a Big Bend arroyo. By the time the newly elected Republican governor hit town, the GOP was approaching a majority in both houses of the Legislature, statewide offices were no longer won or lost in Democratic primaries, and the state's electoral votes had not gone to a Democratic presidential candidate since 1976. Given that trend line, it would not have been unreasonable for Bush, as head of his party and chief executive of his state, to assume he had the muscle to work his will with the agenda on which he had successfully campaigned.

Still, his advisors reminded him that two Democrats—House Speaker Pete Laney and Lt. Gov. Bob Bullock, who presided over the Senate—still controlled the fate of legislation and that he would need a good liaison with both. With that in mind, Bush made a bipartisan hire: Cliff Johnson, a conservative East Texas Democrat who had served in the House, on the staff of Republican Gov. Bill Clements, and on the Texas Water Commission before turning to lobbying and consulting. He knew the legislative nuances and was friends with Laney and Bullock.

As Bush told the story, he noticed one day that Johnson had a Bullock campaign sticker on his pickup truck. After stewing about it for a few days, the governor approached his aide and asked, "Why do you have that Bullock sign on your bumper? I mean, after all, you work for me. Why not a Bush sticker?"

"Governor," Johnson said, "you're new here . . ."

"Yes, I am."

". . . and you just don't understand. In Austin, everybody works for Bullock."

Johnson may have mined hyperbole for emphasis, but it served its purpose. "I quickly learned about power," Bush confessed.

How that power came to be is a compelling enigma.

By almost any measure, Robert D. Bullock would appear to have been a man marked for rapid political extinction. Ravaged by manic depression, sleeplessness, alcoholism, chain-smoking, chronic health problems, multiple marriages and divorces, ethical myopia, fits of fury that approached lunacy, and other demons that those around him could only imagine, he still pulled off an unprecedented political winning streak: Over four decades, he ran eight races for three different offices and never lost—never came close to losing—and accrued a measure of political power that a string of governors could only envy.

Bob Bullock somehow managed to navigate his way through some rapidly changing and politically dangerous state and national crosscurrents. He was born and began his political career when Texas and other southern states were still racially segregated. Yet he embraced the civil rights revolution that Lyndon B. Johnson engineered after Johnson's landslide election in 1964, following President John F. Kennedy's assassination in 1963.

The escalating Vietnam War unleashed a fury on college campuses that led to the widespread feeling that if 18-year-olds could be drafted to die in foreign countries on behalf of the United States, they should be able to vote. As the state's chief election officer at the time, Bullock helped facilitate not only giving 18-year-olds the right to vote in Texas, but also to do so where they attended college rather than in their hometowns. That made him a hero to younger voters, who found their political voice over an increasingly unpopular war.

When the Sharpstown stock fraud and banking scandal in 1971 rocked Texas government to its roots, with disclosures that Texas leaders got loans for sweet quick-profit stock deals in return for passing banking bills sought by Houston real estate and banking mogul Frank Sharp, Bullock somehow survived—even while his boss, Gov. Preston Smith, was one of those implicated and was subsequently defeated for reelection to a third two-year term.

Bullock was a fervent Democrat in the early 1970s, even an outspoken advocate for the doomed Democratic presidential ticket in 1972 of George McGovern and Sargent Shriver.

In 1974, the year the Watergate scandal in Washington forced Republican President Richard Nixon to resign, and again temporarily stalled Republican growth in Texas, Bullock was elected to his first statewide office as the state's tax collector. In that job, he was a pioneer for affirmative action in hiring women and minorities, even before it had a name.

Bullock also won the comptroller's office in the first election in which terms for most Texas statewide officials went from two years to four, and in nonpresidential election years. That unhooked Democrats from the increasingly treacherous national elections. Every four years thereafter, Bullock was almost routinely reelected—even as the once monolithic Democratic Party began a steady decline. It was helped along by the fact that Texans named Bush were on the ballot in five of the eight elections from 1980 through 1994, which meant that for the most part, the national Democratic Party took a pass on competing in Texas, and left Texas Democratic candidates to fend for themselves. In 1990, Bullock sought and won promotion to lieutenant governor, a powerhouse position due to the Texas Senate's tradition of granting enormous power to its presiding officer. Bullock's victory came even while Republicans were winning some other statewide offices above and below him on the ballot.

In 1994, the final time Bullock faced Texas voters, he was reelected easily, even while George W. Bush was winning his first election as governor by unseating popular Democratic Gov. Ann Richards. Bullock was the highest-ranking Democrat elected that year; Democrats have steadily lost every statewide election since. By 1999, when Bullock left office, Republicans had captured every statewide elective office.

Most of the time no one seemed certain where Bullock fit on the philosophical spectrum, and it didn't much matter. He began his career as a segregationist Democrat, evolved into a liberal populist who supported George McGovern for president, and ended his years embracing the fundamentalist Christian, tax-cutting, deficit-spending Republicans personified by George W. Bush. But no metamorphosis diminished his political power or popularity with voters. He never attained the state's highest office—in fact, he never officially strived for it. But from 1956, the year he first ran for public office and won election to the House, through 1998, when impending death from a lifetime of bad habits and reckless behavior forced his exit from the Capitol, Bullock cast a presence over state government that, some of his contemporaries would say, had not been seen since Sam Houston.

Significantly, his ascendancy and longevity spanned a period when political life expectancies in Texas were such that a talented, promising young pol could get through a career quicker than a runway model. The shift to a Republican majority, the changing demographics of the state's urban centers, the decline of the oil economy, and an accompanying drain on the state budget—those factors and others conspired against job security for officeholders. Brighter stars than Bullock's rose over the Capitol, but most flamed out and fell to the status of footnote.

As the new century arrived, not many old political junkies were found sitting around the campfires of their winter years swapping stories of Price Daniel, Preston Smith, Ann Richards, Dolph Briscoe, Bill Clements, or Mark White, let alone Bill Hobby or Ben Barnes. But Bullock's star lingered, and his ghost was equally persistent. For years after his death, it was a popular pastime in Austin for those who had worked for him, served with him, suffered through him, learned from him, loved him, loathed him, or puzzled over him to gather around each other, hoist a glass in his memory, and relive the days of genius and madness.

"All the Bullock stories you hear, most of them are true," Pete Laney once said, "and you don't have to embellish 'em."

A future president would not have eulogized him as the "largest Texan of our time" if his only contribution had been to supply conversational sustenance for the happy-hour crowd. Bullock stood out from the pack because he disdained the pack and gave it a one-finger salute at every opportunity. In a time when slick media imagery, consultant-driven campaigns, and poll-conscious, politically correct public posturing was turning the Texas governing class into a monochrome polyester blob of nervous, tepid conformity, Bullock at best was brash, driven, and impatient, practicing zero tolerance for indecision and inaction—or obstinacy when it abetted either. At worst, he was simply abusive, abominable, and all-around insufferable.

"He was the most atrocious human being who ever lived," said A. R. "Babe" Schwartz, a liberal Democrat who represented Galveston in the House and, later, in the Senate during the formative years of Bullock's rise to power.

Bullock did little to discourage such characterizations. He had the instincts of a gunfighter, and a personality to match. Early in his career, while speaking to reporters, he sardonically referred to one gubernatorial candidate (a fellow Democrat) as a "son of a bitch," an epithet he frequently invoked, as years later when, in the heat of an argument, he addressed the state's attorney general (also a Democrat) as "You skinny-assed son of a bitch." Scolding an African American state senator (a Democrat) who balked at compromise on a racially sensitive bill, Lt. Gov. Bullock firmly urged him to "show some leadership . . . you black motherfucker."

How did such atrociousness survive and prosper for so long? The short answer is *because it worked*. Other tactics probably would have served him equally well, but intimidation was Bullock's way. Though physically unimposing—5′9″ in his prime and shy of 150 pounds—he was a bully, but not without redeeming qualities, if results can be considered redemption. He reformed election laws, initiated a performance review to periodically evaluate state agencies, was the first elected state official to establish an equal employment opportunity program, restructured school funding to equalize the revenue available to poor and rich districts, pushed through the Legislature a bill creating the state's first water conservation and management plan, and was one of the early officials to fully computerize his agency—to name a few.

Early on, Austin's best and brightest civil servants, mostly young, idealistic reformers, some of them graduates of the Lyndon B. Johnson School of Public Affairs, were his eager subordinates and students, largely because they saw in him the drive and audacity to somehow make government better. His two terms in the Texas House of Representatives were scarcely distinguished, but in later years he revealed a flair—more like a compulsion—for taking relatively obscure political posts and pushing them to places they had never been before.

"He knows how to bring things together," said Ralph Wayne, a former state representative who later was Bullock's chief deputy comptroller for a while. "Sam Houston was that way. Sam Houston was a different person. He heard a different drummer. Sam Houston used to drink; Bullock used to drink. Sam Houston was creative; Bullock is creative. Sam Houston tried to forge a consensus, and Bullock is a person who builds consensus and gets things done. That's a great strength of leadership."[1]

Until Bullock took the job, Secretary of State was a position that most Texans probably knew little about or had no clear notion of its function, except that it had something to do with counting votes and certifying elections. For some young pols, it had been a way station on the road to higher office, because it generated statewide name recognition and because it provided entrée to the state's political apparatus. It took Bullock only a few days into his tenure to lift that agency out of obscurity and onto the front pages of newspapers across the state. Stories abounded about the wars Bullock was fighting with both political parties and the changes in election laws, particularly to the benefit of younger voters, he was helping to bring about. Likewise, the office of Comptroller of Public Accounts. Before Bullock, few probably knew its purpose or even how to pronounce it. Within five months, he had loosed on the state his storied "Bullock's Raiders"—lawyers, accountants, and assorted other tax cops—who shut down businesses and confiscated inventories in the first serious effort in at least half a century to collect delinquent taxes. Millions poured into the state treasury, and Bullock became a bona fide folk hero.

The idealistic young reformers knew that signing on with Bullock was an opportunity and an education—if anyone in Austin knew more about state government, top to bottom, he or she had not yet been identified—but they soon learned that it was also a walk through the valley of the shadow. He drove his staff as hard as he drove himself, insisting that they be available to him around the clock. He flooded their inboxes with memos of criticism, praise, and demands. He set impossible deadlines, fired aides on a whim (often rehiring them just as quickly), read compulsively, thirsted for personal and bureaucratic gossip, worked while he guzzled whiskey at his favorite downtown saloons or in his office, and kept everyone around him panting from exhaustion.

Some, unable or unwilling to sustain the pace, drifted away and sought saner employment. Others were driven away by another Bullock hallmark, the tendency to make his own rules, the law be damned. He was targeted by a Travis County grand jury for improper use of the resources of the comptroller's office, was investigated by the FBI, and even admitted to illegal campaign fund-raising while he worked for Gov. Preston Smith—much later, of course. It was a quirk of his peculiar morality that allowed Bullock to believe that if his actions resulted in some public good, then the actions therefore were good, even if they were outside the law.

"Yeah, I'm a crook," he said after being caught using a state airplane for personal purposes, "but I'm the best comptroller this state ever had."[2]

Sam Houston was not the only towering Texas historical figure to whom Bullock was often compared. Sam Rayburn, former Speaker of the U.S. House of Representatives, was another. In a 1998 interview, David Sibley recalled his election to the state Senate in a special election in 1991 and his subsequent meeting with Bullock, who was presiding over that body for the first time. Bullock was already a minor legend in Austin because of his controversial years as comptroller, but Sibley, a Republican from Waco, 35 miles from Bullock's hometown of Hillsboro, found that watching him up close was more fascinating than he had anticipated.

"He can be the reincarnation of Rhett Butler, in every way a southern gentleman," he said. "He can be crude, he can be intimidating, charming . . . and he can do all that in a period of a minute and a half. It's extraordinary to sit there and watch him. People spoke of (how) Sam Rayburn (was) when he got mad. His whole demeanor would flush; he'd look almost dark—not red but dark. And when Bullock is mad, the same thing happens. His whole demeanor changes. It's like watching a storm blow in, the fury and the power of it all."[3]

Most often, though, "the largest Texan of our time" was likened to the largest Texan of an earlier time: Lyndon Johnson. Both came from small towns and returned to their rural roots as often as possible—Johnson to his ranch on the Pedernales River, and Bullock to his retreat near Llano; both sought absolute control over their political environments, demanded and gave absolute personal loyalty, wanted to be loved but settled for being feared. Both understood the power of information and of the purse, the necessity of compromise and bipartisanship, and the ways of manipulating legislators. Both were bullying but thin-skinned, had bawdy senses of humor and explosive tempers, and engaged in obsessive, self-destructive behavior (Bullock continued to smoke even after the removal of most of one lung, and LBJ, who gave up smoking after a heart attack, resumed the habit once he was out of the White House); both were willing to risk their political fortunes on things they thought were right, things good for the country or the state. Johnson wagered his on a series of civil rights acts and the Vietnam War, and the repercussions ended his presidency after five years. Bullock persistently argued for a state income tax, a suicidal tack in tax-averse Texas. He lost the debate—Texas still has no income tax—but then carried out a slick reversal that stole the issue from Republicans who had hoped to use it to beat him.

Most notably, both were meticulously well-organized workaholics in a ceaseless race with the clock, as though driven by the dread that in the next instant the curtain might fall and the show would be over. "LBJ wanted to do everything yesterday," said his longtime aide and spokesman George Christian. Bullock was no less impatient. When his staff informed him that the comptroller had the statutory authority to seize the property of tax-delinquent businesses, he rejected the argument that it would take a couple of weeks to start the process.

"Let's start tomorrow," he insisted.

There were stark dissimilarities in the two men, and they help explain why Johnson went as far as his profession could take him, while Bullock—possessing many of the same skills, smarts, ambitions, mannerisms, strands of temperament, and visions—went no higher than a state-level second tier. Johnson's powers of persuasion were crude but smooth. "His way of doing things was a heck of a lot more sweetness than intimidation," Christian said. "Bullock would intimidate. He would just level your ass."[4]

By dispensing with sweetness and niceties, Bullock sculpted a personal mythology that was not entirely accurate. He was feared because no one knew what form his wrath might take. He kept voluminous files on friends, enemies, contributors, lobbyists, bureaucrats, and legislators. Few of them doubted that he had the power to make their lives uncomfortable and send their pet bills to the shredder. He had the perverse curiosity of a gossip columnist. He knew the secrets—some of them, at least—of reporters, staff members, and other bureaucrats and was not averse to suggesting that he would use what he knew as payback for perceived criticism, disrespect, or disloyalty. But there is not an abundance of evidence to indicate that he truly coveted retribution. He had frequent opportunities to "get" those who had crossed him, but, with a few notable exceptions, he opted for magnanimity—after letting the offending party know he could have done them in, had he chosen to do so.

He also possessed a personal generosity that, while it could have been taken as a kind of *Godfather* affectation, appeared to be genuine. He offered jobs to the down-and-out, cash to the needy, sympathy and support to friends battling their own demons. When an aide lost a teenage daughter to a traffic accident, Bullock sent to his home a jumbo-screen television to help ease the grieving. When that same aide quietly retreated to Padre Island for a few days of solitude, Bullock tracked him down and showed up at his door to inquire about his well-being. When one of his journalistic antagonists, whom Bullock once denounced as "a goddamn drunk," checked into a rehabilitation clinic to dry out, Bullock called him daily to console and encourage him. He waged a long and bitter feud with former Lt. Gov. Ben Barnes, but when Barnes was forced into bankruptcy a few years after leaving office, Bullock dropped by his office with a $10,000 offering.

What drove Bullock, besides genius and madness? Growing up in Hillsboro, a dusty, central Texas cotton town, he was more of a troublemaker than the stuff of a future star. A notorious prankster, daredevil, and mediocre student ("I never got a grade higher than a C in my whole life," he once said), the young Bob Bullock showed little potential. Bright but bored by convention and hell-bent on raising hell, he appeared to his neighbors—and some family members—more likely to be destined for reform school than law school, much less the State Capitol. Even as a young adult, with a law degree and a fluctuating interest in politics, he was edgy and unfocused. "If you can change Bob Bullock, you'll be the first man who ever lived that could do it," his brother-in-law, Will Bond, told Lt. Gov. Preston Smith, who had just hired Bullock to help in his 1968 campaign for governor.

"Previous to being associated with me, he had one foot on gravel," Smith would say later, taking a large measure of credit for solidifying the ground beneath the fledgling young politician.[5] In truth, no one ever changed Bob Bullock; Bullock merely changed venues. The difficult kid from Hillsboro became the difficult adult in high office. In government, he found his true calling, his life's focus. He made government better, but one foot was forever on gravel, the bad boy with him to the end.

As he lay dying shortly before his 70th birthday, he summoned longtime friend and trusted aide Tony Proffitt (whom he had fired and rehired numerous times) and asked a final favor. "I want you to go to your office and write my obituary," he said.

"Don't talk that way," Proffitt said, "It's . . ."

"No, it's time."

Proffitt returned later in the day with a lengthy exposition on his friend's life and career. Bullock read it, asked for a pen, and began crossing out phrases, sentences, and whole paragraphs.

"What are you doing, Bob?" Proffitt asked. "Everything in there is true."

"I know it," Bullock groused, "but this is going to be a paid obituary, and I don't want the goddamn *Austin American-Statesman* to make money off of me."[6]

CHAPTER I

THE USUAL SUSPECT

There is no official record of who planned the caper and who pulled it off, but if it did not bear Bobby Bullock's fingerprints, it had all the signature markings—the trademark planning and daring—of a Bobby Bullock escapade.

The victim was a local cop who was fond of idling away slow evenings over coffee and doughnuts at Andrew's Café on the Hillsboro town square near the courthouse. The teenage boys who also idled around the square, always in search of something to relieve the boredom, duly noted his routine. The officer would park his old Ford—this was during World War II, when new police cars and sophisticated communications equipment were in short supply—on the street beside a call box mounted on a telephone pole near the restaurant. If his services were needed, the call box would ring.

One evening, while the officer partook of coffee and doughnuts, someone wrapped one end of a log chain around the rear axle of the old Ford and secured the other end to the telephone pole. A few moments later, the call box rang. The officer ran outside, grabbed the phone, and heard an excited voice from the other end: "There's a big fight going on at the Bluebonnet Café on Rose Hill." Rose Hill was a couple of miles south of town. The officer had no way of knowing that the call originated at a pay phone a block down the street. He jumped into the car, revved the engine, and popped the clutch. The car lurched forward, but the entire rear-end assembly stayed behind.

Endangering an officer of the law, not to mention the destruction of public property, is a serious crime, but this one went into the *unsolved* file. The boys on the street scattered, and the culprits were never identified. Not positively. No one said it was Bullock; at least, no one swore it was. The fact that Bullock's closest childhood friend, Robert Dohoney, told that story for an oral history project for the Bullock archives at Baylor University might suggest that he suspected that his pal was a party to the prank, which would not have been an unreasonable suspicion. It was Bullock, after all, who teamed up with his friend, the future celebrity physician Dr. Red Duke, to topple a Confederate statue by chaining it to a car.[1]

Whenever anything unusual happened in Hillsboro during the 1940s, there was, as a rule, one usual suspect. "Will Gallagher, the marshal, would always look for Bob first," said Tom Bullock, who, like just about everyone else in Hillsboro, would later wonder how his little brother got so far.[2]

Throughout his political life, Bullock spoke often of his profound love of Texas. Later in his career, he ended every speech with the words "God Bless Texas" and distributed bumper stickers expressing the same sentiment. He sometimes told friends that he regretted that his Texas roots did not run deeper. He was a first-generation Texan, and just barely that. But for a homesick mother, he might have been a Yankee. In 1911, his mother, Ruth Mitchell, made a trip to Connecticut to visit her sister. While there, she met Thomas A. Bullock, a civil engineer from New York, whose passions included opera and the New York Yankees. They were married three weeks later, and at the bride's insistence, took up residence in her hometown of Gainesville on the Red River 65 miles north of Dallas. Ruth, known to her family as a "dominant and forceful" woman, not only wanted to live in Texas, but in small-town Texas. After a few years of following jobs from Gainesville to Mexico to Dallas—and having two daughters and a son along the way— the Bullocks settled in Hillsboro, where their youngest child, Robert, was born on July 10, 1929.

There was nothing in particular to draw them to Hillsboro, except that it was rural, quiet, and safe, and the town just happened to be shopping for a civil engineer. Although pastoral, Hillsboro was far from being a backwater. Just 63 miles south of Dallas and 35 miles north of Waco, the town was established in 1853 as the governmental seat of Hill County. For most of its history, cotton and railroads were its lifeblood, but by the beginning of World War II the population was approaching 8,000, and light manufacturing—mattress makers, dairy processors, printers, ice houses—brought new economic impetus. Hillsboro also had established, as part of the public school system, one of the first municipal junior colleges in the state. And it had the interurban, an early

20th-century light-rail commuter network—nearly 500 miles of electric trolley lines in Texas—clustered mainly around Dallas/Fort Worth and Houston. The interurban provided passenger service to places heavy rail carriers did not. One of the largest systems linked Dallas, Fort Worth, Cleburne, Denison, Corsicana, and Waco, and dozens of smaller towns along the way.

Even with those modern amenities, Hillsboro maintained its bucolic tempo—the languid, insipid drone that is often the background music of life beyond the exurbs, the kind of music that inspires restless and inventive youths to elaborate schemes to escape the tedium. Bobby Bullock was restless and inventive.

"It was a nice place to live," Bullock said in a 1998 interview. "Everybody knew one another, nobody locked their doors. There's certain values you get from living in a small town and from your family. I haven't always followed them, but I knew when I wasn't following them, and I knew when I wasn't doing right. I got into a little trouble up there."[3]

In boozy bull sessions during his time as comptroller, he would confess that he had once urinated in the pepper sauce in the school cafeteria, causing classes to shut down for a day while everyone got health tests and tetanus shots. He also owned up to having shot a neighbor's house full of holes, but the owners, being absent, were spared injury. Small-town legends have been made of lesser stuff. Of course, his confessions were proffered long after the statute of limitations had elapsed—a practice that would repeat itself throughout his public life.

Childhood friends remembered him for pranks generally less malicious. "He was always like a little dog that keeps jumping in your lap and messing up your pants . . . but you love him," said Dohoney, a retired District Court judge, whose lifelong friendship with Bullock began with a fight on the playground at Franklin School. They were six years old, and the fight proved to be a ritual of bonding. In the years that followed, they joined the same Boy Scout troop, played sports together, worked summer jobs together, rode bikes, played golf, double-dated, and learned to drink whiskey together. Both joined the Air Force, became lawyers, participated in each other's weddings and, for a while, shared a duplex in the neighborhood where they grew up. Like most of Bullock's friends, Dohoney was occasionally the target of Bullock's practical jokes and, like the others, he laughed about them and forgave his friend.

Dohoney's wife, Betty (née Smith), grew up next door to Bullock. "I didn't like him," she said. "He was always pestering me. He used to peep in my windows." They had one date, or what passed for a date among the teenagers too young to drive: a bicycle outing with equal numbers of boys and girls paired into couples. "We mutually agreed that we would not date again."[4]

To most of his peers and no small number of his elders, however, Bullock was the irresistible rascal, the charming, unpredictable, risk-taking, and immensely entertaining bad boy. He reveled in racing his Cushman scooter up and down Waco Street, as the highway from Waco to Dallas was called inside Hillsboro, when the interurban trolley passed through, brushing as close to it as possible.

The boys admired him; the girls clamored for his attention. As payback for his pestering, his friends more than once abducted him and deposited him far enough from town that the walk home would teach him a lesson. It never worked. "We would dump him in the boonies, and the girls would follow [to retrieve him]. He'd beat us back to town," said Frasier Blount, a tall and massive man (nearly 300 pounds in his youth) who was known by the nickname Flab.

Although he was a few years Bullock's senior, the two were close—sometimes cohorts and sometimes antagonists, as in the case of the storied church house chase. It began on the sidewalk outside Brown's Corner, a drugstore and popular gathering place for Hillsboro's youth. Blount and the usual crowd were there that Sunday night when Bullock ran around the corner, hit Blount with enough force to knock the wind out of him, and kept running. Blount pursued him up Elm Street and was gaining on him when Bullock ducked into a Presbyterian church, where services were in progress.

With Blount close behind, Bullock sprinted down one aisle, crossed the altar behind the preacher, turned, and sprinted up the other aisle toward the entrance. Another block up the street, Bullock darted behind a house, turned to check Blount's progress, and ran into a clothesline that slammed him to the ground. Blount got his revenge, and the evening ended in a draw.

That relationship of fond antagonism was interrupted when Blount left town to serve in World War II, but it resumed as soon as he returned home and got a job as a mailman. One day, as he did on his route every weekday, Blount approached the two-story Bullock household, crossed under the porte-cochere—a kind of carport with a screened-in room on top—and was about to deposit the family's mail when a No. 2 washtub of water poured down from above.

While Blount sat on the curb sorting through and drying the wet contents of his letter bag, Bullock taunted him from atop the porte-cochere.

Finally, Blount jumped to his feet and charged into the house without knocking, turned, and headed toward the stairs to the room above the driveway.

"Go get him, Flab," Bullock's mother yelled.

"I'm gonna," Blount vowed. But not then. Bullock, smaller and faster, made his escape, and Blount's retribution had to wait. Dohoney remembered that a few days passed before the mailman caught Bullock off guard and "knocked the fool out of him."

Not all the fool. On another day, walking down a side street between two larger avenues on his route, Blount heard an engine behind him. It was Bullock, driving his brother-in-law's car.

"Hop on that fender and I'll give you a lift," Bullock said.

Blount slid onto the left front fender. Bullock accelerated the car and just as suddenly applied the brakes, sending Blount sprawling in the street. Blount managed to get to his feet and land a bruising blow to Bullock's arm as he sped away.[5]

A few years later, the two teamed on an elaborate practical joke that was remembered by Hillsboro old-timers long after Bullock was dead.

Home for the weekend from Texas A&M University, Dohoney encountered Bullock on a downtown street and became an intended victim of that scheme.

"Say, there's a girl out on this side of Bynum I'd like to introduce you to," Bullock told him. "She's really a nice girl, beautiful girl, really beautiful girl."

"Okay," Dohoney said.

That evening, Bullock picked him up and headed out Highway 171 toward Bynum, eventually turning onto a county road for a short distance, then turned again onto a dirt road.

"That's the house down there," Bullock said.

As they approached, the door was flung open and a young man came running out, followed closely by Frasier Blount, waving a shotgun.

"You stay away from my daughter," Blount yelled, and then fired the shotgun into the air.

Bullock said, "Uh-oh, we're too early, we're too early."

The joke on Dohoney was spoiled, but he was certain that Bullock and Blount had lined up several other victims that evening, other young men to be lured to a vacant house near Bynum on the pretense of meeting a "beautiful girl" only to be confronted by a raging 300-pound, shotgun-toting *father*.

"He was going to do that to me!" Dohoney said.

Some of Bullock's penchant for pranks and mischief may have arisen from boredom, but some of it may have been inherited, oddly enough, from the mother he had described as "dominant" and "forceful."

Blount recalled an incident when Bullock's older brother, Tom, was playing in the yard with a friend. Ruth opened the door and said, "Boys, come on in here. I've got a Coca-Cola for you." They sipped their colas, and when the glasses were almost drained, the friend found a pair of false teeth in the bottom of his glass. Fake false teeth, of course.

Whether his tendencies were hereditary or environmental, the young Bullock's reputation was well established by the time he was 16, the year his father died and left him at a crossroads. No one knew which fork he would take. Mostly, he showed signs of being out of control. Childish pranks had grown into crimes and borderline crimes. Tom Bullock had not been markedly successful at keeping a leash on his son, and his passing might have liberated the teenager to follow his darkest impulses. Bullock himself acknowledged as much years later, after Hill Junior College placed his name on a new athletic building: "I'm so happy that they named a gym after me instead of a prison."[6]

However, there was another strong father figure across the street, and he quickly assumed the role from which Tom Bullock had departed. Will Bond, who ran a hardware store and was Hillsboro's unofficial political powerbroker, was married to Bullock's older sister, Louisa, and had always been close to his brother-in-law. When Bullock was a child, he was often chauffeured around town on the handlebars of Bond's bicycle, and later, Bond's car was usually available to him. Not long after Tom Bullock's death, Bullock and his mother, for financial reasons, moved in with Will and Louisa. His mother kept the house they vacated and converted it to two apartments that could generate income.

Bond, too, could not wholly restrain the teenager (it was on Bond's watch that Bullock and a group of friends were caught stealing watermelons), but almost by acclamation, the citizens of Hillsboro deemed him the decisive factor in shaping Bullock's future. "He could have gone either way," Dohoney said. "Will Bond kept him from going to prison."

Because of him, Bullock also got a whiff of the political air that saturated the streets of Hillsboro like lint from the cotton gins. Bond never held elective office—he served for many years as chairman of the State Welfare Board—but he had powerful connections, and few aspiring local politicians filed for office without first consulting him, seeking his advice and his approval. Bond was particularly close to Lyndon Johnson, who stayed overnight in the Bonds' home when his campaigns for the U.S. Senate took him through Hillsboro. After Johnson was elected to the Senate in 1948, he offered Bond a job in Washington, but it was declined.

During those years, Bullock and his brother were exposed to the campaign hoopla (brother Tom, a saxophonist, had a band that helped draw crowds for LBJ's appearances) and were privy to the private talks Bond and Johnson had over dinner and drinks. Neither of the youngsters showed much interest in politics, except for the rousing spectacle of a friendly crowd and a good stump speech, but one of them, subsequent events would reveal, was learning something, was absorbing the nuances of campaigning, the fine touches—firm handshakes, name recall, swift command of facts and issues, grace before hostility, blustery persuasion—that were the primal components of the stump.

Except for his proclivity for mischief, Bullock was little different from other small-town high school boys. He was mediocre in the classroom but stellar on the football field, where, as a running back for the Hillsboro Eagles, he earned the nickname "Bullet Bob." After graduating in 1947, he enrolled in Hillsboro Junior College and again was academically undistinguished but dedicated on the football field. Still swift but too small to make the starting lineup, he spent most of his time on the bench. But, in testimony to his popularity and leadership abilities, he was elected co-captain of the team and remained a crowd favorite.

At one game, the fans, possibly recalling his high school exploits, began chanting, "We want Bullock! We want Bullock!"

After a couple of minutes, Coach Lloyd Raymer became impatient. He walked over to the bench and told his backup ball carrier, "Bullock, go up in those stands and find out what those people want with you."

In the stands that day was Cecil Stubblefield. He recalled that late in the game the coach relented to the crowd's demands and sent Bullock into the game. "He scored a touchdown," Stubblefield said.[7]

Off the field, junior college was a repeat of high school. During basketball season each year, the college was host to a women's basketball tournament that drew teams from throughout the state. It was a major event, and local merchants found ways to cash in on it. Chuck Farhat, a hulking Armenian who owned a small hamburger joint across the street from the college, did pretty well most years by putting someone in charge of his café while he opened a temporary burger stand at the gymnasium.

One year, he left his café to the care of Bobby Bullock and another student, Bobby Younger, a decision he quickly came to rue.

As he dished up a hamburger at his temporary venue, the customer asked, "How much is it?"

Farhat quoted the price.

"That's way too much," the customer said. "They're not charging near that at your place across from the college."

"What do you mean?"

"Well, they're fixing something called a Chuckleburger. It's got double meat, double everything, and they're not charging that much for it."

Chuck was not amused. After recruiting someone to watch his burger stand, he hurried back to his café and charged through the door, cursing at the top of his voice. Bullock and Younger narrowly escaped through the back door.[8]

Bullock left Hillsboro Junior College in the spring of 1949 with an associate arts degree and, as far as anyone could tell, no clear plan for the rest of his life. The front pages indicated that geopolitics would dictate his immediate future, as it would that of most of his peers. In the spring of 1950, the year of the war in Korea, Bullock and Dohoney had reached adulthood in an uncertain time. They were draft age, but neither relished the prospect of infantry hardships. They had solemn discussions of the Air Force.

While they contemplated military service and awaited the inevitable, they engaged in the time-honored rituals of drinking, carousing, and courtship. Childhood shenanigans were behind them, but their reputations were slow to fade.

One evening, they drove to nearby Itasca to pick up their dates, two young women they barely knew. Amelia and Julie Ann Hooks were from a prominent and prosperous family, and they were very attractive. That was all the two young men needed to know. The girls knew more about them. After dinner and a picture show, they drove back to the Hooks' home at 10:30 and parked in the driveway, Dohoney and Julie Ann in the front seat, Bullock and Amelia in the back. The party was cut short when Amelia broke the silence.

"Don't you do that," she snapped, and landed an audible slap to Bullock's face. "My mother told me all about you."

Dohoney disengaged from Julie Ann, looked into the back seat, and started to laugh, but quickly felt the hot sting of Amelia's palm on his cheek. "My mother warned me about you, too," she said. The sisters scrambled out of the car and into the house.[9]

Bob Bullock and Amelia Hooks were married a few months later.

CHAPTER 2

POLITICAL BAPTISM BY GARDEN HOSE

A melia Bullock gave birth to a daughter, Lindy, the following year, the year her husband entered the Air Force for a tour that would last three-and-a-half years. Apart from the uncertainty, the war imposed few hardships on them. Bullock was stationed at Lackland Air Force Base near San Antonio, where he was a supply clerk and made frequent trips on transport planes carrying materials to U.S. combat forces in Korea. It was in that job that he began to display the organizational efficiency, if not the manic drive, that would become a hallmark of his later political life. "He spent the entire war there," said Dohoney, who was stationed at nearby Kelly Air Force Base. "He was a good organizer. I think he was so good the officer in charge wouldn't let him go anywhere else."[1]

Discharged in 1954, Bullock returned with his wife and daughter to Hillsboro, his future still uncertain. His older brother, Tom, had become an architect. That profession held no interest for Bullock. Neither did the hardware business run by his brother-in-law and surrogate father, nor the pharmacy, which was run by Will Bond's uncle. Bullock enrolled in Texas Technological College in Lubbock (later renamed Texas Tech University), where he settled on a major in business administration.

Along the way, he kept up with the hometown news through his mother and stayed in touch with old friends through terse memos, which, like his organizational talents, also were portentous of his management style in later government service. Learning that his old friend, Frasier Blount, now married, was a new father, Bullock dashed off a memo of congratulations: "Mother informs me that you are the happy father of a daughter," the note said. "I hope she's like her mother instead of you. Otherwise, she'll be the ugliest, sorriest jackass ever born."[2]

After Tech, he entered Baylor Law School and, by his own accounting, was an average student, even earning mediocre grades in ethics. "Law school was real hard for me," he acknowledged. While he commuted to law classes, the Bullocks resided in Hillsboro in the house his mother had converted to two apartments after his father died. The Dohoneys occupied the other apartment. Although he was yet to show an interest in politics, Bullock occasionally showed flashes of the political creature.

A particularly illuminating incident occurred while Bullock and Dohoney stood in the yard of their duplex on a sunny afternoon as a neighbor approached on the sidewalk with her young son. Bullock quickly turned and ran into the house.

"Amelia, Amelia," Dohoney heard him yell, "what's Jane's little boy's name?"

"Dennis," Amelia said.

Bullock came back outside. "Hi, Jane," he said, and then bent over the child and added, "And there's little Dennis."[3]

Knowing names—acquiring all manner of personal information—would become another essential Bullock political trait, but at the time he was thinking little about politics and much about getting through law school. It is likely that he was having doubts about the practice of law, doubts that his restlessness and impatience were compatible with the plodding requirements of that profession, especially in a small town.

His brother-in-law may have shared those reservations. In a different setting, Will Bond might have been described as a ward heeler, the Democratic Party's establishment point man and mediator in Hill County—the organizer, the crowd gatherer, the arbiter and interpreter of political trends and drifts. Like Lyndon Johnson, candidates for state or national office courted him. When he attended political functions in Austin, governors and wannabe governors circled around him. Anyone thinking of running for office in Hill County consulted him first. If Bond said he couldn't win, he didn't file. His blessing, though, was often enough to create an immediate front-runner.

After the 1955 legislative session adjourned, Jim Carmichall, who had held the District 54 House seat for only a couple of terms, announced that he would not seek reelection, creating an open race in the Democratic primary the next spring.

"Bobby, you might want to take a look at the Legislature," Will Bond told his brother-in-law near the end of 1955. "You're studying how to interpret laws, but you need to know a little bit about how they're made."[4]

Bullock did, and at the age of 26 was the first candidate to announce that he would be a candidate for that seat. Although living in Will Bond's house had indoctrinated him to the ways and means of campaigning and governing, there were things, little things, he did not know. "I thought the Legislature met every year," he said in an interview years later.[5] He knew the pay was meager, but the opportunities were abundant. It was good, free advertising for someone entering the law business, plus the ranks of lobbyists were glutted with ex-legislators with law degrees. A well-connected lobbyist could easily earn more than a bored lawyer.

Still, it was not the most pleasant time to launch a political career. Cold War Red-baiting, labor strikes on the Gulf Coast, early whiffs of the coming civil rights storm, and other controversies had inspired a rabid, sometimes violent backlash wherever they surfaced. The 1950s was a decade, wrote George Norris Green in his 1979 book *The Establishment in Texas Politics— The Primitive Years, 1939–1957*, when extremism seemed almost to govern the state.[6]

The most prominent of those issues was school desegregation and how to prevent it.

In 1954, the U.S. Supreme Court ruled in *Brown v. Board of Education*, a Topeka, Kansas, lawsuit challenging racially segregated schools. Holding that such public educational systems were unconstitutional, the court ordered the practice to end. The language was clear, and it didn't take a legal scholar to perceive that no loopholes were provided by the High Court. Still, local school boards and state politicians, particularly in the South, had little inclination to acquiesce meekly. Some Deep South states even threatened to abolish their public school systems rather than integrate them. Texas Gov. Allan Shivers, who had strayed from the Democratic Party in 1948 to support the Dixiecrat presidential bid of South Carolina Sen. Strom Thurmond, initially was more temperate, saying that Texas would submit to the court's edict, but that full integration of schools might take years. In fact, it took decades, due to the persistent resistance at every level.

A handful of school districts in Texas quietly integrated their classrooms, but across the state, candidates for the Legislature were printing literature and buying newspaper space to declare their commitment to segregation.

As the width and depth of the voters' rejection of the court decision became evident, Shivers rediscovered his Dixiecrat leanings, with nudging from the Republican gubernatorial candidate, Tod Adams—though Shivers, raised in deep East Texas, didn't need much. A month after *Brown v. Board of Education*, Adams met with the State Republican Executive Committee and declared that, "regardless of the nine politicians on the Supreme Court, if I'm governor, we'll continue to have segregated schools."[7]

About that same time, Shivers reconsidered his "submit" statement. Stumping for reelection in Lufkin, in a region of East Texas where segregationist sentiments ran deep, he told an audience that the Supreme Court had made an "unwarranted invasion of the constitutional rights of the states, and one that could be disastrous to the children and to the teachers of both races."

Then he added, "My administration has already told the local school districts that, as far as the state of Texas is concerned, there are no changes to be made in the way we are conducting our schools."

Even Shivers's opponent, Ralph Yarborough, a populist former district judge with solid support among blacks, making his second race for governor, felt it necessary to ride the tide. At a speech in East Texas, he said he opposed "forced commingling" of the races and favored "separate but genuinely equal schooling."

Race wasn't the only issue in election year 1954, but it was the only one that mattered. It was during the peak of the Red Scare rhetoric, and the Shivers camp equated integration with communism. It made for ugly politicking. Shivers and Yarborough worked that turf with putrid one-upmanship, each blanketing black precincts with circulars boasting of their racial tolerance and littering affluent white neighborhoods with circulars accusing the other of being too sympathetic to black causes. Yarborough, driven more by political practicality than conviction, was no match for Shivers, who also stole every page from the Red-smear playbook of Sen. Joseph McCarthy. But in the July 28 first primary, he ran strongly enough to force Shivers into a runoff (two lesser candidates, including one who lived under a viaduct in Dallas, were eliminated). And so the race-baiting continued into the late summer. (Texas primaries were held in July and August until they were moved to May and June in 1959, to accommodate Lyndon Johnson's desire to be re-nominated to his Senate seat in 1960 before seeking the nomination for president at the Democratic National Convention in July.) Shivers's headquarters hit the low note by mailing to newspapers a retouched photograph of Yarborough in which a darkened skin tone, flattened nose, and modified cheekbones made him appear to be a black man. Shivers slipped by Yarborough in the August 25 runoff and trounced Adams in November. The following year, Shivers appointed the Texas Advisory Committee on Segregation to develop solutions to the "school crisis." The only solution offered by the committee, consisting mostly of segregationists, was to threaten to withhold funding from school districts that had already integrated.

Throughout 1955 and 1956, the heat of the race debate did not abate, but rather intensified, as more school districts voluntarily desegregated and others were placed under court order to do so. Burning crosses, threatening lawmen, and carrying placards that read "A dead nigger is the best nigger," an angry mob of about 400 gathered around a school in Mansfield, near Fort Worth, to prevent court-ordered integration. Shivers termed it an "orderly protest" and dispatched Texas Rangers to assist the mob in blocking black students from attending the white school.[8]

There was little doubt that *Brown* would preoccupy the Texas Legislature when it convened in January 1957.

If school desegregation was a burning topic in Hillsboro when the political season dawned in January 1956, it was not evident on the pages of the *Hillsboro Evening Mirror*. Shivers, whose administration had scandal problems, decided against trying to extend his tenure of more than seven years, so the political news centered mostly around whether U.S. Sen. Price Daniel would run for governor, whether Lyndon Johnson would agree to be a favorite-son nominee for president at the party's national convention, whether Ralph Yarborough would run for governor or senator, and how the state would deal with its latest insurance scandal.

Reporting on racial matters was limited to a screaming headline about a local black man who was placed under citizen's arrest at gunpoint by the father of a white teenage girl with whom he had flirted, and a small *Associated Press* report from Columbia, South Carolina, quoting W. A. Criswell, pastor of the mammoth First Baptist Church of Dallas, as saying integration "is not acceptable." As for the desegregation of Texas schools, there was one brief account of a civic club speech by State Atty. Gen. Will Wilson, who was asked to explain the concept of "interposition." Simply put, he told the Kiwanians, it is a state's attempt to enforce the language of the U.S. Constitution's 10th amendment, which reserves for the states any powers not expressly granted to the federal government. For reasons never fully explained, "interposition" was a straw that segregationists grasped at as potentially the most promising weapon against *Brown v. Board of Education*. Did anyone seriously believe that states could convince the Supreme Court that the Supreme Court had unconstitutionally co-opted states' rights? Certainly not everyone. Another small article in the *Hillsboro Evening Mirror* in the spring of 1956 quoted Republican gubernatorial hopeful J. Evetts Haley as vowing to deploy Texas Rangers to enforce segregation in the state's schools. Guns would be more effective than legal briefs, he reasoned.

Bullock had announced his candidacy for the State House late in 1955. He tackled campaigning with a zeal and intensity he had seldom exhibited in his previous endeavors, except, perhaps, for his dedicated waywardness. It was a time when door-knocking and pamphleteering were the standard campaign tools, and Bullock placed the greater emphasis on the former. He prepared an uninspiring poster, a photograph of himself in a dark jacket and tie with the message:

> VOTE FOR BOB BULLOCK
> *For Your State Representative 54th District, Hill County*
>
> I am a native of Hill County, and a graduate of the Hillsboro public schools. I attended Texas Technological College and am presently attending Baylor University Law School. I am married and have one daughter. I am a veteran of the Korean War, having spent 45 months in the United States Air Force. I have made every effort to qualify myself to be your representative. Your support sincerely appreciated.[9]

It was in the door-knocking, rather than pamphleteering, that he excelled. Although young and self-financed, Bullock had Will Bond's counsel, and more. He understood the value of personal contact. Usually accompanied by his wife and always wearing a suit and tie, he knocked on every door in Hill County twice. At least that was his claim, for which Amelia vouched and which no one challenged.

A memorable and oft-told story of that campaign involved an elderly man who apparently was a devoted supporter of one of Bullock's opponents. Canvassing a neighborhood on the west side of Hillsboro, Bullock encountered him in his front yard watering shrubbery with a garden hose.

"I'm Bob Bullock, and I'm running for state representative," the candidate said. "I would appreciate your support."

The old man turned to face him. "You the one running against old Pete?" he asked. Ludd W. "Pete" Harris of Whitney, who had served one term in the House in the early 1920s and two terms in the early 1940s, was considering another comeback.

"Yes, sir," Bullock said. "Mr. Harris is a fine man, but I'm running anyway."

The old man said nothing. He scowled for a second and then slowly turned the garden hose on Bullock.

Bullock calmly retreated to his car, drove home, changed into a dry suit, drove back to the neighborhood, and continued knocking doors where he had left off.[10]

As it turned out, Harris decided not to run. But, typical of the race for an open seat, competition was inevitable. Early in 1956, three others entered the race: Sam Tinner, a restaurateur; Herbert "Pete" Polgue, a pre-law student at Texas Tech; and Gordon Conner, a Covington businessman. If any had to take positions on the inflammatory issues of the time, it was done in private, on a doorstep or over coffee, and therefore lost to history. Except for a brief report when each declared his candidacy, the local newspaper gave no coverage to the legislative race.

His primary opponents appeared to be at least as qualified as he—one was considerably older, and at least two probably had deeper pockets—but none spent heavily on local media, and the ads published in the *Hillsboro Evening Mirror* were starkly generic. One of Bullock's few newspaper pitches stated merely that he "has never before sought public office . . . directs and finances his own campaign . . . has conducted a clean, open, and diligent campaign, and . . . is obligated to no clique or special interest and will, if elected, faithfully serve all the people and not just a select few."

The Democratic primary was held on July 28, a Saturday. Sunday's banner headline in the *Evening Mirror* shouted that "Bob Bullock Wins Without Run-Off." He had received 4,044 votes; Polgue got 1,123; Tinner and Conner got fewer than 900 each.

With no Republican opponent to face in the general election in November, Bullock had his seat in the Legislature.

CHAPTER 3

IN THE ORBIT OF POWER

I f there is a charge to the air around the State Capitol when the Legislature returns to town for a new session, it may be because even the gods cringe in apprehension at what may be wrought. In January 1957, the atmosphere was more electric than usual. That was partly because new political leadership was on the scene. Gov. Shivers, whose final years as governor were tainted by a series of scandals, did not run for an unprecedented fourth term. He was replaced by U.S. Sen. Price Daniel, Sr., another conservative Democrat, who barely won a rancorous Democratic runoff. Populist Yarborough came within 3,171 votes of almost 1.4 million cast of making his third race for governor the charm. He got 49.9 percent. The House of Representatives was preparing to elect Rep. Waggoner Carr of Lubbock as its new speaker, and the state's political climate was white-hot over the upcoming special election to choose a successor to complete the final two years remaining of Daniel's six-year term in the U.S. Senate. The only one of the three top leaders who had held his job before was Lt. Gov. Ben Ramsey, a former state senator and Secretary of State, who had presided over the Senate since 1951. Publicly, the legislative leaders were saying they wanted appropriations to be the first order of business, but members, particularly those in the House, had other ideas. As the session opened, most of the corridor buzz was about the "manifesto."

Circulated by Rep. Joe N. Chapman, of Sulphur Springs, the manifesto was a blunt call to arms against integration in all its forms, but especially in the classroom. "We pledge our vote and influence and call on all other members of the Texas Legislature to join with us in faithfully discharging our duty

to Texas by supporting appropriate legislation designed to carry out the prin-
ciples of states' rights and constitutional law," the document said.[1] *States'
rights* had become code for *right to racial segregation*.

It was the precursor to a satchel of bills that the hardcore segregationists
from East Texas, with generous help from the Dallas delegation, planned to
introduce when the doors opened. The language of the manifesto was only
mildly controversial. What was striking about it was the political threat the
authors had attached to it: *Names of those who signed it and those who did not
would be made public*. Among the 150 House members, only a handful could
safely defy the segregationists. One who did was Galveston Rep. A. R. "Babe"
Schwartz, the only Jew in the Legislature. "Everybody in the Legislature was
a good ol' boy, but became assholes after *Brown v. Board*. It made a radical out
of me," Schwartz said.[2]

One of the early signers was Rep. Bob Johnson, a Dallas attorney who
had won his seat the previous year by attacking the "socialistic tendencies of
the federal government . . . because of the influence of several minority
groups."[3] Unlike many freshmen backbenchers, who prefer to lie low until
they have negotiated the learning curve, Johnson arrived with his own anti-
integration resolution to fulfill his campaign promises. He advocated constitutional amendments and legislation to allow students to attend the schools
of their choice; using the doctrine of interposition in the fields of education,
oil and gas, insurance, transportation, sedition, and medicine and health;
outlawing the National Association for the Advancement of Colored People
(NAACP) in Texas; and toughening the laws against inciting and agitating
for desegregation.

Johnson became an eager ally of the East Texans, who had drafted nearly two dozen bills that would, among other things, bar NAACP members
from public employment and fine anyone who hired them; withhold accred-
itation and funding from any school that integrated (more than 100 districts
had already done so); and allow parents to withhold their children from integrated schools and provide grants for those children to attend private schools
so that, in the words of one advocate, "no child, white, nigger, or otherwise,
would have to go to an integrated school." In all, 12 segregationist bills were
introduced, and they dominated the session. In the House, resistance to
them was minimal, but the Senate was another matter. Attorney General
Will Wilson declared them unconstitutional, a conclusion shared by Charles
Alan Wright, the noted professor of constitutional law at the University of
Texas, but they were ignored.

Although Bullock became close friends with fellow freshman Johnson and several members of the East Texas delegation, there is no record that he joined the strident civil rights debate. As the segregationist bills ground through the lawmaking machinery, Bullock—to the benefit of his long-term political viability—was content to be seen and not heard. Most mornings of the session, he arose by five-thirty, drove to Waco for a class or two at Baylor Law School, drove back to Austin by eleven for a day's work in the House, joined the after-hours drinking and poker sessions with other legislators and lobbyists, and managed a few hours of sleep before the drill was repeated. Years later, other participants in those after-hours diversions would remember him mostly as an enthusiastic drinker and decent poker player.

Bullock later would describe himself as "liberal" that first session, "a Ralph Yarborough man," he told the *Texas Observer* in a 1972 interview. Besides being pro-labor, he signed on as coauthor of a water conservation bill, a teachers' pay raise bill, and a measure to increase old-age assistance from $58 to $60 per month. He also authored a constitutional amendment allowing the state to provide free medical assistance for needy children and for the elderly and disabled, a measure that was approved by voters later that year by a vote of 380,313 to 244,915, or more than 60 percent.

At that time, those kinds of issues—not segregation and desegregation—were the fault lines between *liberal* and *conservative*. Whatever his true feelings about the segregationist bills—years later he would say that he didn't "believe any of that crap"—Bullock took the perfunctory and politically safe course: he voted for every one of them. Eleven of the bills passed the House, but in the upper chamber there was daring opposition. Six senators staged a 36-hour filibuster and managed to kill all but two of the bills. One of the survivors allowed for students to be assigned to schools based on 17 vague and highly subjective criteria, including "academic preparation, mental energy, psychological qualification, threat of friction, home environment, and morals"—factors that could be interpreted in such a way to ensure that black students would still be assigned to black schools and white students to white schools. The other provided for "local option," a curious attempt to let local school districts decide whether to obey the Supreme Court.

But the issue was far from settled. With the beginning of the new school year in September, an epic showdown took place at Central High School in Little Rock, Arkansas, where, under a seven-year desegregation plan worked out by the city and school board, nine black students were to begin attending classes with the 2,000 white students. Instead, Gov. Orval Faubus sent

National Guard soldiers with rifles and bayonets to surround the school and keep the black teenagers from entering. In response, President Dwight Eisenhower placed the Arkansas National Guard under federal control and sent in a battle group of the 101st Airborne Division from Fort Campbell, Kentucky, to enforce the desegregation order. Thus, governors, mayors, and school boards throughout the country were put on notice: armed resistance would be met with armed force; there would be no local option, no *interposition*.

Eisenhower's stated and demonstrated determination was little deterrent to hard-core segregationists throughout the South. In November, with the turmoil and violence of Little Rock still making news, Gov. Daniel called a special session of the Texas Legislature and had his own bill ready for consideration. Along with it, he sent a message to the Legislature, delivered by his executive assistant:

"I hereby submit the subject of further providing for the maintenance of law, peace, and order in the operation of the public schools without resort to military occupation or control. In this connection, there are four vital objectives for the well-being of our state and our people. One, the protection and continuation of our public school systems. Two, the preservation of good relations among all our citizens. Three, the maintenance of law and order. Four, the preservation of the rights and responsibilities of our state and local governments. All four of these objectives have been threatened and endangered in a neighboring state by the occupation of a public school with military troops. This should never be necessary in Texas and should not be permitted to occur."[4]

In a few years, it would seem remarkable—although it did not at the time—that Daniel made no effort to encourage peaceful compliance with the Supreme Court's order. Instead, his message seemed to tacitly condone resistance to integration, and his bill would have required local officials to close their schools if federal troops arrived to oppose that resistance.

The Senate had a similar bill, and the House had two. As the four bills were whittled and consolidated into three, opponents suggested that Atty. Gen. Wilson review them for constitutionality. Rep. Jerry Sadler, one of the House sponsors, replied, "I don't want Will Wilson and some NAACP lawyer passing on the bill."[5]

Will Wilson said the bills were constitutional. On December 11, Gov. Daniel signed three bills sent to him by the Legislature. One allowed, rather than required, local school boards to close their schools if federal troops attempted to enforce court-ordered integration and provided for state funding to continue so that districts could set up segregated, makeshift classes away from the school. Another set aside funds for the attorney general to assist local school boards defending desegregation lawsuits. The third, though clearly aimed at the NAACP, would have forced any organization to reveal its membership rolls if it "engaged in activities designed to hinder, harass, and interfere with" the duties of the state to operate and control public schools. Even the filing of a federal court lawsuit would have triggered the disclosure provisions of that law.[6]

Although his first year in the House had been eventful—even marginally historic—it did not appear to ignite in the young representative from Hillsboro a lust for lawmaking. He filed for reelection in 1958 and, drawing neither a Democratic primary opponent nor a Republican challenger in the general election, was free to bear down on the study of law and earn his degree. He also spent a little time helping friends he had made in the House win reelection or dispensing advice to old friends running for the first time. He went to Newton to help Sam S. Collins win a seat in deep East Texas. He stayed at Collins's home for several days and counseled him on campaign strategy.

"He was savvy politically," Collins said. "He knew people. He helped me a lot in my first term."

What Collins remembered most about that 1959 session was helping Bullock shepherd through the House the "grits enrichment" bill requiring processors to fortify their product with vitamins and minerals—as was done with cereals. Grits were, and are, a staple of the East Texas diet, and the effort to legislate improvements to their nutritional value was strongly supported by school home economics departments and other health advocates in Collins's district. While hot topics such as a sales tax or hunting regulations provoked little or no correspondence from his constituents, grits brought an avalanche of mail—relatively speaking.

"I got 60 or 70 letters on grits," Collins said.[7]

Compared to 1957, Bullock's second regular legislative session was without passion and adrenaline. If grits was the high point, that alone may have been enough to drive him from politics. More than likely, though, it was personal finance and parental responsibility. He was 29 years old, his daughter was seven, and Amelia had given birth to a son, Robert Douglas Bullock, Jr.

Legislators at that time were paid just $25 per day for living expenses—but only for the first 120 days of the regular session. Legislative days beyond that, including special sessions, brought no state reimbursement. In 1957, the legislators met in special session from October 14 to December 3. Like many legislators who weren't wealthy, earning a living while trying to write laws and represent constituents was a stretch for the young representative.

After law school, Bullock went to work for Donald Eastland, a childhood friend who had hung out his shingle in Hillsboro a couple of years earlier. But for a young man of Bullock's restive—sometimes driven—temperament, the routine was unsustainable. Customers were not exactly lined up at the door when they arrived at the office each morning, and some days the phone never rang. Boredom grated on Bullock as much as the erratic income.

"Bob was always restless," Eastland said. "If a client didn't walk through the door by ten o'clock, he would jump up and say, 'I'm outta here,' and disappear for the rest of the day."

Their work spanned the humdrum spectrum of small-town intercourse: wills, divorces, real estate, feuding neighbors, and police blotters. Their most memorable case, one that Bullock would often recount in later years, was to represent an accused arsonist who sat in the courtroom compulsively striking matches until Eastland disarmed him. The perp was convicted and sent off to jail.[8]

Within a few months, Bullock also was gone from Hillsboro. After the 1959 legislative session ended, plus three special sessions that lasted into August, a Harlingen law firm hired him to work on a Rio Grande Valley water lawsuit. Although he didn't last long in South Texas, that experience may have educated him to the inadequacy of the state's water laws, a condition he would one day strive to correct. While there, he was confronted by what would become a momentous distraction. Byron Tunnell, an East Texas representative with whom he had become friends when the two were freshman legislators in the 1957 session, was convening a group of confidants and advisors at a house on Caddo Lake on October 21, 1959, to discuss his race for House speaker in 1961.[9] Tunnell, likeable and impeccably dressed (he always wore white ties), had only two terms under his belt, but he was better than a long shot. At that time, House speakers did not dig in for long reigns. With the exception of United States senators and members of the Texas Railroad Commission, whose terms were for six years, statewide officeholders served two-year terms, making the tempo of musical chairs far more accelerated than it would later become. One or two terms as speaker, and you're ready to move on to higher office—lieutenant governor, railroad commissioner, or one of the other rungs on the gubernatorial ladder.

Bullock attended the Caddo Lake sit-down and, the next day, resigned his House seat, spent a couple of months tidying up his commitments in Harlingen, and moved to Tyler to become Tunnell's law partner. During that period, Bullock also purchased an interest in Longview's storied Reo Palm Isle ballroom, which booked such headliners as Elvis Presley and Willie Nelson. But politics, not the hospitality business, remained his preoccupation.

Although Bullock told friends he had no interest in ever again seeking public office, he was launched on a circuitous odyssey that would eventually return him to politics—if he ever really removed himself from it. While he may have thought he was through with elections in which he was the candidate, he continued to be drawn by the gravitational pull of public issues and powerful people.

By the summer of 1960, however, it was clear that the speaker's race was a two-man brawl, and Tunnell was seated at ringside. Rep. Wade Spilman of McAllen, in South Texas, and Rep. Jimmy Turman, a more liberal representative from Gober, in Northeast Texas, had taken over the battlefield—it was, literally, a battlefield, and a particularly nasty one. Tunnell would have to bide his time. He gave his endorsement to Spilman and returned his attention to his law practice.[10]

Bullock made plans to sever the partnership and make another move. Tunnell still had speaker potential in the near future, and being in Austin would better position Bullock to aid in that effort. If Tunnell assumed the House leadership, life could, indeed, be good for his good friend and former law partner. Until bigger game could be bagged, Bullock would work as a lawyer and lobbyist for the Texas Automobile Dealers Association, working out of a small office in the Driskill Hotel. Compared to the Big Four lobbying associations—oil and gas, the chemical council, railroads, and the manufacturers—it was a minor-league gig. But if political aspirations still skulked somewhere in his subconscious, the TADA was not a bad place to spend some time. It gave him access not only to legislators but also to a broad, grassroots network of businessmen. Every town of any size had an auto dealer. And, Bullock got to spend some time understudying TADA head H. C. Pittman, from whom he learned a lot.

When the 1961 session convened, Bullock spent generous time at Tunnell's office, drinking whiskey and talking strategy for another run at the speakership. Often joining in those sessions was a strapping, ambitious young freshman House member from West Texas named Ben Barnes. Their paths had crossed a few years earlier, but now they formed a quick bond, a friendship forged by a shared passion for politics, liquor, and women.

CHAPTER 4

WITH FRIENDS LIKE THESE

ew, if any, Texas political figures have ever come out of the starting blocks faster and more forcefully than Ben Barnes, who was elected to the House in 1960 at the age of 22. By the time Barnes was 32, Lyndon Johnson was so enamored of him that he pronounced him a future occupant of the White House.

Born Benny Frank Barnes on April 17, 1938, Barnes grew up in the Comanche County map specks of Comyn and De Leon, 100 miles southwest of Fort Worth. He graduated high school in 1956, and at the age of 19, while a student at Tarleton State University, married his 17-year-old high school sweetheart. Six months later, with a baby on the way, the couple relocated to a garage apartment in Austin, where Barnes would carry a full load of classes at the University of Texas and work full time for the Texas Department of Health, a job he landed with the help of his home county's state representative, Ben Doyle Sudderth.

Through the state job, he began to meet the players in state government. One of them was first-term Rep. Bob Bullock, who helped Barnes's wife, Martha, find a job after their baby was born. Another, and more important at the time, was former Rep. Bert Hall, who had overlapped with Bullock during Bullock's first term, but who quit the Legislature to work at the Health Department. Barnes, as part of his record-keeping duties, detected what he believed was an illegal slush fund. "I got very uncomfortable when I saw all these checks made out to liquor stores and motels," Barnes was quoted in Jerry Hall's manuscript about Barnes's life. "Bert and I began to discuss it."[1]

They approached Truett Latimer, the Abilene representative who chaired the Appropriations Committee. "Bring me some proof," he told them. They did. On a late-night visit to their superiors' office, Barnes jimmied open a desk drawer, retrieved the evidence, and turned it over to Latimer, who later held open hearings on the matter. Three top Health Department officials were then given a choice by Travis County Dist. Atty. Robert O. Smith: face criminal charges or pay the money back and leave the state. They took the second option.

If Barnes had not already decided to enter politics after college, that incident was the catalyst for one of the most spectacular and tumultuous journeys in Texas political history. In his manuscript, Jerry Hall quoted Barnes: "Everybody always says they are running to make a difference. I already made a difference in state government. I liked it, and I wanted to be in a position where I could do more."[2]

As luck would have it, Rep. Sudderth decided not to seek reelection in 1960. Barnes, with a business degree in hand and a year of law school behind him, walked into Sudderth's office and told him he was running to replace him. Sudderth was surprised. "Young man," he said, "I have to tell you, I don't think you have a prayer of winning." Sudderth said he'd already endorsed Ike Hickman, a World War II veteran from the district's population center of Brownwood.[3]

Through tireless campaigning (as Bullock had done in Hillsboro, Barnes —usually accompanied by his wife—knocked on every door in Brownwood), no small amount of charisma, and maybe a little fading gridiron glory, he defeated Hickman, by a vote of 8,023 to 4,293—almost a two-to-one ratio— and faced no Republican opposition in the general election.

One of his first tasks as a new legislator would be to cast a vote in the speaker's race. His political sensibilities drew him to the more conservative Spilman, to whom he pledged his support even before he had arrived in Austin. Spilman assigned him to a variety of tasks in the leadership battle, but it was a losing cause. Turman won narrowly, and Barnes was in the perilous position of beginning his maiden session under a speaker he had opposed. He wasn't alone. Among dozens of others guilty of the same impolitic behavior was Byron Tunnell.

Rather than attempting to make amends with Turman, Barnes relished antagonizing him. He refused to go along on key bills that Turman was pushing and, worse, he flagrantly enlisted in Tunnell's move to unseat the speaker. After the session ended, he tagged along with Tunnell and Bullock as they careened around the state seeking the support of House members and raising funds. A speaker's race was not as easy as calling members and asking for their votes. A serious contender had to conduct what was essentially a statewide campaign, visiting many of the 150 House districts to personally solicit the backing of the representatives or candidates.

One of those trips took them to Brownwood, Barnes's home turf, where they met with Herman Bennett, a wealthy commercial real estate developer who had been one of Barnes's backers in his House race. In Jerry Hall's account, Tunnell accepted a fat envelope from Bennett and placed it in his coat pocket without checking the contents.

"Where's mine, Mr. Bennett?" Barnes laughed. Bennett spoke privately with his secretary, and she left the room, returning promptly with a similarly fat package for Barnes.

Outside their benefactor's office, Tunnell opened the envelope and found a stack of $100 bills. Anticipating the same, Barnes ripped open his envelope and found it was stuffed with postage stamps. Bennett knew where the power lay, and Barnes learned he had not yet reached that level.[4] Bullock didn't get so much as a stamp, but he gained valuable experience in one area of politics where his expertise was lacking. Because his first race for the House had been self-financed and the second, in which he had no opponent, required little money, he was not a practiced fund-raiser. Watching Tunnell pocket a wad of unmarked bills forked over by a donor he had known for a few minutes made an impression. For access to power, cash was readily available, anonymous, and easy to spend, with little accountability.

Tunnell secured the pledges he needed, but the victory turned out to be easier than he had expected. Turman did not seek reelection to his House seat and instead ran in 1962 for lieutenant governor, practically leaving the speaker's gavel in Tunnell's pocket. By almost any measure, Bullock was well positioned to advance any ambition he possessed. His old friend and former partner would be the next speaker of the House of Representatives. His new friend, Ben Barnes, was a rising star who, still in his early 20s, had become a close confidant to the man who would become the next governor and, perhaps, go on to national office. Barnes, in fact, had been among a handful of friends and advisors present at the initial brainstorming session for the candidacy of John Connally.

Connally, a shrewd, urbane Fort Worth attorney known to have been one of Lyndon Johnson's behind-the-scenes chief operatives, was serving as secretary of the navy in the administration of President John F. Kennedy when he decided to enter the race. Although he had been elected student body president of the University of Texas in 1938, he was something of an anomaly: a candidate who had not paid his dues in the Legislature or a secondary state office; and a big-city contender in a state with a historical preference for rural governors, although Connally had grown up in Floresville. His name recognition was limited; an early poll showed that only one percent of Texas voters had heard of him. (He undoubtedly received some residual benefit from the fact that Tom Connally—no relation—had represented Texas in the United States Senate from 1929 into 1953, after a dozen years in the U.S. House.)

John Connally's political organization was nonexistent, but his timing was impeccable. By 1961, Texas's revenue resources were tapped out, and a new vein had to be located. The Legislature that year passed, and Daniel reluctantly signed, a bill creating the sales tax, which guaranteed there would soon be a bevy of new faces in high places. It not only cost many legislators their jobs, but probably stripped Daniel of his as well. Connally led the field of six candidates in the Democratic primary (Daniel ran a distant third) and narrowly beat Houston labor attorney Don Yarborough in a runoff. Though they were not related, Yarborough had the same last name as Ralph Yarborough, who had won the 1957 special election to serve out Daniel's senate term and had been reelected in 1958 to a six-year term of his own. In the general election, Republican Jack Cox, a lawyer from Breckenridge, ran a surprisingly strong race, getting 45.6 percent, which was widely interpreted as further evidence that the Democratic Party's dominance in Texas was in a gradual but perceptible decline.

Connally took office in January 1963, along with a new lieutenant governor, Preston Smith, a former senator from Lubbock, and Tunnell, the new House speaker. It was the beginning of a rancorous period between the governor's office and the Legislature, one that would test loyalties, cost friendships, and hasten the state's political realignment.

At first, Bullock watched it all from the bleachers. If he cashed in on his advantageous position and access to some of the most influential legislators, it wasn't apparent. He remained in his job at the TADA and began to build a reputation for political savvy and for an erratic temperament. Soon after taking office, Connally, acting on Barnes's recommendation, appointed Bullock to a seat on the Texas Historical Commission, which he held for a short time before resigning in anger at Connally over what Barnes later described as a minor and utterly forgettable issue. Bullock maintained his friendship with Barnes, however, and was instrumental in advancing Barnes's political career.

As the 1963 legislative session progressed, Barnes's association with Connally strengthened, even as the governor's relationship with the Legislature, particularly Lt. Gov. Smith, deteriorated. Connally, self-assured and convinced of his own intellectual superiority, was disdainful of what he considered lowbrow rubes in the Legislature who thwarted most of his legislative proposals, particularly those that created revenue demands that might result in higher taxes.

Connally saw himself as a visionary on a mission to drag Texas into the 20th century, and he viewed Tunnell and Smith as troglodytes clinging to a time that had long passed. At the fore of his vision was creating a system of higher education that could compete with more-enlightened states, such as California and Massachusetts. Brainpower brought business, he believed, and brainpower had to be homegrown as well as imported. "We can make Texas first in the nation in education, in industrial growth, in the broadening of job opportunities," he said, in announcing his candidacy.[5] He vowed to be the "most sincere catalyst in improving education beyond high school."[6]

Smith and Tunnell were not impressed. As Ann Fears Crawford and Jack Keever pointed out in their biography of Connally, the Legislature was still populated by fossilized populists who believed higher education was "elitist" and clung to the "conservative bias against funding public school programs that many considered as 'frills and fads.'"[7] (Funding of public education has long been a grudging endeavor; in 2005, after the Legislature failed to produce a school finance bill, House Speaker Tom Craddick reminded reporters that since 1948, no such bill had been passed in a regular session without the duress of a court order.)

In his first term as governor, Connally fumed as Smith and Tunnell cut $13 million from his higher-education budget. In subsequent sessions, Smith and the Senate blocked Connally's proposals for four-year terms, annual legislative sessions, and constitutional revisions. In 1967, after the Senate slapped down his $143 million tax bill, Connally proposed a one-year budget that required no tax increases. It was an unprecedented move, and it angered Smith so much that when he learned that nine senators had gone to the governor's office to discuss the plan, he adjourned the Senate "just seconds before they arrived to make a quorum."

For obvious reasons, Bullock stayed outside the Connally-Smith fray. He was a lobbyist and could afford no powerful enemies. His first impression of Connally, the fledgling candidate, had been mixed. TADA invited Connally to a breakfast meeting in its boardroom and, Bullock told Keever for his

Connally biography, "He stood up and made a speech, and it was the worst I ever heard. I never knew a man who knew less about state government." Two months later TADA invited him back for a second look and, Bullock said, "I never heard a man who knew more about state government. What happened was he had started taking crash courses from people who knew about state government."[8]

From all indications, Bullock's friendship with Barnes, who was emerging as Connally's protégé and closest confidant, was genuine—not the contrived relationship of a lobbyist courting favor. Both were smart, serious students of governance. They shared idealism as well as an intuition for the processes, possibilities, practicalities, and limitations of government.

One evening during the 1963 session, Barnes left the Capitol and walked the half-dozen blocks to Bullock's office in the Driskill Hotel. They poured whiskey and kicked back for their usual bull session on politics.

"When Tunnell's time is over, I'd like to be House speaker," Barnes confided.

Neither knew when that would be. Tunnell was in his first term, and there was no reason to think he might not go for a second. An open challenge was not an option. Not only had Barnes helped him win the post, a coup attempt against a speaker was certain legislative suicide.

Bullock stood up and said, "This is what you do."

He walked to a typewriter, sat down, inserted a sheet of paper, and began typing: "In the event Byron Tunnell does not seek another term as speaker, I pledge my vote to Ben Barnes for speaker." There would be no offense to Tunnell, and Barnes could get a jump on any opponents whenever a vacancy occurred.

He handed Barnes the paper. "My car is downstairs at the curb," Bullock said. "Bob Armstrong is in his office. Go over there and get his signature."[9]

Barnes did as he was told. Armstrong, a House member from Austin elected in a special election in 1963, who would later become the state's land commissioner, signed the pledge. Bullock had created the concept of what became known as the second pledge, and it would become a House tradition.

A year and a half later, in September 1964, Bullock left the TADA and once again took a turn at the private practice of law, but the experience appeared to sour him on the profession for all time. He moved to Houston to take a job with Wanda Petroleum Co., a Houston pipeline firm with large operations in Louisiana, where civil statutes are heavily influenced by the French who had settled the region. He soon bailed out and returned to Austin, telling a friend, "The Napoleonic Code was something I never figured out . . . It just ate me alive, and I didn't like it."[10]

He turned to freelance lobbying, and work wasn't hard to find. He was bright, aggressive, well connected, and wise to the legislative process. Businesses ranging from whiskey sellers to car- and truck-rental companies to light manufacturers paid for his influence and expertise. "I took whatever came along," he said.[11]

Significantly, his advice to Ben Barnes had paid off. Before the 1965 session convened, Gov. Connally, who had long since bonded with Barnes like a conjoined twin, was deeply frustrated by the legislative leadership, which he deemed ignorantly obstructionist. After the frustrations of the 1963 session, Connally realized he direly needed more allies at the top. He was powerless to effect a change in the Senate, where Smith was dug in for a long tenure as lieutenant governor, but he could finesse things in the House. Barnes had collected enough *second pledges* to be elected speaker, but Tunnell had to be nudged out of the way. Connally found the opportunity when a seat opened up on the Railroad Commission.

Would a House speaker bail out to take what to many seemed like an obscure and archaic post overseeing railroads? The Railroad Commission was archaic in name only. It had long since evolved from its original purpose of keeping railroads from gouging farmers into regulatory oversight of the state's most important economic activity: oil and gas. A House speaker had limited life expectancy, but a railroad commissioner had a statewide constituency, a durable power base, a living wage ($18,500 at the time, almost quadruple the $4,800 annual salary to which legislators had been raised), a six-year term, and a ready-made ability to raise campaign cash from the oil and gas industry. Beauford Jester, the governor whose death propelled Allan Shivers to the governorship, had been elected governor in 1948 while serving on the Railroad Commission. And, former Lt. Gov. Ben Ramsey had resigned after a decade of presiding over the Texas Senate to accept appointment to the commission from Daniel in 1961.

Connally made the offer, and Tunnell clearly was interested.

Bullock learned of it almost immediately. He was in Arlington, consulting with one of his beer clients, Carling Black Label Co., when he got a phone call from Frank Erwin, a longtime Connally crony who was emerging as a

ham-fisted and megalomaniacal member of the University of Texas Board
of Regents. "Byron Tunnell needs you," he said. "Connally has offered the
Railroad Commission to Tunnell."

When his private plane landed in Austin, Tunnell was waiting for him.
Tunnell told Bullock that only Connally, Erwin, and Atty. Gen. Carr knew
about the offer. He also told Bullock he was undecided.

"Take it," Bullock advised him.[12]

Tunnell called Connally that night and accepted. It would be a closely
held secret until the next day. Only one other person was brought into the circle. Erwin notified Barnes, who not only had 102 *second pledges*, but now had
a time advantage over other potential contenders.

Before anyone else could mobilize, Bullock, Barnes, and a few Barnes supporters set up a war room in the Driskill Hotel, near Bullock's office. They
waited until Connally officially announced Tunnell's appointment and
Tunnell announced his resignation from the House and then began working
the telephones, contacting members to shore up the pledges already in hand
and scavenging for more. Bullock also paid $800 for telegrams to follow up the
phone calls. By an overwhelming majority, Barnes became speaker, at age 26,
the youngest in Texas history.

Bullock's lobbying prospects suddenly looked brighter. Not only was
Barnes presiding over the House, but Bullock's old friend and colleague Bob
Johnson, who had marched in the segregationist army of the 1957 session, was
now House parliamentarian and director of the bill-writing Texas Legislative
Council. As the interpreter of the rules of the House, the parliamentarian
could exert considerable influence on close calls. But, Bullock was about to
discover that friendships do not always translate into influence. That session,
the state's beer wholesalers were pushing House Bill 82, which would, among
other things, redefine malt liquor so that it would be treated for tax purposes
like beer.

The liquor lobbyists opposed the measure, but presumed they would be
outvoted. They hired Bullock to try to gut the beer proposal. Bullock prepared
an amendment to do so, and took it to Barnes. Barnes hesitated, telling his
old friend that his amendment was unacceptable because it was not germane
to the original bill. Bullock persisted, and Barnes referred it to Bullock's buddy
Bob Johnson, the parliamentarian, who agreed that, indeed, it was irrelevant.
Bullock's $50,000 vanished. He was furious.[13]

That, from all indications, was the beginning of a long and bitter feud
that both amused and mystified the Austin political crowd. Neither Bullock

nor Barnes ever spoke publicly about their feud or its origins—there was frequent gossip that it was over a woman—but for three decades it was the stuff
of almost constant speculation, partly because the hostility between the two
men occasionally would be played out on a very public stage.

For Bullock, it was a pivotal point in his zigzag political path. With the
conservative wing of the Democratic Party congealing into two camps—one
belonging to Connally and the other led by Lt. Gov. Smith—it was an easy
choice for Bullock. If ever he returned to politics, it certainly would not be
through the Connally camp. For better or worse, the war with Barnes had
decided it for him. As it turned out, it was for the better.

CHAPTER 5

THE PATH BACK TO POLITICS

Hillsboro is 135 miles north of Austin, but in the mid-to-late twentieth century, it sometimes seemed that no place in Texas was closer to the Capitol. Over the years, what came to be known as *the Hillsboro Mafia* made the move south to take up high positions in state government. Robert W. Calvert started out on the board of education and went on to be speaker of the House, chairman of the state Democratic Party, and chief justice of the State Supreme Court. John Whitmire, who served in the House from Houston before becoming a fixture in the Senate, grew up in Hillsboro, where his father was the Hill County clerk. Sam Johnson, a Texas Supreme Court justice in Austin who later served on the federal appellate bench, and Frances Tarlton "Cissy" Farenthold, later a state representative from Corpus Christi and a two-time candidate for governor, had Hillsboro roots.

But the one who played a premier role in putting Bullock back on a political path was Crawford Martin, an attorney 13 years his senior who, like Bullock, came from a politically connected and active family, graduated from Hillsboro Junior College, and first won elected office at an early age. Immediately after returning from Coast Guard service during World War II, he was elected mayor of Hillsboro, and a few years later, in 1948, won the state senate seat once held by his father. He served there for 14 years, building a solid populist reputation (he pushed for insurance reform, securities regulation, and the registration of lobbyists), and eventually was elected that chamber's president pro tempore. He left the senate in 1962 to make a run for lieutenant governor, but ran fourth in the primary behind Jimmy Turman and

Preston Smith, who won the runoff. But, as Martin finished up his senate term in 1963, he moved within the Capitol to be the new Gov. Connally's secretary of state, a job he accepted as a way station en route to higher ground.

In 1966, Atty. Gen. Waggoner Carr was leaving that job to be the Democrats' nominee against Republican U.S. Sen. John Tower. Martin, with three years' exposure as secretary of state and Connally's vigorous endorsement, left the governor's staff in 1966 to run successfully for attorney general. He immediately set about implementing a plan to expand the range of that office by creating new divisions of emphasis and responsibility: antitrust, crime prevention, water control, and consumer protection. His first efforts were focused on the high-profile problems of drug abuse and organized crime, but he considered consumer protection nearly as important and potentially more valuable in proving the worth of his reforms. For a director of that division, he went back to the Hillsboro Mafia. Martin and his family had been close friends of Will Bond and family, but more than camaraderie led him to offer the job to Bullock.

As a House member, lobbyist, and lawyer, Bullock had become a serious student of the workings of state government. As in his "second pledge" advice to Barnes, he showed a talent for sizing up strengths and weaknesses and seeing to the center of issues. He also possessed an obsessive attention to detail, a fetish for organization, and an intimidating tenacity—the qualities Martin deemed essential to getting the results he envisioned from the new consumer protection division.

Bullock took the job, but despite his and Martin's friendship and long family ties, theirs was a star-crossed union. Martin was a Connally-Barnes insider, and Bullock felt he had been dealt out of that hand. He began serious work on a nationwide lawsuit against major pharmaceutical companies for fixing the prices of antibiotics, but he kept an eye on other aspects of the attorney general's office.

If lobbying had infected him with a cynicism toward government, a few months as an assistant attorney general only hardened it. He would later admit that those months were an eye-opener, "seeing all those wrong things being done."[1] What he saw also bred a peculiar resentment of the way kinships and friendships of politics influenced the interpretation of law.

"When John Connally asked for an opinion, there was no question how it would go," Bullock later told Molly Ivins of the *Texas Observer*. "The only question was how many copies of the opinion he wanted. In so many cases, you can write it so you can do what you want to do."[2]

The indignation was odd because, in the same interview, Bullock told how he, as a lobbyist, had gone to his friend, Atty. Gen. Waggoner Carr, to resolve a problem for his car- and truck-rental clients. Carr gave him a favorable legal opinion that, even to Bullock, seemed a munificent interpretation of the applicable statutes. "The law was no more on our side . . . I mean, that was no more the law than I'm the man in the moon. But it was the prettiest decision you ever saw in your life."[3] And, of course, Bullock had gotten incensed at Ben Barnes because Bullock's parliamentarian friend Bob Johnson had refused to bend the rules to find his whiskey amendment germane.

As he prepared his antitrust case against the drug companies, Bullock's festering antipathy toward the Connally crowd hardly abated. What began with his grudge against Barnes probably spilled over to just about everyone with whom Barnes was associated. That included Crawford Martin. It was natural that Bullock would gravitate toward the party faction led by Lt. Gov. Preston Smith, who was a recurrent irritation to Connally, and, by extension, to Barnes. Smith, after all, had beaten Connally's man Martin for lieutenant governor. Connally could control the House through Barnes, and he could have his way with the attorney general, but his legislative proposals still were at the mercy of Smith, who rarely showed mercy.

In 1966, Connally was so frustrated by the limited powers of the governor and bored with the ceremonial requirements of the job that he waffled at running for a third term. When he finally decided on another reelection bid, some pundits speculated that he did so mostly to hold the job for Barnes. His youthful protégé had the savvy to be governor, Connally believed, but needed a couple more years of seasoning.

Smith's ambitions were well known—he often told friends that he had wanted to be governor since he was nine years old—and Connally did not relish that prospect. "Preston Smith wouldn't even make a good county commissioner, much less a governor," Connally said.[4]

Two years later, being governor had lost its last shred of appeal, but Connally, uncertain that Barnes would enter the race, again was waffling between getting out and staying in. In the summer of 1967, while the newspapers oozed speculation about Connally's future, Preston Smith launched his campaign. Three terms as governor was enough for anyone, Smith said in his press releases and stump speeches. He dredged up words Connally had used when he ran against three-term governor Price Daniel in 1962: "I feel very strongly that no man, or no one group of men, or no one clique of people should dominate the political life and political thinking of this state. And you are going to get that any time you have a four-term governor."[5]

Smith had the beginnings of a campaign organization—a speechwriter, a public relations team, and a scheduling assistant. He also borrowed a page from the Bob Bullock playbook and solicited secondary pledges from influential Connally supporters, such as members of the State Democratic Executive Committee. It was an effective ploy. But, when Connally bowed out in late August, Barnes, to his disappointment, opted not to run to replace him. Connally then anointed as his successor Eugene Locke, an old friend who had been his campaign manager and close advisor and was a former deputy ambassador to Vietnam. A few of Smith's secondary pledges reneged, telling him they felt obligated to support Connally's choice. But some key players—Will Davis, chairman of the State Democratic Executive Committee, and Frank Erwin, Connally's good friend and chairman of the UT Board of Regents— stayed with him.

The field would eventually include ten Democrats, six of them serious contenders rushing to fill the vacuum created by Connally's absence, and four also-rans. Smith's serious opposition included Dolph Briscoe, a wealthy rancher and former three-term state representative from Uvalde; Waggoner Carr, trying to make a comeback after losing the U.S. Senate race in 1966; Don Yarborough, making his third race for governor; John L. Hill, who had been Connally's replacement for Martin as secretary of state; and Locke. Pat O'Daniel, Edward Whittenburg, Johnnie Mae Hackworthe, and Alphonzo Veloz would be cameo actors.

By getting in early, Smith had a slight advantage, but his campaign style took away some of the edge. To various extents, the others relied on radio and television advertising, which were emerging as the chosen media of campaign efficiency. Locke and Hill had catchy radio tunes that Smith disdained as "empty jingles" and "phony image" building. But Jerry Conn, Smith's speechwriter and later his biographer, noted that Locke's jingle had taken him from an unknown to a household name in just a few weeks.[6]

Smith, by contrast, appeared determined to confirm Connally's perception of him as a rube by running the only way he knew how: under-funded, under-staffed, and relying heavily on the labor-intensive tactic of making as much personal contact with as many voters as possible. In the beginning, Smith tooled around the state solo in a white Chevrolet, haunting civic clubs, diners, street corners, churches, school events—anywhere voting-age flesh congregated.

He was old-fashioned, but no amateur. As a state representative in 1945, Smith began keeping an index file of supporters and sugar daddies. He continued expanding the file when he ran for lieutenant governor in 1950, finishing third in the Democratic primary; for his races for the Texas Senate; and then for his three successful elections for lieutenant governor. By the time he entered the governor's race, the catalog had grown to 60,000 names and assorted personal details. He seemed determined to call on each and every one. It was an inefficient and laborious regimen—eating on the move, touching up speeches between stops, scheduling on short notice, studying maps for the shortest route to the most towns—and promised the smallest bang for the buck.

In September, Smith's friends recognized that those methods were woefully inadequate and intervened to get him on track. As told by Smith in his interview for the Baylor University oral history project, three of them—former House speaker Claud Gilmer, former senator and gas lobbyist Preston Mangum, and Allan Shivers's former public relations specialist Weldon Hart— paid him a visit.

"We are for you, but we just don't think you can win the race traveling by yourself," Gilmer told him. "You need someone to drive for you and help with the details of your campaign."

"I have no idea who I might get," Smith said.

"Get in touch with Bob Bullock," one of the men suggested. "He can run your campaign. Then get whoever you want as your personal assistant."[7]

Smith was acquainted with Bullock, but had had no contact with him since Bullock's days with the Texas Automobile Dealers Association.

"I'm for you and would like to work for you," Bullock said when Smith contacted him a few days later. "But right now, I just can't get involved in a campaign. I've got some bills that have to be paid."

Smith reported back to Gilmer, Mangum, and Hart that for financial reasons, Bullock was not available. Five days later, Bullock showed up at Smith's office, ready to work on the campaign.

In later years, Bullock would claim that he supported Smith so strongly that "I worked for him free," but Smith's interview for the Bullock oral history project at Baylor University hinted at a different scenario.

"I never asked him how he resolved his overdue accounts or whatever they were," Smith said a few years after Bullock's death.[8] The words suggested that if Smith didn't know exactly how Bullock's financial problems disappeared so quickly, he had soundly based suspicions.

There was no indication that Bullock left the attorney general's office under unfriendly terms, but, given Martin's alliance with Connally and Bullock's alienation from Barnes, it was not surprising. His friendship with Martin would publicly dissolve later, but when he left to formally join the Smith camp, Martin had high praise for the legal foundation Bullock had laid against the drug companies. When the case was finally settled, Martin credited Bullock with recovering more than $4 million for Texas consumers and hospitals.

Going with Smith was a gamble, however. For one thing, the office of lieutenant governor wasn't a surefire catapult to the governor's mansion. At the time Smith began his campaign, only three lieutenant governors since statehood had been elected governor—all in the mid- to late 1800s. Seven others became chief executive through resignations, abdication, impeachment, or death. Twelve lieutenant governors made the race for higher office and failed. By signing on with Smith, Bullock could have been boarding a leaking boat. But if the craft stayed afloat, his options for future government service would be considerable.

After hiring Bullock, Smith recruited Lubbock businessman and close friend Larry Teaver as his second campaign aide. In the Baylor University oral history, Smith was generous in his praise of both men. "Without them, I don't think I ever would have been elected governor of Texas," he said.

While the campaign didn't take on a more modern approach—Smith described it as the last pure people-to-people gubernatorial campaign in Texas—it definitely became more efficient.

Bullock set the pace and intensity level. "Bob was a stickler for details," Smith said. "The little things are the things that made him so important to me because he never overlooked any little thing."[9]

Applying the manic work habits for which he became legendary, Bullock had the team up at four o'clock every morning and on the road by six in order to meet their quota of ten towns a day. Steering committees were established in 567 towns with populations of more than 500, and Smith and his entourage visited each one at least once. Along the way, Bullock was expanding Smith's card file and adding new details about the individuals and their towns. He carried with him stacks of phone books, Texas Almanac sketches of communities on the day's list, and a roster of the "players and money guys" waiting at the next stop. He and Teaver also attempted, with considerable success, to orchestrate each appearance. They fed questions to audience members, who, flattered by the opportunity to address the candidate, gladly echoed them.

Bullock also was meticulous about stationing a local supporter immediately ahead of Smith in the reception lines to make certain the candidate could greet everyone by name.

"Mrs. Jones, this is Preston Smith, candidate for governor," the local would say.

"How do you do, Mrs. Jones?" Smith would say, affecting an ersatz familiarity.

The pace was frantic but was paying off. They put 55,000 miles on the Chevy, fondly nicknamed "White Lightning," and, working with Janelle Sherry, an itinerary secretary based in Austin, Bullock and Teaver began to coax Smith out of the car and into airplanes. "I shook more hands than any candidate that ever ran for office," Smith bragged.[10]

If the campaign had a glaring weakness, it was Smith's preference for working the back roads and small towns, places where he felt most comfortable, rather than the big cities. Driving back to Austin after a brief visit to Dallas, Bullock nagged his boss about the lack of a campaign office there. It was Locke's hometown, and they considered him their strongest primary opponent. "Governor, we've got to get somebody up there and open a headquarters," Bullock told him. Smith ignored him. "We at least need to have a presence there, a place where somebody could get bumper stickers, you know, a coordinator and all that."

Bullock carped so incessantly that a few miles north of Waco, Smith pulled to the side of the road.

"Bullock, get out," he said.

"How come?" Bullock asked.

"You think we have a problem not having a campaign office in Dallas, go back and open one," Smith said.

Bullock got out of the car and hitchhiked back to Dallas. A few weeks later, he called Smith and said, "You got one."

"Okay, come on back down here," Smith said. "We need to raise some money."[11]

So impressed was Smith by Bullock's organizational skills and devotion to minutiae that he told him, "Bob, you ought to consider running for office again."

Replied Bullock: "You couldn't pull me into a race with a span of mules."

Bullock also became a hard-nosed fund-raiser during that campaign and, with Smith as his mentor, he learned that ethics and legalities were no impediments to that effort. He was fond of telling one particular story of campaigning with Smith in South Texas, where voting fraud had made Duval County synonymous with political corruption. In this story, Bullock and Smith were accompanied by George Parr, the "Duke of Duval," a rancher and banker who was widely credited with putting Lyndon Johnson in the U.S. Senate by padding Johnson's vote with 203 votes from people who voted in alphabetical order, in the same handwriting and blue ink, from the infamous "Box 13" in Alice. Of those votes, Johnson got all but one, and had his 87-vote "landslide."

As they drove through the tiny county seat of San Diego, Parr handed Smith a check for $5,000.

Smith looked at it and said, "George, I can't take this check. It's written on the school district."

Parr insisted that they stop at the next bank. He went inside, cashed the check, returned to the car, and pushed the laundered wad into Smith's hands. At some future time, school district auditors might detect the odd transaction, but for now, Parr trumped any public body in Duval County.[12]

The May 4 Democratic primary gave Yarborough—a liberal who had narrowly lost to Connally in the Democratic runoff of 1962, and lost badly to him in 1964—top seed with 421,607 votes. But Smith ran a solid second—just 34,732 votes behind, or less than two percent, and more than 120,000 votes ahead of Carr, who finished third.

Swimming against history, Smith found himself in a position to become the first lieutenant governor to be elected governor in the 20th century—provided he could knock off Yarborough in the runoff. There would be a Republican on the ballot in the general election, but the GOP was still a minority party and generally was thought to be mere token opposition. Smith's campaign was invigorated and scratching for new tactics. It was still grassroots, people to people, but there was limited time to press the flesh. The airplane was put to more frequent use, and Bullock came up with a novel appeal. With his card files, phone books, and other resources, he selected 47,000 people across the state with the last name "Smith" to receive a personal letter from the candidate: "Don't you think it is about time one of us was governor?"

In the runoff, Smith won handily: 767,490, or 55.3 percent, to 621,226 for Yarborough. Compared to the total of 1,388,716 cast in the Democratic runoff, and the 1,750,652 in the first primary, the Republican primary turnout was feeble. Only 104,765 votes were cast. Paul Eggers picked up 65,501, enough to take the nomination. The numbers, though, were deceptive. Historically, the Democratic primary was the only one that counted, and therefore many voters who were Republican in spirit shunned that party's bland primaries to vote in the other's, to ensure that the most conservative Democratic candidate was left standing. With a conservative Democrat pitted against a conservative Republican, nobody lost except the liberals. Too, nominal Democrats in 1968 had a greater imperative to influence that party's primary. Nationally, Democrats were shredded by issues such as the Vietnam War, civil rights, women's liberation, campus revolution, the counterculture, and others. It was the year of the pivotal Tet Offensive and Lyndon Johnson's decision to leave the White House. America was growing weary of protest and conflict.

Preston Smith sensed what was happening. New Left, antiwar senators such as Eugene McCarthy and George McGovern, who had spoken out against Johnson's Vietnam excursion, were positioning themselves to challenge his likely heir, Vice President Hubert Humphrey. "The change in the Democratic Party began in the presidential race that year," Smith later reflected. The Supreme Court's *Brown* decision had kick-started the Republican rise in the South; Johnson's civil rights legislation gave it traction, and his abdication, leaving the party open to New Left squatters, gave it horsepower. Some of that turmoil was certain to slosh down to state and local elections.

Even though Humphrey won the Democratic nomination, despite the antiwar protests at the party's convention in Chicago, Alabama Gov. George Wallace's American Independent Party candidacy provided another outlet for protest. In Texas, Humphrey won a narrow plurality, with 1,266,804 votes to Republican Richard Nixon's 1,227,844—a lead of 38,960 votes. Humphrey had 41.1 percent, Nixon 39.9 percent. Wallace's 584,269 Texas votes gave him 19 percent.

Smith got 1,662,019 votes in the general election, enough to win comfortably, and 400,000 votes ahead of Humphrey. But it wasn't the skateboard ride his predecessors had enjoyed. The shocker was the number of votes that went to the Republican, Eggers: 1,254,333—outpolling even his party's presidential candidate.

No Republican candidate for governor had ever come close to that tally. Just two years earlier, in a non-presidential election year, John Connally had swamped his GOP opponent, T. E. Kennerly, 1,037,517 to 368,025. The 1968 results demonstrated that the GOP was regaining some of the momentum that it was exhibiting in 1962, before it was abruptly halted by the 1963 assassination of President John F. Kennedy, and LBJ's 1964 landslide.

Something profound was stirring in the precincts, giving off the odor of the future. It is possible that at the time no one picked up the scent better than Robert Bullock.

January 1969. A new governor. A new lieutenant governor. A new House speaker. But not exactly a new day in Texas politics. In fact, old frictions surfaced even before the new faces were inaugurated. The first was over the details of the inaugural balls—a total of six scattered around Austin. Bowing primarily to the governor-elect's tastes, the planners enlisted country singers—Glen Campbell, Jimmy Dean, Buck Owens, and Charley Pride among them—for five of the galas, and the sixth would offer rock 'n' roll for the younger crowd.

Barnes wanted an act of greater stature, namely Robert Goulet and his wife, Carol Lawrence. They would lend a more sophisticated air to the ball, he argued. In the words of Jerry Hall, a reporter who had agreed to be Smith's press secretary: "Country had not yet become cool." Smith held firm. "I've never heard of this fellow *Goo-let*," he said.

The remark was passed along to syndicated columnists Rowland Evans and Robert Novak by someone—it wasn't hard to guess who—wanting to let the nation know that a "cornpone" politician was about to become governor of Texas. After he had been governor for a few years, Smith had breakfast with Novak and told him he had intentionally mispronounced the singer's name. "Besides," he said, "I saw him on television the other night, and he forgot the words to the Star-Spangled Banner."[13]

CHAPTER 6

"JUST A WASHED-UP LOBBYIST"

J ohn Connally did not leave office in the best of moods. His chosen successor, Barnes, had opted instead to become lieutenant governor. His second choice, Eugene Locke, had made a dismal showing in the Democratic primary, finishing fifth. Instead, he was being replaced by an unpolished bumpkin for whom he had nothing but contempt. *Wouldn't make a good county commissioner.* Connally had a parting shot left in his pistol, one that may have just grazed the new governor but hit his favorite staffer square in the ego.

Before he was sworn in, Smith offered Bullock and Teaver jobs on his staff. During the campaign, Bullock had made a reputation for fund-raising, so much so that he was gradually being perceived as Smith's "bagman." Smith valued his organizational abilities just as much. In the governor's office Bullock's responsibilities would be primarily legal and administrative, which included the function of appointments secretary. It was an important job, one that would give Bullock large influence over the shape of state government. In consultation with the governor, he would select and vet individuals to fill about 1,500 appointive positions, many of them high profile—and highly sought after. The boards of regents for the University of Texas, Texas A&M, and the University of Houston were among the most coveted. The Texas Parks and Wildlife Department board, created at Connally's behest by merging the Parks Commission and the Game and Fish Commission, was another. Such appointments are not only one of the few ways the constitutionally weak governor can etch a lasting signature on agencies, programs, and policies, they also reward past contributors and affect future fund-raising.

Connally's exit slap at Smith was a practice known as midnight appointments—11th-hour moves by a departing governor to project his influence over state government beyond his tenure in office. It also deprived the new governor of some of the spoils of victory. It was not unheard of, but not common either. At any given time, three or four hundred vacancies may have existed, many of them on small, obscure boards or commissions. If a governor loaded up a few on his way out, it usually caused some controversy. But Connally pushed it to the point that eventually midnight appointments were outlawed. Connally—knowing he had his man Barnes presiding over the Senate that would have to confirm the appointments—was more audacious than his predecessors. He made a slew of such appointments, and few were obscure. "He appointed the plum jobs," said Randall "Buck" Wood, who at that time was a 23-year-old lawyer working in the secretary of state's office. Connally made three appointments each to the UT and A&M boards, and "Smith was very upset about it. Bullock was absolutely furious."[1]

Wood had never met Bullock, but he was about to. Unwilling to let the midnight appointments stand, Bullock prepared for a legal battle. Having a secretary and no other staff, he placed a call to Martin Dies, Jr., the new secretary of state, whose office was next door to the governor's.

"You got a young lawyer over here that I've heard some good things about, and he's got some experience," Bullock said. "I need him right now because we've got some problems on these appointments and I want some research done."

Dies summoned Wood and told him, "Go over to the governor's office and see Bob Bullock."[2]

It was the beginning of what would be a professional and personal relationship that would endure for as long as Bullock lived. In future years, Wood would work for Bullock, run personal errands for him and, even after leaving government and establishing a private law practice, be available when Bullock called with a crisis. The predicament that day early in 1969 was finding the legal ammo to fire back at John Connally.

Wood walked into Bullock's office and introduced himself. "You wanted to see me, Mr. Bullock?"

"Drop the Mr.," Bullock said.

As Bullock began to explain the project, Wood realized he had "walked in on a private war." Connally was attempting to continue to perpetuate his power, he thought, and Bullock was adamantly determined that would not happen. He was, time would reveal, even more determined than Smith to prosecute the war.

The A&M appointments were relatively easy to challenge. They were illegal because the terms of the regents had not expired. Therefore, there were no vacancies. UT was another matter. "The language of the constitution and statutes regarding UT were more obscure," Wood said.[3]

The simplest resolution would have been for the Senate to reject Connally's 11th-hour appointments, but, with Barnes presiding over that chamber, such an outcome was unlikely. Wood suggested another strategy: Smith would appoint three new members to the UT board, creating competing slates. One of Smith's appointees would have legal standing to file a declaratory judgment action, leaving it to the courts to resolve the matter. Bullock agreed, and so did Smith, at least initially. They selected three candidates, but before he made their appointments official, Smith blinked. He chose another battlefield, one where his chances of success were no better than they were in the Senate: The attorney general's office.

Bullock and Wood were incredulous. Requesting a formal opinion from Crawford Martin was tantamount to surrender. Martin, they believed, owed his job to Connally and had spent six years writing favorable opinions for his benefactor. Why would he not now be able to give a sympathetic read to the law? As if on cue, Martin ruled that Connally's appointments to the UT board were legal. His formal opinion was not binding—did not have the force of law—but it effectively ended the war. Smith still could have pursued a remedy in the courts, but without the support of the attorney general, it would be with a severely weakened hand.

Bullock, seething over his boss's capitulation, nonetheless plowed ahead with screening candidates for other appointments. Smith was impressed with his work. "Bob Bullock was extremely effective in selecting the right people," he said.[4]

Not in every instance. In the administration's early days, Bullock urged Smith to hire a Mexican American for his staff. At that time, Hispanics held few high-level positions in government but were a growing segment of the state's population. Attention to demographics, Bullock was learning, was smart politics.

The first person he selected was personable and intelligent and had an impressive resume. Smith accepted the recommendation without challenge. "We appointed him, and he was working, and then it turned up that he had been involved in two or three bank robberies," Smith said. "When we found out and confronted him, he resigned without any problem. We found another man who was just about as good."[5]

Appointments to minor boards and commissions seldom draw much attention—not much more than a short press release condensed in the appointees' hometown newspapers. Not so with the newly established Board of Psychologists. Prior to the 1969 legislative session, there was no regulatory board for that profession and, consequently, it was a field populated by competent professionals as well as many with questionable credentials and reputations. The psychologists had tried for years to establish a certification board that would filter out the riff-raff. They finally got it, but there ensued heated lobbying skirmishes to win seats on the nine-member board.

Buck Wood, whom Bullock had drafted once again to vet candidates, recalled what happened: "There were two groups—those who were the professional Ph.D. psychologists, and then you had the quacks, as Bullock termed them. There was a whole segment of people who had been counselors and had been calling themselves psychologists. They were afraid they were not going to get certified, so they wanted some representation on the board. One of Bullock's good buddies, a former lobbyist, was representing the less elite of the practicing psychologists. So he came to see Bob [and] brought a list of people. He wanted a majority on the board, or as many as he could get. Bullock trusted his buddy. On a board like that, Smith wasn't going to spend a lot of time thinking about it. So Preston announces these appointments. There's no fanfare or anything. He just signs the appointments and sends them over to the Senate. Well, the reputable psychologists went crazy. It turned out that two or three individuals that Bob had gotten Preston to appoint had horrible reputations . . . all sorts of complaints against them, really bad stuff. Amazingly enough, it made a big news splash. It was very embarrassing. Preston had to withdraw a number of them. Bullock really fell out of favor."[6]

His influence inside the governor's office may have been diminished momentarily by the episode, but Bullock's value to Smith remained indelible. He was a crackerjack fund-raiser, and he was the keeper of the treasured card files. What had begun as Smith's catalog of 60,000 names—the core of his political power—had, over time, become Bullock's. He reorganized it, adding details and thousands of new names. And he stayed in touch with the major players and moneymen.

As Smith's first term was ending and his reelection effort was cranking up, Bullock made a trip to Houston for a series of meetings with potential contributors and returned in a state of high excitement. He called Wood into his office and hoisted a large briefcase—some said he actually carried the kind of bag that doctors used to make house calls—and emptied the contents onto his desk. "I think this is the most anybody has ever raised in one fund-raising trip in the history of Texas," he boasted.[7]

Wood was impressed. He assessed the mound of cash and checks and esti-mated it could have totaled $75,000 or more, a hefty wad in 1969.[8] He began to think that Bullock was marked for something higher than a gubernatorial assistant. It wasn't just his prodigious fund-raising, but his eagerness to spend long hours exploring the problems of state government and to find quick fixes.

"You ought to think about running for office," Wood told him as their friendship grew stronger.

"Aw, I'm just a washed-up lobbyist," Bullock said, in one of his frequent moments of self-effacement. "Besides, I couldn't get elected to anything after all those racist bills I voted for back in the fifties."[9]

Wood wasn't the only one impressed by Bullock's fund-raising prowess. Dick Cory, a 26-year House member who was already in the House when Bullock and Bob Johnson got there, told of a South Texas hunting trip he went on that included them. They and three others decided to wet their whis-tles after a hot afternoon of walking around fields chasing birds. They stopped in a bar to get some drinks and food.

"Johnson leaned over to me and said, 'Watch this,'" Cory recalled years later. "Then Johnson said to Bullock, 'Bob, you know that job you've got now? By the end of this year, you should be independently wealthy. And by the end of next year, you should be headed for prison.' Bullock jumped to his feet, upended the table, and drinks and things went all over everyone. When we all started laughing, Bullock realized he'd been had."[10]

Carlton Carl, who'd started work in the governor's office as a student intern, said those who worked with Bullock in Smith's campaign generally had their drink tabs picked up by Bullock.

"There was a lot of cash money in the Preston Smith campaign," Carl observed.[11]

Texas, in the sixties, was still living on its natural resources and not much else. When oil revenues were up, the treasury was flush. When oil prices tanked, the budgets got lean and the Legislature had to pass some kind of tax bill—usually one barely enough to provide minimum services. Outside Texas, the state was often regarded as a backwater that ranked near the bottom in almost every category of state services, from education to public health to welfare. Spending was generous only in those areas—highways among them —favored by the lobbyists who dictated legislation, or by the few powerful legislators who could earmark spending for their districts. Smith's first term was a lean period. The sales tax enacted in 1961 was only two percent, and the political carnage that followed its passage discouraged any thought of increasing it. Likewise, any mention of a state income tax was tantamount to stepping in front of a speeding truck. The trick for the governor and lawmakers was to come up with a tax bill that "wouldn't get you beat," in Wood's words.[12]

Patching loopholes and tweaking fees were not the answers. Bullock, though not specifically charged with developing Smith's legislative agenda, went looking for potential revenue. He found it on the Gulf Coast, where the state's refineries were concentrated. At that time, Texas churned out about half of the refined chemicals consumed in America. Bullock reasoned that since about 80 percent of Texas's output was exported to other states, it provided an opportunity to collect taxes from out of state. He persuaded Smith to propose a 1.5 percent levy on all refined chemicals, which would include everything from gasoline to the base ingredients for paints and plastics. The tax on Texas consumers of those refined products would be small, but the money that could be raked in from other states, it appeared, could be enormous.

In the governor's office, the full impact of the tax was mostly guesswork. Smith's staff was small and had little expertise in such matters. Legislators also had small staffs and limited resources. The proper official to turn to for research was the state comptroller, the tax-collecting and revenue-estimating arm of government. But that office had been mired in the Dark Ages for as long as anyone could remember. Economic forecasting, like enforcement, was in short supply. The only place the governor and legislators could get expert counsel on the wisdom and likely consequences of their actions was from the industries they were taxing and regulating. Individual lobbyists could be called on, as could the Texas Research League, an innocuous-sounding outfit that was actually founded and funded by businesses and industries.

Smith's bill was drafted and introduced in the House, where it was assigned to the revenue and taxation committee. When hearings were held, the refiners produced a witness to shred the legislation. The tax, he argued, would "stack" or "compound" in ways its proponents had not envisioned. If a refinery produced a certain chemical, it was taxed. If that chemical was then cooked into another chemical or combined with other chemicals for a different use, it would be taxed again. That process could be repeated several times. The expert witness held up a bucket of paint and recited the various chemicals that went into the end product and the number of times those ingredients would be subject to the new tax. The result, he said, would be to double the cost of a bucket of common house paint. Explain that to your constituents.

The bill was dead, and it became the stuff of jokes for the rest of the session. Although he also laughed about it, Bullock was embarrassed. Not angry, but definitely wiser. "I think that experience taught Bullock that he never wanted to be on the short end of information again," Wood said. "It's something that followed him all the rest of his life."[13]

CHAPTER 7

A TURNING POINT IN HISTORY

D ue in no small part to Bullock's prodigious fund-raising, Preston Smith's return to the governor's office in 1970 was essentially a repeat of his first success, but he continued to make minor political history by being the first Democrat in Texas history to draw no gubernatorial primary opponent. In November, he again faced Paul Eggers and, again, won by about 158,675 votes of 2,306,765 cast—or 53.4 percent.

As was customary in Texas, the voters had given him his second term and, in all probability, a third was in his future. That *probability*, however, did not take into account a securities and banking scandal that had been simmering for a few months and was about to wreak carnage in the corridors of power. It came to be known simply as "Sharpstown," and its impact was such that two decades later, Houston author Mickey Herskowitz, in his book *Sharpstown Revisited*, termed it a "turning point in Texas history."[1]

In 1969, the year Preston Smith first moved into the governor's office, some events occurred that caused state and federal banking regulators, as well as the U.S. Securities and Exchange Commission, eventually to take a close look at the wheeling and dealing of Frank Sharp, a Houston banker, financier, and insurance tycoon. His empire ranged from shopping malls to banks to country clubs to real estate developments. What attracted the attention of regulators were some curious loans his Sharpstown Bank had made to important people so they could buy stock in his Bankers National Life Insurance Co. Then, the government believed, Sharp manipulated the stock price to ensure that those powerful people turned a quick and handsome profit. Sharp's motive? To gain passage of legislation favorable to his banking business.

Among those who had cashed in on Bankers Life stock were Gov. Smith, who pocketed $62,500, and Gus Mutscher, Ben Barnes's successor as speaker of the House, who picked up $30,000. There were others scattered through Texas's political ranks. Until the investigations became public, none of the beneficiaries found it noteworthy that they would be so generously rewarded by a fatcat with a legislative agenda.

In the summer of 1969, during a special legislative session called by Smith, the House passed a resolution praising Sharp. At the same time, Fort Worth Rep. Tommy Shannon, a Mutscher lieutenant, introduced the two bills Sharp wanted passed. They would have created a privately funded insurance system to be regulated by the state banking commission, not the Federal Deposit Insurance Commission. It would have radically altered the way banking business was done in Texas. Banks could have offered insurance on deposits up to $100,000—the FDIC cap was $15,000—and the banks, such as Sharp's, would have been the winners. It also would have required banks to have just 10 percent in reserve to protect loans, instead of 25 percent under the federal system. This would allow Sharp to loan himself more of his bank depositors' money to build more projects faster—loans that would be overseen by state regulators, not the feds.

Near the end of the special session, the bills easily passed both houses. By the time they reached Smith's desk, however, the larger banks had organized an intense lobbying front against them. Among the opponents was former Gov. Allan Shivers, himself a big banker. Smith wilted under the firestorm and vetoed the bills. Persuading him to take that action may have been the biggest favor a lobbyist had ever done for him. It helped remove some of the bribery suspicion surrounding his $62,500 profit.

But, the death of Sharp's bills did not halt the federal investigations. In January 1971, as Smith was being inaugurated for a second term, the SEC filed suit in Fort Worth, alleging securities fraud and misrepresentation by Sharp and 27 others, including corporations. The most prominent political name on the list was former House Speaker and Attorney General Waggoner Carr, but the federal actions sent tremors through Austin and the offices of every pol who had ever met Sharp or held stock in his insurance company or voted for his bills. While not accused, Smith and Mutscher were among those mentioned in the SEC complaint. No one knew if other indictments would follow or who else might be smeared, fairly or unfairly, once the cases got into court.

Depositors made a punishing run on Sharp's bank, and it was officially closed a week after the SEC action, but the bank was a peripheral matter.

Rumors and speculation had it that the Richard Nixon administration was hell-bent on bringing down potent Texas Democrats, and the sweetheart stock deals, which reeked of payoff, might be used to bag a bunch of them, if not by convicting, then by discrediting them.

As the 1971 session moved along, the fog of Sharpstown wafted through the Capitol like a sulfur cloud, and reputations crumbled like stale biscuits. A group of rebellious representatives who became known as the Dirty Thirty tried to force the House to investigate its leaders' roles in Sharpstown, but Mutscher, who had a despotic hold on that chamber, quashed the uprising. They had little effect—at that time—except to keep Sharpstown in the news. However, as the session moved along, so did the authorities. In the next round of indictments, Mutscher was indicted for bribery by a Travis County grand jury at the behest of District Attorney Bob Smith. When Mutscher was convicted, on March 15, 1972, he resigned as speaker. He was replaced by Rayford Price of Palestine who, ironically, would lose his legislative seat in a Democratic primary runoff.

To some who made a living trying to read the political tea leaves of Austin, it appeared that fallout from the scandal had spilled over to the governor's office. Specifically, the tea readers found omens in a pair of appointments Smith made that summer.

Larry Teaver, who had taken over as appointments secretary after Bullock moved on to chief counsel and campaign manager, was appointed to a seat on the State Insurance Board. By itself, Teaver's appointment raised few flags. Besides his real estate development business, he also was an insurance agent. But, a week later, a vacancy developed on the Ninth Court of Civil Appeals in Beaumont. The governor placed a telephone call to Martin Dies, Jr., his secretary of state, to ask if he was interested in the judicial slot. He was. Smith then placed a call to Bullock, who, despite a few fumbles with appointments and false starts on tax schemes, had served him well.

"I'm going to appoint you secretary of state," he said.

"You've got to be kidding," Bullock said.

"No. I think, Bob, you'll do a good job," the governor persisted.

After a pause, Bullock said, "Well, governor, I would sure appreciate it. But . . . I know a lot of people have helped you more than I did who are more qualified to do this."

"Well, but you're the man I want, Bob."[2]

The deal was done. Once again, Bullock found himself in a position not just of influence, but of potential future political bounty. As the state's chief elections officer, he would be in contact with local election officials in every county, as well as the leaders of both political parties. As the keeper of corporate records, he would have direct contact with countless honchos of business and industry. Additionally, he frequently would act as Smith's personal representative, standing in for him at various ceremonies and functions. Several secretaries of state had gone on to statewide elected office: Ben Ramsey to lieutenant governor, and Gerald Mann, John Ben Shepperd, and Crawford Martin to attorney general, just to name some of them. Wrote Sam Kinch, Jr., longtime *Dallas Morning News* reporter: "In short, Bullock had an appointive job that . . . yielded countless names, telephone numbers, and addresses of thousands of Texans. The fact that he kept and used all of that information, and kept building on it, was a key to his political success."[3]

Immediately, there was two-pronged speculation, one about Smith's future and the other about Bullock's. Under the headline "Aides' Departure Indicates Smith Won't Run Again," *Houston Chronicle* reporter Bo Byers wrote:

> Departure of two of Gov. Preston Smith's top administrative staff members—both by appointment from the governor—indicates Smith has abandoned a 1972 race for reelection.
>
> Smith probably will continue to suggest a third-term bid as one of the possible alternatives in his plans for the future, but few will take him seriously—if they had done so up to now.
>
> Teaver and Bullock were two of the key men in Smith's campaigns for governor in 1968 and 1970. It is highly unlikely he would have moved them from their staff positions . . . if he planned to run again next year.[4]

At the same time, there were reports in the major Texas newspapers that the nomination was destined for trouble. The *Dallas Times Herald* called it a surprise "because Smith conceded last year Bullock could not be named to any job that requires Senate confirmation because of his deep differences with Lt. Gov. Ben Barnes."[5] Too, Bullock had told friends that he would be named executive director of the newly created Texas Vending Commission.

If appointed to any other agency or commission, Bullock's term would have been for a set period and could have extended beyond Smith's service as governor. The secretary of state, however, serves at the governor's pleasure, and thus Bullock would exit in tandem with his boss. For that reason, Smith may have believed that the Senate would more easily confirm him without resistance from Barnes. One senator, Charles Herring, who represented the Austin district in which Bullock lived, would have had veto power over the appointment, but he told reporters, "I will not object. It is traditionally the right of the governor to appoint anybody he wants as secretary of state. The secretary of state is the right arm of the governor."[6]

Still, the buzz was that Barnes would use his considerable powers to defeat the nomination. The Legislature was not in session, and would not meet again until 1973, unless Smith called a special session, which seemed unlikely because of the Sharpstown hangover. Whenever the subject came up, Bullock advised Smith against calling a special session because he feared that maverick legislators might use it to impeach the governor.

There also could have been a survival impulse to his counsel. Until the Senate acted on his nomination, Bullock was the secretary of state, free to do his job.

Inside the secretary of state's office, longtime employees greeted the arrival of their new boss with trepidation.

After the surprise announcement was made, Sybil Dickinson, who had worked there for more than 20 years and often behaved as though she were the secretary of state, walked into Wood's office with an unhappy look.

"Randall," she said, "We've got a problem. Bob Bullock doesn't know anything about secretary of state."

"Well, there's not much to know," Wood said. True. It was the highest appointive position in state government, but one of the least demanding. The office practically ran itself.

"Oh, this is going to be horrible," she said.

"I know Bob," said Wood, who was then director of elections. "We get along fine."[7]

His reassurances calmed her only a little. Because of his work for Smith —raising funds and attacking the governor's political opponents—Bullock had gained a reputation of being somewhat unsavory, a bagman, a hatchet man. His mood swings, his erratic veering from project to project, his growing practice of calling associates and underlings at three or four o'clock in the morning, created the perception of a loose cannon. Wood had come to know him well, and even as he tried to soothe his anxious co-worker, he sensed that the office was about to change, that Bullock, now running his own show, was not one to preside over a sleepy hollow. It was an accurate perception.

Bullock hit the door with a frenzied thirst for information. He wanted to know everything at once. He constantly pumped employees for information about their jobs, quizzed the attorneys about the range of laws that affected the office and, drawing on advice he had picked up earlier from H. C. Pittman at the auto dealers, he believed an education came in with each day's post. He would spend hours reading the mounds of mail—much of it dull and routine, such as Uniform Commercial Code submissions or mundane corporate filings.

As much mail went out as came in, and it was far too much for one man to sign personally. As had been the custom, an employee asked Bullock for copies of his signature to be etched into a printing block. Bullock tersely refused.

Bullock called Wood and his assistant, Don Ray, into his office and asked about the signature stamp business.

"Bob, there's a lot of stuff that goes out of here every day. Most of it is just routine. It's cover letters. You know, 'Here's your corporate charter' kind of stuff," Wood said.

Bullock bristled. "I'm going to sign the stuff that goes out of here," he said. "You bring it in here and put it on that table right over there and I'll sign it."

Bullock was proud of his signature. Over the years, he had spent countless hours practicing and perfecting it. He didn't just dash off a quick scribble; he created art. For a week and a half, he was mostly sequestered in his office, signing stacks of documents and falling further and further behind while his amused underlings speculated on the life expectancy of this new policy.

Wood arrived for work one morning and had just sat down at his deck when he heard Bullock bellow, "Buck!"

Wood walked to his door.

"Tell somebody to get in here and get this shit off my desk and get it out of here," Bullock said. "I don't want to see any more of this stuff ever again."

Wood broke into laughter.

"I know you and Don are sitting out there watching me and knowing this wasn't going to work."

"Yeah, Bullock, we tried to warn you," Wood said. "You weren't interested in listening, so we figured we would let you find out on your own."

Wood braced for one of Bullock's explosive tirades, but it never came. Instead, he joined in laughing at his own folly.[8]

A pattern began to emerge in Bullock's behavior. Anger, whether justified or not, would erupt like a geyser and abate just as quickly. No one was certain whether the outbreaks were genuine or a contrived part of a developing management scheme. Maybe he read this in a book. A terrified worker is an efficient worker. As often as not, the displays of temper occurred when they were least expected, and failed to appear when they were most expected.

A prime example recalled by Wood:

After settling in as secretary of state, Bullock decided that he wanted the huge card file of political information that remained in the governor's office. It belonged to Preston Smith, but Bullock had played a large role in compiling it. Smith wanted to keep the material, but agreed to let Bullock, who was still his chief fund-raiser, copy it. By Smith's estimate, there were 200,000 four-by-six cards, and duplicating them would be no small undertaking. The secretary of state's office had the latest Xerox copiers, but they were slow and labor intensive. Four cards at a time had to be placed on a curved glass under which a scanning light made a lethargic pass. Several seconds would pass before the reproduction was disgorged.

Bullock assigned members of his staff—state employees working on state time—to perform what was essentially a political task. At that time, his office employed several part-time workers called *charter boys*, whose jobs were to copy and file corporate charters, amendments, and other documents. Once the card file reproduction began, the charter boys often found that they could not do their jobs because the Xerox machines were not available. That went on for weeks. One young man, a law student, was annoyed by the delays and also believed it was an improper use of state workers and equipment. After a couple of weeks, he expressed his frustrations to a friend, another UT student who happened to be a reporter for the *Daily Texan*. Soon, the young journalist was in Bullock's office asking questions about the card file and the improper use of state workers and equipment. After his story was published in the campus newspaper, it was picked up by the state's major dailies. Bullock erupted, partly over the embarrassing news stories and partly over what he perceived to be the disloyalty of an employee. He ordered Don Ray to find the leaker and fire him.

It could have been anyone in his office or the governor's. Ray made inquiries but got nowhere. The young charter boy assumed he would eventually be identified and decided to confess. He told Ray he was probably the source for the story. It was not malicious, he said, he was just blowing off steam with a friend and did not realize it would turn into a news story.

"Well, I suspect this is the end of your tenure, but just sit right here," Ray said.

He walked over to Bullock's office and said, "Bob, I found your leak."

"Have him come in here," Bullock snapped.

The young man haltingly slid into Bullock office and was treated to an exhibition of howling rage. "Loyalty means something," Bullock preached, with veins straining against the skin of his forehead. "I give you a job over here, and you do this to me. If you're going to do the rest of your life like this, you're going to find it doesn't work."

The lecture went on for several minutes and, inexplicably, Bullock abruptly became calm and forgiving.

"You know, when I was your age I'd probably have done the same damn thing," he said. "Get your ass back to work."[9]

As expected, Bullock was quickly bored by the perfunctory, routine duties he had assumed. He was not a good speaker and disliked those occasions when he was called upon to stand in for the governor. He fidgeted for a cause, a war to fight. He didn't have to look far. In fact, he didn't have to look at all. The cause came to him, in the form of a series of lawsuits challenging the constitutionality of the Texas election code. As chief elections officer, he was the defendant. Oddly, it would be the incident that would supply the first building blocks of his future political base.

It happened like this:

In June of that year, President Richard Nixon certified the 26th Amendment to the U.S. Constitution, lowering the voting age from 21 to 18. Anticipating that event, the Texas Legislature amended the election code to require single voters under the age of 21 to register in the counties where their parents lived, which meant that college students or military personnel would have to go back home to vote. The stated motive for the new law was that concentrations of students in college or military towns would give them "undue political power."

Establishment politicians, particularly conservatives, had reason to fear what, to many, appeared to be an uncertain future. In those days, college students tended to be more liberal and more politically active than their parents, and they had the numbers to make themselves heard. Across the country, students were rallying behind antiwar candidates and the Democratic Party was in a clear leftward drift. Conservative Democrats in Texas were determined to hold the line in their state.

However, lawsuits challenging the constitutionality of the new provision began showing up in federal courts around the state, naming the secretary of state as defendant. The first to be heard was filed in Denton, home of North Texas State University, by two 19-year-old students, Steve Muncy and Wesley Ownby, whose parents lived elsewhere. Ownby would have been forced to register and vote in Las Vegas, New Mexico, or go through the cumbersome absentee voting process.

Bullock not only announced that he agreed that the provision was unconstitutional, but he made a trip to Sherman to testify against the state in a hearing before U.S. District Judge William Wayne Justice, who declared the act "null and void and in violation of the Fourteenth and Twenty-sixth Amendments to the U.S. Constitution."

Bullock may have angered the establishment in Austin, but he had made loyal friends among a large bloc of newly enfranchised voters. Moreover, he had revealed a streak of the maverick he had always been and the reformer he was becoming.

To the dismay of his friends, he was revealing another streak, one that they interpreted as a classic symptom of manic depression. Besides chain-smoking and polishing off a fifth of Old Charter a day, he was beset by mood swings that reached soaring highs and abysmal depths. One day he would be withdrawn and morose and steep himself in problem-solving. The next, he would be flying, and in those periods, life was one long party of all-night drinking and carousing and reckless behavior.

One night, during a bourbonized domestic quarrel, his wife ordered him out of the house and he drove to the apartment of his friend and advisor, Carlton Carl, to spend the night. Carl was away, and Bullock couldn't get into the apartment, so he crawled into the back seat of what he *thought* was his friend's 1966 Chevrolet Bellaire. The next morning, he woke up as the car was motoring up Interstate 35, the driver unaware that he had a passenger. Bullock sat up and startled the stranger by announcing, "Hi there, I'm Bob Bullock, your secretary of state."[10]

CHAPTER 8

SPOILING FOR A FIGHT

I n the process of winning the hearts and minds of young voters, Bullock was coming to the realization that he could make a difference, a fact that both emboldened and energized him. It seemed there was no fight he wouldn't start or one that he would not join with relish, even those not squarely on his turf.

Six weeks into his tenure, he weighed in on the losing side of the fray over the election of a new state Democratic Party chairman. Along with Gov. Smith, Bullock supported Agriculture Commissioner John C. White, but the post went to a John Connally loyalist, Roy Orr, a conservative Democrat and the mayor of the Dallas suburb of DeSoto. It appeared to be another victory for the Connally faction and defeat for Smith's side.

Bullock, his friends and enemies were learning, was not a good loser. Three months after Orr assumed the party post, he had to confront Bullock again. A member of the Dallas County Commissioners Court died, and County Judge Lew Sterrett appointed Orr to fill the vacancy. It was the statutory responsibility of the secretary of state to determine the eligibility of a newly installed officeholder. If Bullock found Orr ineligible, he could refuse to certify him, thereby preventing him from performing his official duties. Bullock could hardly conceal his eagerness to force Orr to resign as party chairman if he wanted to be certified as a commissioner.

Newspapers reported that Bullock had assigned his entire legal staff to researching the question: Is there a potential conflict of interest if a political party boss also serves as a county commissioner with powers over election machinery? "I don't know whether he is eligible or not," Bullock said. "My whole staff is studying it."[1] It was not a trivial issue, but the law was imprecise enough to invite a range of interpretations. Section 3.04 of the election code, which prohibited county party chairmen from holding public office, said nothing about state chairmen.

With national elections a year away, many Democrats—especially liberals—had reason for their reservations about Orr: He had worked behind the scenes to oppose reform rules that promised greater participation in the party for women, young people, and minorities. Too, they had reservations about Orr's loyalty to the party and his ability, or will, to help the Democrats' national candidates carry Texas in 1972. John Connally was cozying up to the Nixon administration and was potentially the ringleader of an exodus to the GOP. Orr was considered a likely member of that pilgrimage. In a news release, State AFL-CIO President Roy Evans said, "We can only reemphasize our belief that Mr. Orr has been put into this office by the John Connally group to be a Trojan horse inside the Democratic Party. He has been and will continue to be a divisive force of questionable value."[2]

Two days after Orr's appointment and swearing in as a county commissioner, Bullock announced that he was withholding certification on the grounds of a potential conflict of interest. Dallas County Dist. Atty. Henry Wade then issued a memorandum at law stating that Orr could hold both jobs, and he told the county auditor to pay Orr his commissioner's salary. After a few days of public verbal exchanges, the issue evaporated.

Bullock had already moved on to angering a broader audience. Potential candidates were shuffling their cards for the 1972 state primaries and Smith, despite the Sharpstown factor, announced he would run for reelection and that Bullock would again be his chief fund-raiser and campaign strategist. Although Bullock was morphing into an unabashed liberal, he was intensely loyal to the conservative governor and pummeled his opponents—Democrat and Republican—at every opportunity. He cranked out press releases slamming Lt. Gov. Ben Barnes for his nonsupport of Smith's legislative agenda and Atty. Gen. Crawford Martin for his vigorous defense of the state's archaic election laws.

But, those he loved offending the most were Republicans. He denounced them as "silly" and "idiotic" and at least once tried to get GOP party officials indicted. That occurred after the GOP offered a $5,000 reward to any candidate who could defeat House Speaker Gus Mutscher or Appropriations

Chairman W. S. "Bill" Heatly. Bullock declared that the offer was a violation of state election law and took the matter to Travis County District Attorney Bob Smith. The GOP withdrew the offer, but not its anger.[3]

Demanding his removal, GOP Chairman George Willeford told reporters, "Over and over he has displayed naked hostility toward our party, toward any one of us who may express our views on any topic. Many other than us have felt the venom of his vicious outbursts."[4]

Replied Bullock, "They're just mad because I caught their hands in the cookie jar."[5]

After the House, dominated by Democrats, passed a laughably impotent new state ethics code, Willeford tried to make political hay of its many weaknesses and loopholes. He dropped the issue after Bullock made sure that the press was aware that nine of the ten House Republicans had voted for the bill and the tenth was absent.

"You take somebody like Willeford and Maurice Angly [a GOP House member]," Bullock said. "I don't believe they represent the rank and file Republicans. I think the average Republican is an intelligent voter."[6]

The warfare continued throughout the fall as Bullock was devoting more and more time to Smith's reelection effort. In January, Willeford again demanded Bullock's ouster, after learning that the secretary of state had accepted a $1,200 loan from Jimmy Day, a vending machine lobbyist. Willeford said the deal proved that Bullock was "totally unfit" for the position he held. In a letter to Roy Orr, state Democratic chairman, he vowed to press the Senate to refuse to confirm Bullock. "I would expect you to agree that Texas needs no more scandals."[7]

Being up to his belt buckle in Smith's campaign, Bullock largely ignored the latest assault—or attempted to. A tough field had lined up for the Democratic primary, and the governor's survival was iffy. Among those he would face were Barnes; former state Rep. Dolph Briscoe, a wealthy Uvalde rancher who had finished fourth in the 1968 Democratic gubernatorial primary; and state Rep. Frances "Cissy" Farenthold, a liberal from Corpus Christi and the only woman in the Texas House.

Although Smith had not been indicted, and the feds had not accused Barnes of wrongdoing in the Sharpstown scandal, it was becoming increasingly obvious that the mood for a housecleaning had seeped into the electorate. The scandal involved complex and arcane transactions that few voters understood, but they understood that it had the appearance of corruption or, at least, tawdriness. Who knew who did what? Frank Sharp's bills had passed the Senate, where Barnes presided, but there was no suggestion that the lieutenant governor had trafficked in Sharp's stock. Smith had allowed Sharp's bills to be considered during a special legislative session. He later vetoed them, but only after being hammered by banking lobbyists led by former Gov. Shivers.

Briscoe and Farenthold could be difficult opponents. Not only had they not been touched by the scandal, Farenthold had been one of the Dirty Thirty House members who led the move to investigate Mutscher. To make matters worse for Smith and Barnes, Mutscher, no longer House speaker and a convicted felon, was running for reelection. Although the felony would have kept him from taking office even if he won, his continued presence in the political mix helped keep Sharpstown warming on the stove. Briscoe and Farenthold also proved capable of keeping the scandal simmering.

In declaring his candidacy, Briscoe said, "This time, the people of Texas have a clear choice between honest and independent leadership and the kind of irresponsible leadership that has brought us to our present state of deplorable affairs. People are generally fed up with what has been going on in Austin."[8]

Also, *Houston Post* newspaper publisher Bill Hobby, a former parliamentarian of the Senate and the son of a former governor and lieutenant governor, was running for the Democratic nomination for lieutenant governor. His opponents were three state senators, including Wayne Connally, the former governor's brother.[9] Hobby, underlining the fact that he hadn't been around the Legislature during the Sharpstown bills, had as his campaign slogan: "Bill Hobby will make a good lieutenant governor. Honestly."

From the beginning, a pessimistic Smith crew knew it was pushing a large rock uphill and tried to deflect the scandal with humor, sometimes with success. In February, Smith appeared at the Austin Headliners Club's annual stag luncheon, an event for roasting politicians, and, reading a speech written by a staffer, said, "Let him who is without stock throw the first rock." One journalist wrote that Smith, never known for eloquence or sophisticated humor, "had the huge crowd eating out of his hand."[10]

While trying to steer Smith through the reelection minefield, Bullock kept his own name in the news with a string of maverick acts as secretary of state. In one, he again testified against the state in a case that led to the end of multi-member legislative districts in Dallas and San Antonio, where they had been used for decades to keep the downtown business establishments —mostly conservative Democrats—in control. By requiring that every state representative in the county run at large, by place, the business slate could stave off upstarts who might run if the county were divided into several districts. The business slate usually had a token black, perhaps someone from labor, but mostly moderate to conservative Democrats with a business point of view. Minority groups, liberal Democrats, and Republicans felt that the system left them underrepresented—and they were right. Republican Fred Agnich, a Dallas multi-millionaire, spent enough of his own money to run against the grain and be elected to the House countywide in Dallas in 1970. But he was unique. All the other Dallas representatives were Democrats.

The system was challenged by minority groups and Republicans.

Lower federal courts ruled in favor of single-member districts, and Atty. Gen. Martin appealed for the state, arguing that single-member districts would place an unnecessary burden on election officials. The tax assessor-collectors of Dallas and Bexar Counties, who at the time had been left with the job of supervising elections stemming from their days of collecting poll taxes, backed him up. It would create chaos, they said, possibly gridlock.

Bullock's analysis for the three-judge court was directly opposite that presented by Martin, his former friend and boss. He saw no problem with the change whatsoever. The court's decision went so far as to cite Bullock's reassurances as a deciding factor in the case, and decided in favor of the plaintiffs. The U.S. Supreme Court decided to let the decision stand.

"It is probable that Bullock had as much as any other single person to do with the demise of multi-member districts in Dallas and San Antonio," Molly Ivins wrote in the *Texas Observer*.[11]

It widened the rift between Martin and Bullock, and it alienated lots of conservative Democrats, but Bullock showed no concern about collecting enemies. In that same article, Ivins quoted Buck Wood: "Bullock's just not afraid of anybody. He's not running for anything, he doesn't plan to run for anything, and he doesn't care who he pisses off." Besides, he had gained a new batch of friends, including a bunch of younger people interested in getting involved in politics. One of them was Texas Aggie graduate Garry Mauro, who was working for the Texas Students' Association and soon found himself in Bullock's orbit.

Just as importantly, Bullock had padded his reputation as a reformer spoiling for a fight. He found his next one in a court battle over the way primary elections were financed. Until 1972, the primaries were paid for by the political parties, which raised the money through exorbitant filing fees. It cost thousands just to enter a race for county commissioner, making politics prohibitive for wannabes of limited means, and thus making reelection easier for incumbents.

A suit filed in federal court in El Paso challenged the filing fee system, and a three-judge panel sitting in Dallas ruled that the system was unconstitutional. The decision was appealed all the way to the U.S. Supreme Court, which had been tossing out fragments of Texas's election laws for three decades (it was a Texas case the high court used to declare the poll tax unconstitutional). The filing fee system met the same fate: the court ruled that it was the responsibility of the state rather than of the candidates to finance primaries. It was a momentous decision, and the timing was awful—just before the 1972 primaries scheduled for May 6. The Legislature was not in session, and there had been no appropriation to fund the primaries.

Smith, fearing an impeachment move against him if he called the Legislature into special session, told Bullock, "Figure out some way to do this."

Bullock went to Wood, his elections chief. "How the hell do we do this?" he asked.

"We can't," Wood replied. "We don't have the money."

"I've got the money," Bullock said. "The governor's emergency reserve fund."

"We don't have the authority to spend it on this," Wood said.

It was a major obstacle. After a couple of days of brainstorming, Bullock and his staff lawyers came up with a strategy that was daring—and also one in which they had no great confidence. Since federal elections also were on the ballot, perhaps a federal court would give the secretary of state emergency authority to fund the primaries. Bypassing Atty. Gen. Martin, Bullock's lawyers drafted a motion and filed it with the same three-judge federal panel that had struck down the fee system. It was an audacious move, and to Bullock's surprise and Wood's, the federal court gave them the authority they sought to restructure and preside over the primaries—without specifying how they would pay for them.

"The so-called Tory establishment was appalled," Wood said. "We made up rules and regulations as to what the filing fees were going to be for every office. We just literally created the entire methodology of conducting and financing the primaries out of whole cloth. There wasn't any other way to do it. We worked nights, worked in bars, we worked."[12]

Once the details were worked out, the regulations were issued and Bullock sent a voucher to State Comptroller Robert S. Calvert, instructing him to pay the amount needed to implement the plan. Calvert, an aging bean-counter who had been comptroller since 1949, and was hardly known for a confrontational style, drew a line.

"We're not going to do it," he said. "We don't think the federal courts gave you that much authority."[13]

Atty. Gen. Martin agreed with Calvert. In truth, the court's ruling had been vague, but Bullock had been running on bluff anyway and saw no reason to stop now. He made the rare move of suing another state agency—the comptroller—in the State Supreme Court.

Again, Bullock got his way. The state's highest court, which had previously held that primaries were strictly party matters, finally agreed that the state had to finance them. Those elections would be conducted under rules and regulations issued by the secretary of state.

By now, the press was starting to pay serious attention to Bullock, and while he was distrustful of reporters, he was becoming increasingly comfortable with seeing his name in the headlines. In fact, he sometimes reveled in it. He bristled at a hint of negativity in stories written about him, but he behaved in a way that guaranteed that reporters would circle around him.

During that intensely contested primary of 1972, he directed a stream of vitriol not only at Barnes, whom he probably considered Smith's toughest opponent, but Atty. Gen. Crawford Martin, who was seeking reelection to a fourth two-year term. Bullock's attacks were so harsh that Smith apologized to both men.

Bullock was plotting another reform of the state's election system, one that struck those close to him as peculiar—a good idea but odd in that it came from Bullock. As a fund-raiser for Smith, he had always been secretive about his activities and sensitive to suggestions that he operated outside the law. Now he championed full disclosure of campaign contributions.

The existing laws were feeble and feebly enforced, and it was easy to conceal the source of funds. Contributions, if the candidate chose to report them, could be identified as coming from an organization—Duval County Committee to Elect Preston Smith, for example—and no questions were asked. Bullock had excelled under that laxity, but suddenly he was anxious to reform it.

"What about all these committees?" he asked his elections chief one day.

Wood was surprised, but welcomed his boss's interest. He explained that when the first reporting law was passed in the 1930s, it contemplated only individual contributions. When the law was recodified in 1951, no one anticipated the rise of political action committees. The law remained silent on that point.

"Why don't we just put out an opinion that says you can't report under a committee name in Texas? You've got to report individual contributions," he said.

His office did not have that rulemaking authority, but, again, bluff had served him well so far. Wood drafted a regulation requiring committees to list the individual sources of the funds they gave to candidates.

It's possible that the reformer impulse was behind Bullock's sudden interest in transparency. But there may have been a less idealistic motivation. Barnes, still regarded as the golden boy of Texas politics, was raising large amounts of money, and Bullock may have wanted to know where he was getting it. It could be useful information, if not in this race, then in a future one. The new regulations were issued and met little resistance. "Most everybody was afraid not to comply," Wood said. "They were afraid Bullock would sue them."[14]

May 6, primary election day. Not a good time for incumbents. The Sharpstown scandal wiped out the entire political hierarchy of Texas. This time, Bullock's masterful fund-raising could not save the governor, and his ruthless rhetoric during the campaign was directed at the wrong opponent, Ben Barnes. The lieutenant governor was never really in the race.

Briscoe led the pack with 963,397 votes, or 43.9 percent—short of the majority he needed to win without a runoff. Farenthold came in second with 612,051 (27.9 percent). Barnes was a distant third with 392,356 (17.9 percent), and Smith was trounced even worse with a mere 190,709 (8.7 percent).

As the vote tallies were counted and the results became obvious, Ralph Wayne, who was working for Barnes, called Bullock at Smith's campaign headquarters. He said, "Well, your man didn't get reelected." To which, according to Smith's speechwriter Jerry Conn, Bullock shot back: "Yeah, but my man has been governor, and yours never will be."[15]

In all, the toll from Sharpstown, aided by legislative redistricting that included the court-forced single-member House districts in major urban counties, came to about 100 officeholders. Atty. Gen. Martin lost his bid for reelection. Speaker Mutscher barely survived—temporarily—by making the runoff in his district, but many of his lieutenants and backers in the House suffered similar or worse fates. Fully half the House and Senate would have replacements come January. With few exceptions—Comptroller Robert Calvert being one—Texas would have a lame-duck government for the next seven months.

There was still work to be done. Smith had to call a special legislative session that summer to deal with important state issues. He called one in June, limited to passing the state's appropriation bill, that lasted three weeks. But that also gave the Texas Senate, presided over by Barnes, the opportunity to consider passing judgment on 28 appointments—one of them being Bullock's confirmation as secretary of state. The Capitol again braced for a savage Barnes-Bullock showdown. Barnes, now 34 years old and stinging from his first political defeat, rattled no sabers, but Bullock went into war mode.

Said an article in the *Dallas Times Herald*: "Bullock has such a talent for making life uncomfortable for his foes that he has become known as a force to be reckoned with on whatever terms are available. [He] applied every type of pressure, subtle and direct, that his combative nature and fertile imagination could devise to win this confirmation. Few senators relished the thought of what he would pull next on them if they opposed him."[16]

The showdown never came. After a brief session, the Senate Nominations Committee approved Bullock with high praise and sent the matter to the full Senate, where Barnes had the 11 votes needed to thump Bullock. Instead, he released his supporters to vote as they pleased, and the confirmation was approved 24–6.

Maybe Barnes was too weary from the campaign and too deflated by his loss to find the vigor for another battle. Or maybe he figured this one wasn't worth fighting. Bullock had held the job for a year and had only another six months before he departed, along with Smith and almost everyone else in Austin. Whatever Barnes's motive, Bullock was surprised by the ease of his endorsement.

"One Senator even called to tell me [the outcome] and said Ben Barnes even made a little talk for me," he said. "I don't know what to say except all this hugging and kissing's about to kill me."[17]

CHAPTER 9

BUSTED BY THE SENATE

Howener sweet the confirmation, it was accompanied by the reality that Bullock, like nearly everyone else in the Capitol, was half a year from unemployment and had a future to ponder. There might be a job for him under the new Atty. Gen. John Hill. Bullock had supported him, mainly through his attacks on the incumbent Crawford Martin. He could return to the private practice of law. Under no circumstance, he declared, was lobbying one of his options. "They couldn't pay me $100,000 a year to go back to lobbying. It's hard work, and I just don't like it. I don't want anything to do with it. It's just a bad business."[1] He was an unabashed "convert to liberalism" now and had lost his taste for persuading lawmakers to make distasteful laws.

Long-range plans would have to wait, though. Bullock was only 43, and he still worked with the intensity of a cruise missile and played with the abandon of a mustang. Able to function on four or five hours of sleep each night, he had long been a fixture at the handful of Austin political-media saloons, chain-smoking and tossing down mass quantities of Old Charter before heading home to read and, occasionally, place phone calls to staffers at obscene hours. His second marriage had ended, and his body was suffering.

The Senate confirmed him on July 6. Two weeks later, he checked into Brackenridge Hospital for treatment of a kidney disorder. While there, doctors discovered a tumor on his lung.

It was enough to take anybody's mind off politics, but 1972 was a pivotal time in the affairs of Texas and the nation. The Democrats had placed liberal Sens. George McGovern and Thomas Eagleton on their national ticket and, not unexpectedly, some of Texas's most influential and conservative Democrats ducked for the exits and slid over to the Richard Nixon camp. John Connally endorsed the Republican president and headed up a state organization called Democrats for Nixon. State party chairman Roy Orr tacitly backed the president by declining to support his own party's ticket. From his hospital bed, Bullock issued an endorsement of the McGovern-Eagleton ticket and scolded his fellow Democrats who didn't. He received a personal call from the vice presidential nominee.

"I just wanted to thank you," Sen. Eagleton said. "I want you to know we are not going to write off Texas."[2]

A few days later, McGovern removed Eagleton from the ticket because of revelations that he had undergone psychiatric counseling. That same day, doctors removed most of Bullock's right lung. It was enough to sideline both men, but only Eagleton dropped from sight. Leaving the hospital and nursing ribs that were broken for the lung surgery, Bullock stepped directly into the most ferocious and acrimonious political fight of his life.

In the same special session that saw Bullock's easy confirmation as secretary of state, Larry Teaver, whom Smith had appointed chairman of the State Insurance Board nearly a year earlier, was denied confirmation—"busted," in the vernacular of the Senate. In appointing Teaver, Smith had promised he would be a consumer champion, which triggered swift opposition from insurance lobbyists, who had become accustomed to selecting the members of the board that regulated their industry.

Teaver's rejection so angered Smith that, uncharacteristically, he called another special session in September, ostensibly for the purpose of passing legislation to reform the insurance rate-setting process. Lawmakers puzzled over the move. Smith had often expressed opposition to special sessions except in the case of true emergencies. How insurance rates were set may have been in need of restructuring, but was it a crisis that justified spending $33,000 a day to haul the Legislature back to Austin for a month? As soon as they hit town, some legislators thought they had unraveled the mystery: Gov. Smith named another trusted aide to fill the insurance board vacancy. "I expect Bob Bullock to be a tough, but fair, consumer advocate," Smith said, again inviting the insurance lobbyists to a duel.[3]

If Smith's dare wasn't enough, Bullock waved his own red flag. "I will not be satisfied until Texas has lower insurance rates than any other state," he said.

Bullock told reporters that he had asked Smith for the appointment. "I've griped about insurance rates. Now I want to get in and solve some of the problems. It may sound corny, but there comes a time when a man ought to put a little something back into the system."[4]

Given Bullock's history of cutthroat campaign tactics and his hatchet man/bagman image, it did sound a little corny, if not disingenuous. In addition to offering an opportunity for putting something back into the system, a seat on the insurance board had long-range career potential. He would serve until 1975—two years after the governor who appointed him had left town—and then he could command top money lobbying for the industry he had regulated.

Bullock wanted the job badly, and he believed that confirmation was doable, if not a done deal. Barnes had only fleetingly opposed him for secretary of state, and maybe, even with the higher stakes in this battle, he would again capitulate. The insurance lobby, among the most powerful and well-heeled in town, would also be a factor, but Bullock had friends there, dating back to his own lobbying days. Surely they would stand with him.

He miscalculated on both fronts. No lobbyists had much interest in the secretary of state, but the insurance crowd had become wary of Bullock because of his coziness with the trial lawyers—the plaintiff's attorneys representing consumers in suits against, among others, insurance companies. Joe K. Longley, the executive director of the Texas Consumer Association and a plaintiff's attorney, called Bullock's appointment "a blow struck for the consumers of Texas."[5] Moreover, it was personal—one grudge match between the governor and the lieutenant governor, lame ducks both, and another between Barnes and Bullock. Barnes believed that Bullock's vicious attacks during the primary campaign had kept him out of the runoff, and he was spoiling for payback.

It would be a short but impassioned war—eight days from nomination to confirmation vote—that would provoke fear, outrage, and, in at least one instance, physical illness.

At first, Robert Spellings, Barnes's administrative assistant, oversaw the effort to block Bullock. Under new Senate rules, the number of standing committees was reduced from 27 to nine and all appointments had to be remade. Half the senators were on their way out and had little interest in the committees. For those who were returning, the assignments were critical to their districts. Speaking on condition of anonymity, senators complained to reporters that Spellings was calling senators and suggesting that Barnes would base his committee assignments on how members voted on Bullock's confirmation. Spellings denied the reports, but they persisted. Barnes professed neutrality. "I'm not collecting votes," Barnes said. He added that if Spellings "or anyone has applied any pressure on anyone, then that's wrong, and that's done without my permission."[6]

Barnes didn't have to do the heavy lifting. In the 31-member Senate, a two-thirds majority was needed for confirmation, meaning that 11 senators could bust the nominee. The insurance lobby was putting forth an extraordinary campaign to deliver those votes. Pasadena Sen. Chet Brooks, a Bullock ally, was one of many who grumbled that he was being swamped with phone calls. "The insurance lobby has activated some people in almost every Senate district," he said.[7]

As the war escalated, Smith, too, used the abundant leverage at his disposal. The special legislative session was called specifically to consider insurance rate-setting, but Smith spread the word that he might open it up to pet bills of senators who fell into line. Moreover, the entire executive branch appeared prepared to dispense other rewards. Sen. Ronald Bridges of Corpus Christi told the *Dallas Morning News* that he was pressed to vote for Bullock in order to get consideration of funds for a branch university campus in his hometown. Smith had previously vetoed funds for that campus.

Sen. J. P. Word, a conservative Democrat and Barnes loyalist from Meridian, west of Waco, showed reporters a telegram he had received from a physician in his district, who was pushing a particular person for the Texas A&M Board of Regents. He called it "blatant" evidence of the kind of pressure he and other senators were suffering. "If we are to hope to get the governor to make this appointment, we are going to have to depend on you and Sen. [Tom] Creighton to support the confirmation of Bob Bullock for insurance commissioner," the telegram said. Word also said he had received information that "favorable action" might be taken on a savings and loan application for a business group in his district if Bullock were confirmed. Sen. Don Kennard, a progressive Democrat from Fort Worth, said he had indirect word that the governor's office would go along with a previously vetoed hospital appropriation for Fort Worth in exchange for a favorable vote on Bullock.[8]

After a few days, Barnes dropped the neutrality pretense. "As private citizen Ben Barnes, I am personally opposed to Bob Bullock serving on the State Board of Insurance, and I have expressed this personal position to my friends and to the Texas Senate," he said. "I do not believe that he is qualified to serve in such a sensitive position. I feel that Gov. Smith should not have made this appointment from within his own political family. I think the people of Texas deserve someone other than a key member of the political team of a lame-duck governor."

Spellings, the aide who had earlier denied pressuring senators to vote against Bullock, also came out of the closet. Bob Bain, of the *Fort Worth Star-Telegram*, reported talking with Roy Orr outside Barnes's office when Spellings walked by.

"Did you bring us any votes?" Spellings asked.

"Votes for what?" Orr replied.

"To bust Bullock," Spellings said.[9]

There were reports that insurance lobbyists had taken over Barnes's office and converted it into a war room. Perfunctory denials were made, but they rang as hollow as sun-dried pumpkins. Barnes pleaded innocent, but nobody believed him. Sam Winters, an attorney and lobbyist for the Texas Life Convention, an association of life insurers, said, with a straight face, that he knew of nobody in the insurance industry who was campaigning against Bullock.

Although he was upfront about his feelings about Bullock, Barnes continued to refute reports that he used committee appointments to lure waffling legislators to his camp. To "prove" the speciousness of that charge, he announced the appointments a few days before the vote. "If I had wished to resort to such a maneuver," he said, "I would have withheld all appointments until Bullock's name had come to the Senate floor and the vote had been taken."[10]

Not necessarily. Both sides had been working the phones and keeping lists of who was on their side, who was on the other, and who was undecided. Barnes was confident that he had the votes to bust Bullock, and he knew who they were. As it turned out, anti-Bullock senators scored well in committee assignments, and pro-Bullock members, well . . . Sen. Brooks was removed from three committees active during that session. Nine of the ten senators dropped from the Finance Committee—the most powerful of them all—were Bullock supporters.

Meanwhile, the nominee himself was dipping into his bag of tricks to sway votes, or at least get opposing senators to hear his sales pitch. Bill Collier, a reporter for the *Houston Chronicle*, was in Bullock's office to interview him about the battle and witnessed the artfulness of a master competitor.

"These senators who won't return my calls worry me," Bullock said. "If there's a quick vote, they can say later, 'Well, Bob, you never came to talk to me.'"

He wasn't going to give anyone that excuse. While Collier sat nearby, Bullock picked up the phone and dialed one of those who had not returned his calls. After a brief hassle with the senator's secretary, Bullock barked, "You tell him that this is about his business as well as mine. There's an IRS man down here going over his campaign expense reports line by line. I thought he would like to know about it."[11]

In Bullock's mind, the war narrowed into one between him and Barnes. Preston Smith, the insurance lobby, all the other players became peripheral. This was a gladiatorial event, *mano a mano*, and only one would be left standing.

Beyond contacting each senator at least once, Bullock went to his extensive card file, scoured it for names of contributors in each senator's district, and pleaded for their help. New intelligence—who's talking to whom, who's leaning which way—came in daily, and senators who needed shoring up were contacted again. To those senators who told him they could not support him, he suggested they *walk* when it came time to vote. The two-thirds rule applies to the number of senators present and voting. If someone *walks*, the math changes.

The lieutenant governor had significant control over the Senate. He not only made committee assignments unilaterally, he determined if and when bills were brought to the floor for a vote. Bullock knew that Barnes, even though he was a lame duck, would use that authority to his own advantage, and he plotted a countermove. "If I can ever get it to where Barnes thinks I'm one vote down, he'll let it come up," he told Buck Wood. "When it comes up, then he's going to be taken by surprise."[12]

Bullock's hole card was his old friend and drinking buddy, Bryan Sen. Bill Moore, one of Barnes's lieutenants. Known as the Bull of the Brazos, the crusty Moore was a crafty politician and a deal-maker with a cracked ethical and moral compass. Barnes had solicited his support in the gubernatorial race, and Moore pledged it on one condition: "Leave my whorehouse alone." It was a reference to the La Grange Chicken Ranch in his district. Moore backed the wrong horse. Gov. Dolph Briscoe would later close "The Best Little Whorehouse in Texas."

Bullock credited his brother-in-law, Will Bond, with bringing Moore into his camp, but there were other reports that early in his Senate career, a grand jury in Bryan was on the brink of indicting Moore until Bullock gave exculpatory testimony that got Moore off the hook. It was a chit that Bullock never called in—until now. Moore pledged to vote for his confirmation.

"Not only do I want your vote," Bullock told him, "I don't want you to tell Barnes about it, ever."

Moore agreed and kept his word. Barnes continued to count Moore in his camp until the day of the vote.

On Friday, September 21, Bullock went before the Senate Nominations Subcommittee, which would make a recommendation to the full chamber. Only four of the subcommittee's members were present. Bullock answered a few tepid questions, and the subcommittee voted 3–1 in his favor.

For another five days, the storm raged. Bullock homed in on the "uncommitted," and Barnes did likewise. Newspapers did their own polls of senators and published lineups that suggested the outcome could fall either way.

Like Bullock, Barnes was redeeming IOUs. According to published reports, he reminded Lufkin Sen. Charles Wilson, who was leaving the Senate for a seat in the U.S. House of Representatives, that he had helped carve out for him a congressional district in the 1971 redistricting. He reminded Barbara Jordan, a black senator from Houston, who also was headed for Congress, how, in addition to helping draw her a congressional district, he had helped her repeal a catalogue of racist laws that had lingered on the books for years. Nerves were stretched like bungee cords on the day the vote was scheduled in a closed-door session. Denied attendance, reporters were reduced to giving secondhand accounts, usually anonymous, of the proceeding. George Kuempel reported in the *Houston Chronicle* that "a hand-wringing" Wilson stopped by Jordan's desk and said, "This is going to be a tough one after all that Barnes has done for us."

Jordan, still listed among the uncommitted, replied, "Senator, you and I have repaid those obligations long ago." Obviously, she had made up her mind, and the line was becoming more clearly drawn.

There was at least one surprise, the one Bullock had planned for Barnes. Thirty minutes before the vote was taken, Kuempel wrote, Moore broke "the news that he was supporting Bullock." Barnes, his source told him, "was crushed."[13]

Even without Moore, however, Barnes had the votes he needed. The session lasted only 25 minutes, and Bullock was busted by a vote of 19 for him and 11 against.

Sen. Wilson, who had voted for Bullock, went immediately into the restroom and threw up.

Barnes was buoyant. He had speared the man he believed had played a large role in knocking him out of the Democratic gubernatorial primary and couldn't resist an oratorical strut, a verbal victory lap. "It wasn't difficult to bust Bullock," Barnes said. "There were more than 11 votes against him." He said four other senators were prepared to vote against Bullock if their votes were needed.[14]

Now it was Bullock who was crushed. "I thought I had the votes," he said with a tinge of humble resignation. "I was counting on five of the senators who voted against me." Then his characteristic imprudence seeped through. "It merely confirms what a lot of Texans think today—that you can't get confirmed unless you're close to the insurance industry or that you're so mealymouthed that you wouldn't say 'mud' if you had a mouth full of it."[15]

Dejection did not adequately describe the emotional toll taken by the defeat. "Not until it was over did I realize how serious Bullock was about this," said Buck Wood, who had helped cajole senators in the run-up to the vote. "He really wanted that job. He fought as hard as he could fight, and he lost. He was really, really devastated. A picture was on the front page of the *Daily Texan* the day after he was busted. He's got his head hung down and his eyes appear to be almost closed. He wasn't depressed, he was beaten. It wasn't a game anymore. It really hurt him. It put Bob into, not one of his manic depressions, but it took the air out of him."[16]

In that mood, Bullock made a list of the senators who voted against him—or whom he thought had voted against him. It included Babe Schwartz, who had actually abstained but was prepared to vote "no" if he was needed. Schwartz, a pro-labor liberal, personally disliked Bullock, but had received pressure from his union constituency to vote to confirm. The others on his list were H. J. "Doc" Blanchard, Ronald Bridges, Wayne Connally, Tom Creighton, O. H. "Ike" Harris, Jack Hightower, Glenn Kothmann, Oscar Mauzy, Max Sherman, Pete Snelson, and J. P. Word.

Bullock folded the list, tucked it into his wallet and, as far as his friends knew, carried it with him until he died, although it is unlikely that he ever needed a piece of paper to jog his memory of the most hurtful moment of his political life. What would he do with the list? He would be leaving government in three months and might never be in a position to exact revenge. But then again, he might.

CHAPTER 10

TEXAS GETS A NEW TAX COLLECTOR

T hroughout the fall of 1972—a time for putting away the dueling pistols and brooding on the future—Bullock occupied himself with weighing career options. He had been divorced from first wife Amelia in 1971, and his brief second marriage—to Kathryn Ann Mitchell— had ended in divorce in August. His remaining political function was to chair the Democratic Unity Day early in October at the request of Sen. McGovern, the party's presidential nominee. It seemed an awkward choice. Bullock had just been through a season of intra-party bloodletting, and now he was charged with establishing harmony, persuading his party to close ranks against the Nixon administration. The *Houston Chronicle* thought the notion was humorous enough that it headlined its story "Battling Bob Bullock to Head Democratic Unity Day in Texas." He made the standard assaults on Nixon's failed promise to end the Vietnam War and his economic polices that resulted in high unemployment and rampant inflation.[1] That done, he went back to avoiding the unemployment lines himself.

Since leaving the Legislature in 1959, Bullock had consistently disavowed ambitions of running for office again. In mid-October 1972, he spoke to a small group of students at a University of Texas *sandwich seminar*. It was an admiring crowd—the student voters who saw him as their voting rights patron. They were curious where he would go from here. Relaxed and mellow, Bullock mentioned the possibility of a judicial appointment. The previous Legislature had created a new district court for Austin, and "I asked the governor to keep me in mind." Another possibility was a business offer extended by a close friend in Dallas, he said. *What about politics?* someone asked. "I don't have any plans to run for political office," he said.[2]

Some of his friends *did* have plans for him to run. Wood, along with his secretary-of-state colleagues Don Ray, Carlton Carl, and Paul Wehrle, went to work on him. The nudging was subtle at first. They approached his brother, Tom; his brother-in-law, Will Bond; and anyone else they thought could influence him. Bullock had been abrasive toward the press, but reporters liked him—he had provided them a deep well of material and no doubt would welcome his continued presence—so Buck Wood sounded them out.

Occasionally, he would tell Bullock that he had talked to one reporter or another about him running for office. Bullock's response was not that of a man who had written off politics. "Well, what did he think?" he would ask. "He would like to see you run," Wood would tell him.[3]

Ken Wendler, the Travis County Democratic Party chairman, joined in the effort, and slowly Bullock let his true interests be known—along with his reservations. He reminded Wood of the racist legislation he had voted for in 1957 and said, "I have gone to White Citizens Council meetings in Tyler. I'm telling you that's not going to work."[4]

There were only three blacks in the 1971 Legislature—Curtis Graves of Houston and Zan Holmes of Dallas, in the House, and Barbara Jordan of Houston, in the Senate. But the complexion of the upcoming session would be far different, thanks to the establishment of single-member districts in the state's most populous counties, redistricting, the Sharpstown scandal, and the newly enfranchised youth vote. It was not a good year for Democrats in general—McGovern's lopsided loss to Nixon enabled Texas Republicans to increase their presence in Austin—but black Democrats made strong gains, winning eight seats in the House even while losing their lone black senator—Jordan—who in redistricting had traded in her Senate district for a congressional one. It occurred to Wood that the black legislators might be a good sounding board on the potential for Bullock's rehabilitation.

"Bullock, why don't you let me put together a group of black leaders in the Legislature and see if they would be willing to meet with you?" Wood said. "Tell them how you feel about it . . . you feel like it was horrible."

Wood contacted a few of them who were in Austin—Eddie Bernice Johnson, Mickey Leland, Craig Washington, and Paul Ragsdale among them—and then went to the Spanish Village, a hangout near the Capitol, to arrange a meeting room. Throughout the process, Bullock called every two or three hours. "You got the meeting set up?" he wanted to know. "Who's coming? Who agreed to come?"

The gathering went better than he expected. Of course, they knew of Bullock's old voting record, but they also knew of his emerging incarnation as a liberal reformer and that the election reforms that transpired on his watch had made their own elections possible. *No big deal*, the incoming black legislators told him. *Lots of bad things happened back then. That's in the past.* The skeleton was out of the closet, and it frightened no one. Bullock was ready to run for office.[5]

But which office?

State treasurer. It wasn't high profile, almost a minor adjunct to the comptroller's office. The comptroller collected the money, and the treasurer wrote the checks. But it was a statewide office and a race that could test his broad voter appeal. Besides, the sitting treasurer was a crook named Jesse James. In the 1960s, James had gone through a scandal nearly as bad as Sharpstown. As treasurer, he also sat on the three-member State Banking Board, and it was an open secret that to get a banking charter, you had to slip $10,000 under Jesse James's desk. He was beatable, Bullock believed, and the job would hardly be demanding. "There's nothing to that office," he told Wood. "They've got 25 employees." He also was intrigued by the idea of issuing banking charters and the clout it would give him with the business community.

Wood and Don Ray had another office in mind: Comptroller. It had hundreds of employees, far more authority, offices scattered around the state, and the power to actually do something. Wood knew Bullock well enough to know that the boredom of the treasurer's office would lead him into trouble. They were getting nowhere until Ray got the statutes covering both offices and made a side-by-side comparison and analysis. The treasurer's powers and duties could have been written on a memo pad. The comptroller's authorities and responsibilities would have filled up a Big Chief tablet.

The office of Comptroller of Public Accounts dates back to 1835 and the Provisional Government of Texas. It was commissioned by the governor and given the task of approving or rejecting claims presented by the state auditor. Ten years later, the state's first constitution and a subsequent statute defined and broadened its scope, "to superintend the fiscal concerns of the state"; to perform official acts previously required of the Secretary of the Treasury under the Republic of Texas; to report annually to the governor on the state's revenues, expenditures of the previous years, and a detailed estimate of expenditures for the coming year; to suggest plans for improving and managing public revenue; to direct the collection of monies due the state. The comptroller, therefore, was the chief fiscal officer of the state and was required also to provide the research and statistics required for revenue estimating, which would determine how much the Legislature could appropriate in the next session. Too, the comptroller was made an ex-officio member of other state boards and commissions.

Perhaps the biggest power was added by the Legislature and voters when Texas amended its constitution in 1942 to require a balanced budget. The amendment specified that the comptroller had to certify that enough revenue would come in to finance the Legislature's budget. That in essence gave the comptroller the power to set a lid on what legislators could spend.

Tucked into the specific obligations of the office were implied powers that were just as significant. If Bullock truly wanted to "put a little something back into the system," this was as good a place as any to start—particularly since the office had hundreds of jobs that could be used for patronage purposes. It was just as easy to hire a daughter of a county commissioner as someone whose father was a telephone lineman.

The sitting comptroller was almost as vulnerable as Jesse James, but not because of a recent scandal. Robert S. Calvert was 80 years old and had held the office since he was appointed to it on January 17, 1949, after his predecessor, George H. Sheppard, died. Calvert had been a bank teller in Sheppard's home town of Sweetwater, and worked as a statistician and later chief clerk in the comptroller's office before being named to succeed Sheppard. Calvert was called "Squeaky" because of a high-pitched voice that, legend had it, resulted from being gassed during World War I. Although his office had broad powers of enforcement, they were rarely, if ever, used, a fact that was brought to light in March 1972 by an interim Senate committee staff report that concluded that Texas was losing at least $12 million a year in uncollected sales taxes.

Dissatisfaction with the comptroller's performance ushered in a season of firsts. Calvert drew his first serious political opposition ever. Six Democrats took him on in the 1972 primary, and for the first time he was forced into a runoff—against James Wilson, one of his former aides. And, owing to the malevolence of that brawl, reporters gave the comptroller's race serious coverage for the first time.

Wilson, 42, dismissed Calvert as a "sick, senile octogenarian" as well as a racist who discriminated in hiring against non-whites and non-Democrats. Calvert called Wilson a "moral reprobate" and gave reporters evidence that his opponent had been married six times—including one marriage that was annulled because, according to the annulment petition, "he was intoxicated on liquor and was so drunk that he did not know what he was doing [but] left his wife as soon as he sobered up."[6] So the old guy with white hair and an ever-present cigar was no gentleman after all. But that nasty runoff—Calvert won with 56.7 percent—may have softened him up for 1974, when he would be 82 years old.

Bullock wasn't sold. He went to his card file, selected the ones he considered most influential, and solicited their input as to which office he should seek. Most of them were businessmen or business lobbyists, and they had become leery of his new liberal persona. They paid taxes and were not eager to see him as the state's chief tax collector. Said Wood: "He got a lot of replies that said, 'Hey, why don't you run for treasurer?'"

Before making his decision, he traveled around the state calling on businessmen he thought were his friends. Some gave him tepid support; some declined to commit. One in particular, sealed the decision for him.

In Houston, he went to see Oscar Wyatt, who owned Coastal States Gas Co., one of the largest producers in the country. Entering his office, Bullock extended his hand over an oversized desk and said, "Oscar, I'm planning on running for comptroller. I want your support. I want your financial help. I want your vote."

Wyatt scowled across the big desk and said, "Bullock, you ain't ever going to be comptroller."

Bullock picked up his briefcase, left the building, and drove back to Austin. "How did it go?" Wood asked him.

"I'll tell you one thing," Bullock said, "I'm running for comptroller."[7]

Sporting an eight-day growth of beard, Bullock called a press conference on December 19 and disclosed his plans, in part. He said he would resign as secretary of state on January 2, two weeks before his term was to expire, to again practice law and to enter a real estate partnership with Ken Wendler, the Travis County Democratic Party chairman and president of Anken Construction Co. Reporters, though, pressed for juicier information. *Do you have any plans to run for office in 1974?* Two months earlier, he had told the UT students he had none. Now, he revealed a change of heart and mind. "I very definitely have some," he smiled.[8]

"Which office?" the reporters asked. Hoping to generate the kind of mystery that would keep his name humming along the grapevine and, at the same time, avoid tipping off potential opponents, he pleaded indecision. "I'm going to just sit back and see who does bad, and I may take a shot at that," he said.[9]

Meanwhile, he would try his hand at real estate, all the while setting up a campaign strategy and organization. He had no reason to expect a tough race, especially if Calvert decided to seek reelection at the age of 82. Bullock had made his peace with prominent black leaders and, even if he hadn't, they would have had a hard time supporting the incumbent. Two years earlier, Calvert had defended himself with utter ineptitude against Wilson's charge that he adhered to racist hiring practices. "I don't think we've had a darkie apply here since I've been in this office who could do the work," he said. "Hell, I'm not a nigger-hater—and I'm not a nigger-lover either."[10]

Surely Bullock would have the black vote, as well as the youth vote, the labor vote, probably the women's vote, the liberal vote, and plenty of conservative allies. He also had his cherished card file and the remnants of Preston Smith's organization. Any other primary opponent would likely be a political newcomer or someone—a legislator or county official—with only a local constituency. Republicans were unlikely to be a problem. Only one Republican in modern times, U.S. Sen. John Tower, had won a statewide race, and it was unlikely that an individual, or the party, would throw resources into a run for what was considered an insignificant prize.

If there was a hitch early on, it was a surprising one. While encouraging Bullock to run, Wood had not thought much about fund-raising. Why should he? Bullock was a master at that. He had been as insistent as a drill sergeant on behalf of Preston Smith, but Bullock went limp when it came to his own cause.

Calling prospective donors, he made small talk before his tepid, mumbled pitch: *I need your vote, and I need your support*, or maybe *I need your financial support*. Wood began to remind him of fund-raising techniques Bullock had once perfected. *Ask for a specific amount, or you'll get lowballed*. Bullock seemed incapable of doing that. Wood often sat by the phone scribbling dollar amounts on a note pad and holding it up for Bullock to read. "He was as shy about it as any candidate I'd ever seen," Wood said.

Sometimes Bullock tried to foist the fund-raising off on Wood or others. "Bullock," Wood reminded him, "you know the rule is that the candidate has to ask."[11]

On June 20, six months before the filing deadline for the 1974 primary, Bullock called a press conference—strange in its timing and texture—to announce that he would be a candidate for "one of the most important, but unfortunately one of the least noticed, offices in Texas." The timing was odd because Bullock was sporting a black eye. Would it have been wiser to wait until the shiner had healed? When asked about the injury, he blithely invoked the language of a cigarette commercial of that era—"Hell, I'm not like John Connally, I'd rather fight than switch"—a reference to the former governor's recent formal leap to the GOP. No, he confessed, the eye was the result of a sailing mishap. "Damn boom knocked me right out of the boat," he said. Eventually, another story seeped into the rumor mill: His wife had punched him after catching him with another woman.

The texture of the press conference was peculiar because of its studied humility. Rather than jumping in with bluster and flair, Bullock seemed almost apologetic. "There is not a great big groundswell for me to run," he laughed. "There haven't been a lot of letters written begging me to run." But, he added, he was doing it anyway because "I care about this state." Citing the legislative report on the incumbent's enforcement laxity, Bullock said, "The present controller has lacked aggressiveness. His office has not taken progressive action in the past 25 years and today is suffering, in my opinion, from bureaucratic rigor mortis."[12]

With that, Bullock began to sketch the political persona he would cultivate for the rest of his time in government: The unassuming, if not self-deprecating, Lone Ranger suffering to lead Texas out of the wilderness; an imperfect private man but selfless public servant with a noble heart.

The press lapped it up and salivated over what the future promised. Art Wiese, a *Houston Post* reporter, wrote in the *Austin Citizen*: "One of the wildest, saltiest campaigns in recent Texas history may already be shaping up for the 1974 Democratic nomination for state comptroller."

Calvert declined to commit to the race and wouldn't comment on Bullock's candidacy. "Anything I said would be bad," he said.[13]

Early in 1974, Calvert bowed out and anointed Hugh Edburg, one of his top assistants, as his chosen successor, but the boss's endorsement was of dubious value. The charges of racism leveled at Calvert had been compounded the previous fall when the federal Equal Employment Opportunity Commission accused him of discriminating against women. Buddy F. Kirk, one of Calvert's former employees, who had quit early in 1973 when he was transferred out of the Houston office for trying to collect sales taxes on luxury yachts bought out of state and delivered to Texas, also filed for the office.

In converse fashion, they were ever-present reminders of Calvert's lapses and shortcomings. Neither had a chance. Bullock had name recognition, a head start, an organization, extensive contacts, and indefatigable drive. Still, he ran like an underdog.

Ken Wendler's interest in Bullock as a partner in real estate development was his fund-raising ability. Wendler owned several parcels of land in Austin, and if Bullock could find investors to help develop them, they had a deal. Bullock would reel in the money, and Wendler would build the buildings or houses.

For a man setting up a run for the sensitive public office of chief financial officer of the state, Bullock went about his private job in a strange way. On Wendler's behalf, he went first to his old friend, Clinton Manges, the South Texas rancher and banker who had been involved in controversy and whiffs of scandals for years. Wendler was uneasy about Manges but was relieved to discover that he did not cast the presence of a crook. Manges was polite and soft-spoken, and Wendler suspected that much of his reputation as a business ogre derived mostly from his ability to outfox some of the state's notable sharpies in the oil business.

One of their first projects was to develop a federally subsidized housing project on property that Wendler owned in Southeast Austin. It became stalled in controversy because of neighborhood opposition at the same time that the Nixon Administration was trying to eliminate its sponsoring agency, the Department of Housing and Urban Development. The *Austin American* added to the difficulty, Wendler said, when the editor, Ray Marriotti, "took after Bullock and me, like we were trying to screw somebody."[14]

In the heat of that battle, Bullock was too busy running for comptroller to be of much value. Instead, Wendler's office became his campaign headquarters. Garry Mauro, who had been a traveling aide with former U.S. Sen. Ralph Yarborough in his comeback try in the Democratic primary in 1972, and later chairman of the Young Texans for McGovern, signed on as Bullock's travel aide. By early 1974, they were, essentially, replicating Preston Smith's campaign techniques. A separate package of material was developed on each town and county, and press packets tailored for each venue were prepared. During the week, they cruised the state in a station wagon and left their campaign material at the small-town radio stations and newspapers. On the theory that down-ballot victories are dependent on the support of local elected officials, they visited every office in every courthouse in Texas. While Bullock glad-handed inside, Mauro worked the square, calling on merchants and placing business cards on the windshields of parked cars.

"He was the most organized person I'd ever traveled with—to the point of obsession," said Mauro, whose admiration for Bullock's painstaking organization was offset by Bullock's erratic temperament and mood swings.[15] "About twice a month, Garry would come into my office and say, 'I have to quit. I can't go on another damn trip with him,'" said Wendler.[16]

Mauro and Bullock returned to Austin each weekend, and on one occasion, Bullock walked into the campaign office and fired everyone except Mauro, who had to take over the operation of the headquarters, leaving Bullock shy a traveling aide. He tried to draft his old friends Buck Wood and Don Ray, who had found other work after leaving the secretary of state's office and were unavailable. Unfazed, Bullock hit the road alone.

If Bullock had a real opponent in the primary, it was his own past. Now and then, his voting record on the 1957 session's rash of segregationist bills came up, and Bullock never tried to evade or minimize it. At a press breakfast in Lubbock, he told a group of reporters, "There are a lot of things I have done in my political career that I'm not proud of. The question is whether I have the integrity to correct those mistakes. I think I have."[17]

The voters agreed. Kirk dropped out of the race—too late for his name to be removed from the ballot—and endorsed Bullock. The count: Bullock, 912,740; Edburg, 280,258; Kirk, 6,549. Bullock got 76.1 percent.

In the general election that fall, Bullock's 1,099,599 votes, or 71.6 percent, swamped Republican Nick Rowe (419,657 votes) and Socialist Workers Party candidate Sas Scoggins (16,383 votes).

CHAPTER II

BULLOCK'S RAIDERS

The clock on the wall of the comptroller's office said it all. It ran backwards. "True story. The clock on the wall, it didn't run this way," Bullock said in a 1995 interview, circling his index finger in a clockwise motion. "It ran backwards."[1]

Backward was a polite way of describing the comptroller's office when Bullock arrived. He found an aging staff of bean-counters in green eyeshades making journal and ledger entries with lead pencils and keeping tallies with antiquated, manual adding machines. The most evident bow to modern technology was in the intake room, where a dozen or more workers sat on stools around a table opening mail—checks from taxpayers—with an *electric letter opener*. Once opened, the checks made their way slowly into the books and into state bank accounts. Crates of unopened checks were stacked nearby, awaiting processing that took weeks. The slow processing time was costing the state dearly in interest that would have been earned had the money been promptly deposited.

Everything creaked: The procedures, the equipment, the employees. Two months before taking office, Bullock put together a three-person team to interview Calvert's top aides and division managers. Because he knew he was going to replace most of them, he sat in on the interviews and questioned each person. Firing workers was not something Bullock enjoyed, especially not in the weeks before Christmas.

"I'm not going to let you wait," he told them. "I'm going to tell you as soon as I can whether you're staying or going." He set a deadline of December 1 to make the decisions. Thirty got the ax, and the few who made the cut would not survive long under the high-pressure management style of the new comptroller. Speed and organization would be paramount, and results would be expected yesterday, if not sooner.

Attracting new talent was not difficult. Bullock's reputation as a "one-man fury of reform," as one aide put it, was widely accepted, and the young idealists—some of whom had worked in his campaign—flocked to him. In some circles the comptroller's office was considered the most powerful post in state government—it was the comptroller, after all, who controlled the purse strings. Properly run, the comptroller's office could have vast influence over nearly every function of government. It was a tempting venue for those eager to make a difference, who wanted to make government better.

Well before he took office in January, Bullock had key staff members ready to walk through the door with him. Buck Wood would be his general counsel, and Don Ray would run his field-office division. He recruited Ervin Osborn, the respected former chief of the Austin regional office of the Internal Revenue Service, to be his chief deputy. He made it clear to them that patience would be no virtue in this agency. It would be expanded, modernized, computerized, and streamlined. Above all, enforcement would be toughened.

"We don't have enough money," he told them. "We can't even hire auditors."

To rectify that, he called on Gov. Dolph Briscoe, Lt. Gov. Bill Hobby, new House Speaker Billy Clayton, and a smattering of other influential legislators to make a case for beefing up tax-collection efforts.

"I've got to have an emergency appropriation," he told each of them, "and I have to have it immediately. The minute the Legislature walks in the door on the first Tuesday after the first Monday in January, I need that money. For every dollar you give me, I'll give you ten."[2]

Whether they believed he could deliver *ten for one* or were just calling his bluff, the deal was done. Bullock had his appropriation as soon as he took office, and things were about to get hectic. Running on one lung, a sea of alcohol, and the gathering forces of manic depression, he tried to engage every task at once—and he had laid out many tasks. His growing flock of fresh-faced, good-government romantics would soon learn that when they signed on with Bullock, they checked their personal lives at the door.

But first there were a couple of housekeeping details to attend. He removed the portrait of Calvert that had been hung by Calvert's staff years earlier, and would not allow it to be replaced with his own. "If they are going to put something up, let it be the state seal," he said. "They [the agency's employees] work for the state and its people. I'm just a conduit."

Next, there was the matter of the agency's name: *Comptroller of Public Accounts*. The correct pronunciation was *controller*, Bullock had long believed. *Comptroller* was an archaic English spelling, which would remain unchanged. But the correct pronunciation, he decreed, would be with an *n* and not an *mp*. To support his case, he consulted the Oxford Dictionary of the English Language and included its definition in a memo, sent to every employee, insisting that henceforth *controller* would be the spoken form. Occasionally, if someone relapsed to the unacceptable enunciation, Bullock would correct them: "If you're going to work in this office, you've got to know what it's called, and it ain't COMP*troller*."

That done, he set an exhausting pace that drove some of the holdovers from Calvert's reign to exit voluntarily. Wood described his attitude as being one of "If you think you can do it in a week, you probably can do it in a day." He hired a press aide to crank out a daily blitz of news releases—about his hires, about problems he was finding in the agency and how he intended to fix them, about matters before the Legislature. Once, he issued a press release to announce that "nothing happened in the comptroller's office today."

Having wiped out the top tier of Calvert's staff, he began working his way through the second echelon, firing those whose work he deemed inadequate or tardy. When he could, Bullock foisted that unpleasant duty onto one of his subordinates. When he had to do it himself, the firings were abrupt and emotionless: *Take your personal belongings and go*. After getting that message without warning, one employee of the revenue-processing division drove to his home, tied a rope to a rafter in his garage, and hanged himself. "The problem was that Bullock couldn't tell the difference between an incompetent worker and an impossible task," Bill Collier, one of his early top aides, wrote in a 1980 magazine article that was scathingly critical of his former boss.[3]

From the first day, Bullock's preoccupation, justifiably, was unpaid taxes. "I want to know how much delinquent tax is out there in the state," he told Ray.

An answer was not readily available, but the scramble was on to find out. Toiling with a decrepit bookkeeping system and an IBM computer for which a program had to be written, it took Ray's staff a couple of months to come up with numbers that appeared to be accurate: 70,000 delinquents owed the state $60 million. Some of the accounts were years old, and the businesses that owed them were long since defunct. Some involved only miniscule amounts, but many of the scofflaws were still around and owed hundreds of thousands of dollars that had gone unpaid for years. That money was collectible, but no one knew exactly how, since it was an activity that had never been exploited. For years, the most vigorous collection effort had been a letter to the offending business. Compliance was voluntary.

Then, researching the comptroller's statutory powers, Ray made a discovery he knew Bullock would love. Leaving his desk, he stepped across the hall to Wood's office.

"Buck," he said, "we got the power to go in and just seize property."

Wood's eyes widened.

"I've been up talking to the head of sales tax, and he said they tried it one time in Dallas. A sewing machine store. They seized a bunch of Singer sewing machines, but they actually lost money on the deal. By the time they sold them . . . they didn't get much for them, and they had [to bear] the cost of selling them . . . so they never did it again. Buck, there are a lot of businesses on this list. We could make it work."

Wood was interested but cautious. "Let's look at this really hard," he said. "Seizures involve due process problems. We've got to have a whole set of documentation. We've got to study the law. We'll want to read some cases. We don't even have a form for seizure notices."

He anticipated a lawsuit from the first raid, and he wanted nothing left to guesswork. He wanted to know the precise extent of the seizure authority, the mechanics and logistics of it. Wood figured it would take at least two weeks to bone up on the subject. "Do me a favor," he told Ray. "Have everything set up before you tell Bullock, because I know what's going to happen. He'll want to do it the next day."

The next day, the red light signaling an interoffice call flashed on Wood's phone.

"Buck, come in here to my office," Bullock said. From the excitement in his voice, Wood sensed what was coming. He entered the office and found Bullock and Ray drinking Budweiser beer. He knew for certain. *We're about to screw up.*

"Don tells me we've got the power to go out and seize this stuff," Bullock said, gesturing to a big stack of delinquencies on his desk. "I've already found five or eight that owe us hundreds of thousands of dollars, and they're still in business. This will get everybody's attention. We'll bring in more money doing this than by sending out hundreds of auditors."

Bullock's mind was racing. He rambled about the value the publicity would have in forcing future voluntary compliance. Ray sat quietly, grinning broadly as Bullock spoke. *Don,* Wood thought, *you and I are the ones who are going to have to do this, and we don't know what the hell we're doing.* Within a few minutes, Bullock had summoned half a dozen other staffers to his office to brainstorm the delinquency list and select targets.

The questions in Wood's mind were compounding. How much notice did the agency have to give the business owner? What documentation was needed? What about security? Did they need policemen with them in case an angry target decided to defend his inventory with force? What's the rush? Nobody's going anywhere in the next two weeks.

Under the statute, similar to one used by the Internal Revenue Service, the comptroller could simply issue a "jeopardy determination" and seize assets and freeze bank accounts on the spot; no 30-day notice, no hearing.

"How about these liquor stores in San Antonio?" Bullock asked. "There are three down there, and they owe us $405,000."

Johnny Gabriel operated the three stores, and not paying sales taxes was only one of his transgressions. Six years earlier, the Alcoholic Beverage Control Board had canceled his package store permits for buying liquor from unauthorized sources. He had no sales tax permit and had never paid "one red cent in sales taxes," Bullock told those gathered in his office.

"I'm going to padlock that son of a bitch," he said. "I can sell that stuff and get my money, right? Get a trailer to haul all that whiskey off. Get somebody to change the locks. Buck, get whatever documents I need to walk in the door and tell the son of a bitch I'm taking over."

"When do you want to do this?" someone asked.

"When do you think I want to do it?" Bullock said. "Tomorrow."

Making the argument of logistical hardships, possible due process requirements, and other ends that needed to be tidied up, the staff convinced him that tomorrow was too soon, but the most time they could buy was three days. Bullock had entered the launch code, and the missile already was rising from the silo.

Three days. It was scant time to prepare all the documents, consult with the attorney general's office, and make arrangements for the manpower and vehicles required to empty three large liquor stores. The attorney general's staff warned of "all sorts of due process problems." Rather than implant caution, that kind of recalcitrance only angered Bullock. "Well, we're going to need you," he told an assistant attorney general in San Antonio. "The day after tomorrow, we're coming down there and we're going to seize these places."

Trucks were rented to haul away the liquor, and arrangements were made to rent storage space at Southern Moving and Storage. The seizure notice was drafted, and extra enforcement officers were dispatched to San Antonio. On the day before the raid was scheduled, an officer in the San Antonio field office was instructed to visit each liquor store, do a walk-through, and make an estimate of the amount of inventory. The stores varied in size, and the enforcement officer had no experience estimating inventory. His guesswork was likely to be tenuous. Wood still wanted more time.

"Buck, you take the big store," Bullock instructed. "Don will get the next largest, and Wayne Oakes will take the third."

Assuming that the element of surprise would be important to avoid evasion as well as minimize hostile resistance, they planned to enter the stores simultaneously when they opened at ten o'clock the next morning. As Wood and his crew arrived at the first store, accompanied by a San Antonio police officer, a bobtail truck was backed up to the front door, prepared to haul away the goods. No customers were inside, just a young Hispanic clerk standing behind the counter.

"This business owes the state $405,000," Wood said, flashing the jeopardy determination papers. "If you pay this amount now, we'll leave. If you don't, we're going to seize the contents of this store."

No emotion registered on the young man's face. He opened the cash register and emptied the contents onto the counter. Smiling, he said, "If you wait until dark, I'll get you some more."

Wood had no idea what he meant. "I take it you don't have the $405,000?"

"No."

"Here's your notice of seizure," Wood said. "You're no longer in charge here."

For the next several hours, it was impossible to determine who was in charge. The store was huge, and the inventory would not fit into a single bobtail truck. Wood ordered another, but he soon realized that even two would not accommodate the entire inventory. He called Ray, who told him that he, too, needed more trucks. Wood called a major moving company, one with real trucks—18-wheeler, semi-trailer big rigs.

"Sure, we have trucks available," the voice on the other end of the line said. "What are we moving?"

"Whiskey," Wood said.

"We can't haul whiskey," the guy said. "You have to have a license to haul that."

That, in the race to pull off the raid, was just one of the snags the tax police had not anticipated. "What do I do to get a license to haul whiskey?" Wood asked.

"It takes federal and state permission."

He placed a call to Bullock and told him the situation. Bullock called Ben Ramsey, chairman of the Texas Railroad Commission, which regulated intrastate trucking, and said he needed an emergency license to haul whiskey. Ramsey said he'd need to check with his attorneys.

Wood imagined that he was wondering *what kind of trouble can I get into*. Ramsey was friendly with Bullock, however, and within an hour, the permits were issued. But, other obstacles presented themselves. Wood had procured a forklift and pallets to transfer the liquor from the storage room, but the door had to be removed to get the vehicle inside. Then, the storage room was too small to get the lift inside. Everything had to be manually loaded onto the pallets. Every available field agent in San Antonio was called to the scene.

Once in the trucks, the cases of liquor could not be stacked more than a few cases high because of the potential shifting and damage that would occur during transport. More trucks were summoned—18 in all just to the largest of the liquor stores.

Finally, the first truck left for the warehouse at Southern Moving and Storage, where another problem awaited. While other trucks were still being loaded, Wood received a telephone call from an enforcement officer at the warehouse.

"There's a problem. I'll put you on the phone with the guy in charge of the warehouse," the agent told him.

"We can't store liquor," the manager told him. "You have to be bonded. You have to have a permit . . . . a federal permit."

Wood called his boss, who had remained in Austin, waiting to see how the seizure went before making an appearance in San Antonio. "Bullock, we have a real problem," he said. "We need a federal permit to store this stuff. I don't have the time for it. Somebody else is going to have to do it."

A couple of hours later, Bullock called and told him the federal permit was in hand. The warehouse manager still was not satisfied.

"This stuff is flammable, and we usually don't store flammables."

Several truckloads of whiskey were idling in the parking lot, and Wood was growing impatient. *The guy is confusing flammable with combustible,* he thought. "Furniture is flammable," Wood snapped. "You store furniture."

At length, the manager relented on that issue but raised another. "I've got pilferage problems," he said. "You're bringing in $30 and $40 bottles of brandy. People will walk off with them."

"Whatever you've got to do, do it," Wood said.

More headaches. At 2 p.m, a constable delivered to Wood formal notice that a hearing would be held at 3 p.m. on an injunction to stop the seizure. That much he had anticipated. He drove to the attorney general's San Antonio office and found a group of nervous assistant AGs. "We don't know anything about tax law," the head of the office told him. "You're going to have to handle this."

Faced with her persistence, Wood agreed. His job was not to try cases, but he knew a little about the situation he was facing. There was, for instance, a provision of the tax law that prohibited a state court from enjoining the enforcement of a tax. At the hearing, the liquor store's attorneys made their case first, then Wood got his shot at the owner.

"You've been sitting on these bills for years," he said. "Why haven't you paid your taxes?"

The questioning was designed not so much to block the injunction, but to get the judge's sympathy and to persuade him that the liquor dealer was not a sympathetic figure. It seemed to work, even before Wood played his hole card.

"Judge, you simply don't have the right to issue an injunction," he said, citing the statute.

Without hesitation, the judge said, "That's right. I don't have jurisdiction. The injunction is denied."

Back at the liquor store, a crowd was beginning to gather. Word of the raids had gotten out and made the noon newscasts. Now more reporters and camera crews were swarming the place. Wood paid the spectators scant attention until five o'clock, when the forklift driver, not an agency employee, shut down his equipment and said, "End of the day. I'm gone."

Wood pleaded with him to stay. "We've got to have you. We'll pay you overtime," he said.

"Can't do it. I've got to pick up my kid."

Wood approached the audience and shouted, "Can anyone here operate a forklift?" He had no authority to hire anyone. No vouchers. No way to follow normal procurement procedures. One man stepped forward. They negotiated a price, and he went to work.

With all the glitches ironed out, Bullock arrived to harvest a public relations bumper crop. He spoke to the spectators and the press about businesses that don't pay their taxes, about his commitment to doing what the comptroller's office had always neglected, about how cheaters are a burden on everyone. *YOU pay the taxes*, he explained, *they collect it from you and pocket it.* He left and drove back to Austin, but work at the liquor store and warehouse went on through the night.

At midnight, the young man whom Wood had served the seizure papers, and who had remained at the store throughout, asked for a favor. He wanted permission to drink one of the expensive whiskies he had never been able to afford.

"You're an employee of the store," Wood shrugged. "If you're willing to take responsibility for it, I don't care."

Pulling a bottle from a shelf, the young man unscrewed the cap and poured a generous shot into a paper cup. He walked outside, sat down on the curb, and had polished off half the bottle by the time Wood and his crew locked the doors and headed home. The sun would be coming up soon.[4]

News of the raid was splashed across the front pages the next morning, and the early reaction was mostly positive. Law-abiding businessmen and businesswomen expressed outrage that the cheaters had for so long defied the law with impunity. The ordinary Joes and Janes loved seeing the big guys taken down.

New targets were selected the day after the first raid, and in the future, the comptroller would ride at the head of the column when Bullock's Raiders came to town. At Norma's Home Folks Café in Dallas, an angry and sobbing Norma Manis confronted the raiders, while television cameras recorded the emotion. Bullock's response: He pointed out that she was driving a Lincoln Continental while owing $45,000 in back taxes. She paid up with a cashier's check two hours later. In Houston, a nervous young manager of a music store tried to explain why he was in arrears to the tune of $8,638. "I don't feel sorry for a damn one of them," Bullock told the reporters who accompanied him there. "They took the nickels and dimes and quarters of the people of the state of Texas."[5]

In the early stages of the crusade, business owners were just as likely to be incredulous as angry. A liquor retailer in Houston laughed when Bullock told him the amount of his delinquent bill, but panicked when Bullock ordered the building padlocked. In Tyler, Bullock told the owner of a small carpet store he would have to pay up or "I'll seize and auction off your inventory." Replied the owner: "If you do, I'll kill you."[6]

Over the next several months, hundreds of seizures were conducted and Bullock's Raiders rode into Texas lore. Lawbreakers of long standing stepped forward and settled their accounts voluntarily rather than risk a visit from Bullock and the press corps that always accompanied him.

After the first one, the raids became easier. Bullock's legal staff had discovered that it was not necessary to haul away inventories and store them. All they had to do was padlock the doors.

CHAPTER 12

A BULLOCK IN A CHINA CLOSET

I n the reorganization frenzy of those first two years, Bullock's demeanor took twists that went beyond eccentricity. He would fire a staff member at night and rehire him the next morning. He herded his top deputies to long afternoon work sessions in nearby taverns. In the office, he alternated between roaring like a hungry lion and secluding himself, poking pins into a voodoo doll representing one of his enemies. Occasionally, he took a chair beside a secretary's desk and sat for long periods, saying nothing, just chain-smoking and staring into the distance.

Always a voracious reader of history and biography, he added the bureaucratic printing output to his reading list. Most days he took home armloads of reports published by various agencies, pored over them until the wee hours, and frequently woke his top aides to give them an impulsive assignment or solicit their thoughts on how to deal with something in the Department of Parks and Wildlife or how to improve Child Protective Services or some other agency beyond his jurisdiction. He insisted that his department heads be available anytime he wanted them—few would dare go to the restroom without leaving word with their secretaries—and each received pagers to make sure they were never beyond his reach. Most days, he was at his desk at seven o'clock in the morning, tapping out memos of instruction or criticism to his aides. Few were spared the "blue zingers"—so called because of the color of the paper they were typed on—and few did not live in dread of them.

His gluttony for knowledge became the stuff of Capitol legend. He created a research department unlike anything that had ever existed in Texas government, one that ranged far beyond revenue estimating and the state's economic trends. Knowledge was coin of the realm, and Bullock was holding all the change. Legislators had previously relied on fragments of information from the various agencies, on the self-serving presentations of lobbyists, or on the business-funded Texas Research League. Now, they could turn to the comptroller for *independent* data—ostensibly untainted by private greed—on almost any subject.

For most of the young liberals who had gone to work for him, it was the most exciting time of their life. It also may have been one of the strangest. During the campaign, he had insisted that everyone who worked for him read and reread *The Little Red Hen* and absorb its message of individual initiative and self-reliance. After taking office, he copied and distributed to each staffer an 1899 essay by Elbert Hubbard called *A Message to Garcia*, a sermon on duty, obedience, and resourcefulness built on a tale from the Spanish-American War. Garcia, it was told, was an insurgent leader working from a hidden base somewhere in the mountains of Cuba, and President William McKinley needed to get an urgent message to him.

From the story:

> Someone said to the President, "There's a fellow by the name of Rowan who will find Garcia for you if anybody can."
>
> Rowan was sent for and given a letter to be delivered to Garcia. How the "fellow by the name of Rowan" took the letter, sealed it up in an oil-skin pouch, strapped it over his heart, in four days landed by night off the coast of Cuba from an open boat, disappeared into the jungle, and in three weeks came out on the other side of the island, having traversed a hostile country on foot and delivered his letter to Garcia, are things I have no special desire now to tell in detail. The point I wish to make is this: McKinley gave Rowan a letter to be delivered to Garcia; Rowan took the letter and did not ask "Where is he at?" By the Eternal! There is a man whose form should be cast in deathless bronze and the statue placed in every college in the land. It is not book-learning young men need, nor instruction about this and that, but a stiffening of the vertebrae which will cause them to be loyal to a trust, to act promptly, concentrate their energies—do the thing, "Carry a message to Garcia."[1]

Bullock wanted only Rowans at his service.

Whenever he came up with a seemingly impossible assignment and a staffer asked, "How are we going to do it?", he or she would fall under an icy stare and the admonition, "You need to go back and read *A Message to Garcia*. Don't ask me how to get it done. That's your job."

After six months on the job, Bullock was getting high marks, even from officeholders who had previously opposed him, even when he butted into matters without invitation, which was often.

On his own, he conducted a "four-year look ahead at revenue prospects and spending trends" and informed legislators that if they didn't plug the out-flow, they would have to pass a $2 billion tax bill in 1977. He suggested that one new tax that should be considered was a corporate *income tax*—the most toxic two words in the Texas political lexicon. Jon Ford, the *Austin American-Statesman's* political editor, termed the four-year projection "unprecedented" and Bullock's lecturing of the Legislature as "audacious."[2]

Whether it was an adrenalin rush that accompanied his surge in fame, popularity, and power; or some bipolar mechanism; or simply booze, "audacious" was an adjective more and more commonly attached to the comptroller's name, especially in his high-profile rankling of fellow Democrats.

Sen. Lloyd Bentsen had his eye on higher office and was pushing for a presidential preference primary in 1976. He and his supporters estimated that it would cost less than $10,000 and would be more efficient and Democratic than the caucuses and conventions controlled by a small number of party members. Though no one asked for his opinion, Bullock issued a press release saying the primary would cost $200,000—an amount likely to erode support for it. He had inserted himself into an issue so politically delicate, Ford wrote, that "previous occupants of the office wouldn't have touched [it] with a 10-foot pole."[3]

He scolded Secretary of State Mark White for his opposition to bringing Texas under the federal Voting Rights Act. He blasted State Treasurer Jesse James for allowing "the worst problem with idle funds of any state in the nation." In his well-publicized view, State Auditor George McNiel, whose auditors had raised questions about some of the comptroller's expenditures, could do nothing right. He particularly ridiculed McNiel for requesting a computer inventory (a 33,600-page printout) of state property that could take weeks of valuable computing time to produce. That information was already available, Bullock said, in the monthly reports his office issued.

"Maybe this is just a continuing attempt on Bullock's part to harass us, since we are the only state agency that has authority to monitor what goes on over in [his] office," McNiel said.[4]

Even John Connally, long gone from state politics and the Democratic Party, did not escape an occasional dart. Three years after Connally had switched parties and joined the Nixon cabinet, Bullock, with no apparent provocation, issued a press release summoning "all Democrats to join me in a silent moment of thanks to Big John Connally for joining the Republican Party."[5]

While Bullock was meddling in the Legislature's business and offending his fellow officeholders, however, he also was bringing important reforms to his own agency. He speeded up the tax hearings process and shortened the time it took to return sales tax collections to cities. Expense accounts were processed promptly, the 128,000 state employees were paid on the day their checks were due and, of course, his aggressive enforcement—led by Bullock's Raiders—was forcing tax delinquents to get legal.

He also made good on his promise to recruit more minority employees, partially by personally calling on the presidents and deans of small black colleges and asking them to submit, for his consideration, the names of their top students. His affirmative action initiative was successful enough that a few months after he took office, a group of black legislators dropped a discriminatory hiring lawsuit they had filed against the comptroller's office before Bullock arrived.[6]

After pointing out those and other early accomplishments to a reporter, Bullock, aware of the considerable buzz about his future gubernatorial prospects, modestly gave most of the credit to his staff, which he described as the brightest group of people ever assembled in a state office building. In a sense, it was a circuitous compliment to himself. He, after all, had shown the superb judgment to hire them.

By the time the raids trickled down to small-change offenders and the interest of the press began to wane, the name *Bullock* had become one of the most—if not *the* most—recognizable in Texas politics. Voters who struggled to name their governor had no trouble identifying their comptroller. "When I ran for the office, most people couldn't spell it, couldn't pronounce it, and didn't know what the comptroller did," he said. "Now, they can spell it. They can pronounce it. And they damn well know what we do."[7]

The genes of populism were still strong in the DNA of Texas, and Bullock, at least in public image, was the purest personification of that strain. When he talked about all the home folks being screwed out of *their pennies, their nickels, their dimes*, one could almost hear the background chorus. The hymn wasn't just for the common voters; Bullock also was singing to the governor and the Legislature, and they were a rapt audience.

The emergency appropriations he had received at the beginning of the 1975 session had paid dividends, and Bullock was not shy about asking for more. Auditors, he argued, were profit centers. *Give me more money, and I'll hire more auditors to snag more revenue for you to spend*, he told the lawmakers. And he used his power over the purse strings to ensure that they would be accommodating.

Meeting for 140 days every other year, the Legislature passes an appropriations bill to pay for state government for the next two years. Under the constitution's prohibition of deficit spending, the Legislature can appropriate only the amount the comptroller says will be available during that period. It is a system that invites the rawest application of political manipulation. Example: His revenue estimators might determine that $10 billion would be available over the next two years. Bullock could tell the governor and Legislature that the number was $9.5 billion, but that he could increase it by a few hundred million with more auditors and enforcement officers. Invariably, he got the money, and in four years, the budget for his office increased from $16.5 million to $46 million.

Bullock also used the strategy to make himself a hero to selected segments of the bureaucracy. He'd frowned on Land Commissioner Bob Armstrong's desire to spend $10 million to acquire what later became the Big Bend Ranch in West Texas. But Lt. Gov. Hobby, according to Bullock's longtime aide Glen Castlebury, thought Armstrong was right. Hobby asked Bullock if he could find an additional $10 million in the revenue estimate. "Bullock never said no to Governor Hobby," Castlebury added.

But instead of granting the money outright, Bullock said he couldn't find $10 million—but he might be able to find $11 million, if $10 million went for the ranch and $1 million for a pay raise for the Texas Rangers. Hobby gulped and took the deal. Then Bullock immediately got the top Ranger on the phone.

"You've just got a $1 million pay raise," Bullock told him. "And don't think for a minute Hobby got it for you."[8]

His burgeoning budgets unleashed a ferocious beast that foraged for new sources of revenue. He toured the tax collection agencies of other states to study their systems in search of greater efficiency, began audits of out-of-state companies that did business in Texas, and acquired airplanes to quicken the tempo of those endeavors. It was no surprise that the beast would, on occasion, bite the hand that created it.

One notable example: Bullock was sued by the Texas Council of Campfire Girls after he forced the organization to pay $13,284.13 in sales taxes on its fund-raising sales of candy. In a suit to reclaim the money, the council argued that if Girl Scouts could sell cookies tax-free, Campfire Girls should get the same treatment. "There is no distinctive difference between a 'cookie' and 'candy,'" the lawsuit said. Maybe no difference in sugar content, but there was a distinction. Bullock pointed to the state statute, which defined candy—but not cookies—as a luxury item and therefore not exempt from taxation.[9] He was correct, but doing battle with Campfire Girls was antithetical to the image of a righteous reformer battling for the little people. Bullock was not displeased, therefore, when the Legislature quickly deflected the heat from him by drafting legislation to remove candy from the list of taxable goods.

In another moment of flawed zeal, Bullock's staff discovered that while auto repairs were subject to sales tax, airplane repairs were not. There were thousands of private aircraft in Texas, and several commercial airlines had maintenance depots in the state. After Bullock had a bill introduced to close that loophole, he received calls from the airline industry, asking for a meeting. A crowd large enough to pack his expansive office showed up, not just to argue against the tax, but to inform him that they had no intention of paying it.

"It would be just as easy for us to repair all these airplanes in Oklahoma City as in San Antonio or Fort Worth," an airline executive told him. If the maintenance operations were relocated, Texas stood to lose thousands of high-paying jobs. Bullock retreated and asked his legislative sponsors to scrap the airplane repair tax bill.[10]

Those kinds of missteps occurred under the pressure to produce more revenue. Slowly, however, some of the young idealists who had signed on with Bullock noticed other, less innocent acts that cast their boss in a new light. They figured out, for example, that the press releases boasting of another wad of found revenue were frequently disingenuous, and the "new" money was illusory.

"In fiscal 1976, Bullock's auditors identified $84 million in new tax liabilities, six times what the old comptroller's staff had come up with in 1974," wrote Bill Collier, a former *Houston Chronicle* reporter who joined Bullock's staff as a public relations aide. "But what we soon learned was that those figures were often based on highly questionable interpretations of tax law produced by auditors who were under the gun to turn out impressive totals. Many amounts couldn't stand up under appeal, and millions of dollars Bullock claimed to be raking in didn't exist. Bullock never provided any figures on how much of that audit money is really collected. The Legislature never challenged him."

Too, they noticed that the comptroller's office was morphing into a kind of employment depository for friends and relatives of legislators or other influential state officials with whom Bullock wanted to curry favor. If someone was down and out, and had the right connections, Bullock would hire him, even if it meant firing a more competent worker. State and federal regulations required that job openings be publicly posted, but those guidelines were largely ignored. "The few postings that were made were jokes—the jobs had already been filled," Collier wrote.[11]

Still, it was a giddy time to work for the comptroller's office, and no one wallowed in the giddiness with as much abandon as Bullock. On a whim, he would throw an office party on a workday or open up his office bar to lubricate business meetings. It was not unusual for Bullock to be drunk when he arrived at work.

Sometimes he took a group of aides out for lunches that began at noon and stretched into the evening. At other times, several assistants accompanied him to a bar at mid-afternoon for a drinking "work" session that ended at closing time. One member of the party was usually sent back to the office to invite women to join them. "The emphasis was on pairing off couples," Collier wrote after leaving the comptroller's staff, "and Bullock presided over these events like Bacchus himself."[12]

When he traveled, Bullock usually selected from the secretarial pool an attractive traveling companion.

Many of Bullock's early excesses slid beneath the radar of the Capitol press corps, which had been admiring of his reform efforts and appreciative of his flair for generating an unending progression of interesting stories, complete with outrageous quotes. His professed dislike and distrust of the press was belied by his insistence on mingling with reporters after work at places such as Scholz Garten, a beer hall where he would exchange gossip with them, share tips on behind-the-scenes shenanigans in the Legislature and, when deep enough in his cups, confess repentantly of his own past sins.

As a legislator he had taken money from the white supremacy lobby, he admitted. As a nightclub owner and operator in East Texas, he had skimmed state tax money, he said. As Preston Smith's fund-raiser and bagman, he had raked in illegal corporate money and laundered it through individual contributors, he said. He would have been caught in the Sharpstown scandal, he acknowledged, except that Smith had neglected to cut him in on the easy money.

The reporters rarely went rushing to their typewriters to file dispatches about the comptroller's unabashed candor, however. Most were stories about crimes on which the statute of limitations had expired and, besides, there was an unwritten code about running with information obtained at the bottom of a bottle. What happened at Scholz's stayed at Scholz's.

The motive for Bullock's candor was not entirely clear. He may have assumed that at some point, possibly when he ran for governor, his entire past would be more carefully scrutinized and old transgressions would surface anyway. Better he reveal them than leave them for a future political opponent's *gotcha* bag. Or, he may have been tapping into a sentiment rooted in religious fundamentalism—the notion that there is no greater tribute to God than a redeemed sinner; the greater the sin, the more glorious the redemption. The tacit moral to his confessions was clear: Bullock once was lost but now he's found, was blind but now he sees. His errant ways were behind him, and he would tell the reporters, "Stealing is out this year, boys."[13]

That prohibition apparently did not extend to questionable use of state funds, the "boys" were discovering. Late in the summer of 1975, two reporters, Sam Kinch, Jr., of the *Dallas Morning News*, and George Kuempel, of the *Houston Chronicle*, independently got wind of what appeared to be just that. Eight state-paid employees worked full- or part-time to create and maintain voluminous files on hundreds of state and national politicians. The archive, which was separate from Bullock's renowned card file of political contributors and activists, might have been a valuable political asset but had little, if anything, to do with the comptroller's responsibilities. The comptroller's office also was paying $600 a month for the Texas Press Association's clipping service, a daily compilation of stories from nearly every newspaper in the state.

After working on the story for several days, Kinch and Kuempel called Bullock's office and requested an interview. It was a major story, and they had it exclusively.

"I'll just take care of you guys," an incensed Bullock told them. "I'm going to call the *Houston Post* and tell them."

"You wouldn't do that, would you, Bob?" Kuempel asked.

"You just wait and see," Bullock said.

In fact, he not only called the *Post* but also the *Dallas Times Herald* and invited their reporters to attend a press conference the next day to discuss the matter. Letting other reporters in on the "scoop" would not deter the negative publicity that was certain to follow, but it would shift the paradigm from stinging exposé to sheepish announcement. It also would let Kinch and Kuempel know that he was not intimidated by their snooping, and that Bob Bullock's scalp would not easily be taken.

Other news organizations began to get wind of the upcoming press conference and made plans to attend, although Bullock had not invited them. To avoid losing their exclusive, Kinch and Kuempel did not wait for the press conference. They rushed their stories into print the next morning, making the crowded interview with Bullock a follow-up piece.

At the press conference, Bullock was asked about the "vindictive" act of tipping the entire press corps off to the enterprising work of two reporters. He expressed astonishment of being so accused.

"How in the world could I punish a newspaper person?" he said.

"Bob," a reporter asked, "are you having any trouble keeping a straight face?"

"I keep files on reporters, too," he said. "I could name your girlfriends and where they live and what flowers you buy them . . . if I wanted to tell that to your wives."[14]

That incident was a turning point in Bullock's relationship with the press. Reporters still valued his proclivity for making news, his tendency toward scandalous behavior, and his deep well of quotable quotes. But they watched him more carefully, were more skeptical of his grandstanding and spin-doctoring. His longstanding dislike of the press was merely fortified. His staff scoured the major newspapers daily, and Bullock sent letters of complaint to reporters—and their editors—for words or phrases he perceived as even mildly negative. He was known to call reporters at five or six o'clock in the morning to complain about their work or to ask why one of his press releases had not appeared in print. But he still hung out with them and drank with them, all the while needling them, wheedling them, or worse.

But they apparently got his attention, because a few months after the stories about his card file ran, Bullock moved the operation to a private office in the Westgate Building, across the street from the Capitol.

At Scholz Garten, not long after his massive archive was revealed, Bullock called Kinch aside and told him he wanted to talk privately on the patio. As soon as they sat down, Bullock pulled a gun from his pocket and placed it on the table between them.

"I sometimes get so mad at you that I want to shoot you," he said, leaning forward until his face was a foot from Kinch's. "I just wanted you to know that."

He glared at the reporter for a few more seconds, stood up, pocketed the pistol, and went back into the bar.[15]

CHAPTER 13

WHISKEY, WOMEN, AIRPLANES, AND GUNS

On Thanksgiving Day 1975, Buck Wood was at home preparing to have dinner with his family. In the 11 hectic months since he had joined Bullock in the comptroller's office, leisure time had been rare, as holidays, weekends, and vacations were secondary to Bullock's whims. Wood had spent months on the road, evaluating the comptroller's field offices around the state and carrying out the unpleasant task of firing employees who did not measure up to the new performance standards that had been put in place. This was an uncommon and welcome day of rest.

In the middle of the afternoon, the phone rang, and Wood was not surprised to hear Bullock's voice. "Buck, I need you to do something."

What now? The office is closed. The Legislature is out of town. No raids are scheduled. "What is it?" Wood asked.

"I need you to go to the store, pick up some sage, and bring it to me," Bullock said.

"Bullock, I'm getting ready to have dinner with my family," Wood protested.

"This won't take long. I really need it."

"Why can't you go get it? I've got a bunch of family here."

Bullock stammered with an answer. "I'm just . . . I'm real busy, Buck. I need you to do this for me."

Wood was baffled and more than a little put off by the request. He continued to plead his own family obligations and press his boss for an explanation. Finally, Bullock blurted out, "Dammit, Buck, I'm trying to cook two

Thanksgiving dinners, and I can't get away." With a little more prodding, Wood learned that one dinner was for Bullock and his wife, Amelia, and the other he would share with Kathryn, the second wife he had continued to see after their divorce and his remarriage to Amelia.[1]

The story is telling because it illustrates the reckless turmoil in Bullock's private life that lapped over into his public life. In his manic states, there was no risk that couldn't be taken, no speed limits, no road guards. In his private life, that was evident with whiskey and willing women; in his public life, it was evident in the manner in which he managed what was becoming a very important state office. Eventually, the public and private would merge into the makings of a full-blown scandal that could have finished him in politics. Women were part of the problem. Airplanes were another.

To that first small plane obtained from the Department of Public Safety, which had confiscated it in a drug bust, he added a Mitsubishi MU-2, which, while larger and faster, soon proved inadequate for Bullock's travels. At a frantic pace, he winged around the country, ostensibly to study the tax-collecting methods of other states. Those information-seeking forays soon became little more than high-altitude parties.

After being told that Louisiana was a model of tax enforcement, Bullock put together a crew—staff lawyers and enforcement experts—and lit out on a Friday for Baton Rouge, the state capital. After spending most of the day there, Bullock's group realized they were in the wrong place; Louisiana's out-of-state audits were handled out of the New Orleans office. Back at their hotel, they gathered in the bar to plan their next move.

"We've got to go to New Orleans," Bullock said. "Let's go this afternoon. We'll spend the night, and we'll go to the audit office tomorrow."

"This is Friday," Wood said. "They're not going to be open tomorrow."

"Wrong," Bullock said. "Their offices are open half a day on Saturday. We'll just fly over there and have a good time."

While they were talking, a young lawyer in their group was busy flirting with their 18-year-old Cajun cocktail waitress, something that had not escaped Bullock's notice.

"Paul, you like that waitress. Ask her if she wants to go with us," Bullock said.

For God's sake, what are we doing? Wood thought. "Paul, don't do it," he said.

"Why not?" his assistant said. "I'll pay for everything."

"Well, it's your poison, but I don't think it's a good idea."

The next time the waitress visited their table, Paul said, "How would you like to go to New Orleans?"

"Yeah, I would like that," she said. Looking down at her abbreviated cocktail dress, she added, "But I don't have any clothes. I'd have to go home . . ."

"We don't have time to do that," Bullock said. "Paul, find out where a dress shop is and go buy her some clothes."

At a nearby shopping center, while Paul and the waitress fetched clothing and the others waited in the car, Wood received a phone call from his wife, telling him that their son was sick and would probably have to be hospitalized. He informed Bullock.

"Drop us off in New Orleans," Bullock told the pilots, "and fly him home and fly back to pick us up."

In New Orleans, the party continued until the cocktail waitress became ill and had to be flown back to Baton Rouge. The plane then returned to New Orleans and flew Bullock's group back to Texas the next day.

The following Monday morning, Bullock told Wood that everyone was too hung over to go to the New Orleans tax office—except him. When he got there, Wood said, Bullock found that it was the wrong division, and that no one there could help him with out-of-state audits. But that conversation with Wood later kept Bullock from being indicted for the New Orleans trip. Bullock's lawyer, Roy Minton, asked Wood to relate the story to a grand jury investigating Bullock's travels. Wood testified to the grand jury that Bullock had told him about the Saturday visit two days later. Asked if he believed Bullock was telling the truth, Wood said yes, that Bullock wouldn't have had any other reason for telling him that at that time.[2]

It became a pattern. Bullock would select a destination—Phoenix, Santa Fe, Denver, sixteen in all before the binge ended—and assemble a crew to accompany him, a crew that usually included his concubine of the moment. His practice was to send his staff to meet with the local officials while he and his female friend took in the sights and saloons. To the professional staff, it sometimes seemed that their primary missions on those trips was not to bone up on the science of tax collecting, but to keep Bullock out of trouble.

At a tax conference in Denver, attended by representatives of the western states, Bullock was manic and restless. Sitting in the hotel bar at eight o'clock on the first evening, he announced, "This place is boring." Turning to one of the pilots, he asked, "Is the plane where we can use it?"

"Sure, I can make a phone call and it will be ready in 30 minutes."

"Call and get it warmed up. We're going to Vegas," Bullock said.

Wood sat quietly, waiting for one of the other lawyers to object. Instead they said, "Let's go."

So, Wood spoke up: "We're not going to take a state plane to Las Vegas."

"You just hide and watch," Bullock snapped at him, flashing a wicked grin.

Wood looked at the pilots and said, "Boys, you ain't taking Bullock to Vegas."

"What's the flying time?" Bullock asked, ignoring Wood's protests.

"We can be there in the morning," a pilot said.

"Call and get us some hotel rooms," Bullock told another of his aides.

"Whoa," Wood said. "We are not going to Vegas." Addressing the pilots, he said, "It's a felony to take that plane to Vegas, and it's going to cost thousands in state money to make that trip. Do you want to be part of a conspiracy to commit a felony?"[3]

Bullock acted angry, but was acquiescent. After lobbing a few choice and profane epithets at Wood, he ordered more whiskey and didn't mention Vegas again. Wood never knew whether Bullock was serious about the Vegas trip or putting him on.

By early 1976, reporters had taken note of the comptroller's frequent travels and were making inquiries, requesting copies of his expense accounts and the flight logs kept by the pilots. Those documents should have told them where Bullock went, why he went, and who went with him. What they got was less than the full story, and a doctored one at that.

After receiving a reporter's request for the documents, Bill Collier, Bullock's public relations chief, looked them over and found stark discrepancies that the newsmen would have easily detected. For example, some of the reporters knew that Diane Daniel, a Bullock employee and the ex-wife of ex-House Speaker Price Daniel, Jr., had made many of the trips, but her name did not appear on the flight logs. The pilots had been fearful of recording the names of Bullock's female companions.

"With Bullock's help, the logs were reconstructed as accurately as possible (or as accurately as he wanted them to be) and forged onto new flight log forms," Collier later wrote. Diane Daniel's name was added to the reconstructed logs, which, invariably and often falsely, reflected that the purpose of the travel was "to confer with tax officials" or "to confer with area taxpayers."

Because state law did not require it, dates of the flights were not included on the forms, making it nearly impossible to verify their veracity. In actuality, according to Collier, some of the trips had been for meeting friends, to conduct private business or to hunt on the South Texas ranch of his friend and former client Clinton Manges. While Bullock played, the planes were not idle: They flew onto and off the ranch daily, delivering the major Texas newspapers to him.[4]

Even with doctored records, reporters were able to piece together the rudiments of Bullock's extravagances and misuse of state funds. Read one early headline: *Bullock Spends Freely on Luxury.*[5] Attempts to explain the travel costs were ineffective; the press smelled blood and was in full arousal. On April 19, 1976, the *Austin Citizen* wrote:

> The *Austin Citizen* today requested access to key state documents from the office of State Comptroller Bob Bullock as part of a three-week investigation into allegations of mismanagement, high living and apparent violations of both the State Appropriations Act and Senate Bill 1. Allegations leveled by former state employees and backed by some documentation include:
>
> - Falsification of airplane flight logs.
> - Keeping more high-salaried employees on the comptroller's payroll than authorized by the Legislature.
> - Using funds allocated for pay raises for employees to hire new personnel.
> - Expensive remodeling and furnishing of Bullock's office in the Lyndon B. Johnson building.

The article noted that in just over one year, Bullock's payroll had ballooned by 50 percent, to 1,877, and that the state auditor was looking into misuse of funds in many of the hires. It mentioned flight log discrepancies and the lavish renovation of his office (a $225 antique clock and the addition of a shower, kitchen, and bar). For several days, the newspaper hammered away at Bullock's spending, reporting that his expense claims topped those of all other elected officials—including the governor—and pointing out that those expenses did not include the costs associated with maintaining two airplanes and four pilots.[6]

Bullock responded with a lengthy, astringent letter to Thomas Reay, executive editor of the five-day-a-week, free-distribution newspaper. "I've had better flyers stuck under my windshield wipers at the grocery store than the pathetic rag you've been littering my yard with," he wrote in part. "When the people of this state want to return to the old days of having a do-nothing Comptroller, a Comptroller afraid to do his job for fear of asinine criticism, when they want delinquent sales taxes they paid to stay in the hands of some disreputable merchant and tax cheaters to get off without paying their fair share, they'll do what you can't do—vote me out of office."[7]

Four months later, with the stories of extravagance still popping up in the newspapers and in Austin watering holes, Bullock ditched his $9,000-a-month leased MU-2. In what seemed to be defiance of the negative publicity and his editorial critics, he replaced it with a roomier $13,999-a-month twin-engine Beech King Air.

For the next few years, Bullock seemed hell-bent on self-destruction. His second marriage to Amelia was spiraling toward another divorce, and drinking was propelling him into curiouser and curiouser behavior. He often carried a handgun and spent long nights at the Quorum Club, owned by his old friend Nick Kralj, a sometime political operative and lobbyist. In a drunken snit one night, he pulled his gun on a young waiter who had displeased him. He put the barrel against the young man's head, cocked the hammer, and breathed hot breath in his face.

Breaking free, the waiter ran out of the restaurant and never returned. Kralj called him to apologize. "Come on back, at least to get your money," Kralj said.

"I wouldn't come down there if you had a thousand dollars for me," the young man said.

Considered an excellent marksman by his friends—some claimed he could put a rifle round through a wild turkey's head at 300 yards—he was admired on a hunt, but he racked nerves in more domestic environs.

At a stag barbecue at Kralj's house, which backed up to Camp Mabry, the National Guard compound in North Central Austin, some of the guests were target shooting with machine guns. Bullock sat at a picnic table behind them. Suddenly, he jumped up, pulled out a pistol, and began firing past his pals at the targets beyond them. On another occasion, Kralj accompanied him to San Antonio, where he was to speak to a group of corporate executives at an elegant museum. As they entered the large reception area, Bullock's pistol fell out of his pocket and went skittering and clattering across the tile floor. Kralj calmly stepped forward, picked it up, and put it in his pocket, as though it belonged to him. Bullock quietly thanked him and proceeded to mingle with the distinguished audience he had come to address.

The story went that Kralj, no stranger to the byways of the wild side, once got drunk with Bullock and the two of them took out their pistols and spent some time shooting at roaches in the Quorum Club. But Kralj said that never happened. "The walls were all stone," he said. "We would have been killed by the ricochets." He said Molly Ivins had written that story two or three times—perhaps told to her by Bullock—and it had become an urban legend.

One that did happen, however, was a night when Kralj had to leave the club to look in on his ailing mother, and left Bullock and George Garland, a Kralj buddy and the head of the comptroller's bingo division, in charge. He gave them the combination to the safe, which contained not only cash, but also guns.

"It wasn't two hours before George was in jail," Kralj said.[8] Bullock and his aide, abandoning their custodial obligation to the Quorum Club, left the establishment and were stopped a few blocks away by a patrolman, who saw Garland pointing the pistol at the driver of another car. He was cuffed and jailed until Bullock showed up with lawyer Roy Minton and bailed him out.

More than two decades later, Bullock told his chief of staff, Bruce Gibson, that back in his drinking days, he once was having a few cocktails with several people in an Austin motel. It kept getting later and later, when the husband of a woman Bullock had been hustling came in the front door. Bullock ducked into the bathroom, but then realized that he was trapped: The husband would be waiting for him when he came out. He saw a window in the bathroom and crawled up and dropped through the window toward the ground.

What he hadn't realized or thought about was that the motel backed up to a drainage ditch—a deep drainage ditch. "I just kept falling, and falling, and falling," Bullock recalled—about a 30-foot drop, into the mud. Bullock then found that the banks were so steep he couldn't get out. He had lost his sharkskin loafers in the mud, and had to walk four blocks in his socks before he could escape from the creek. "I kept seeing the headline, 'Comptroller Dies in Creek,'" Bullock told Gibson.[9]

To his employees, Bullock's conduct at work was as disturbing as his after-hours shenanigans. His demands grew more intense, often irrational, and although he was under closer press scrutiny, he was more brazen in the uses of the powers of his office. Some staffers tried to alert him that he was risking legal trouble by using his secretaries to do work for his 1978 campaign, but he ignored them or, in some cases, drove away those confidants who were trying to keep him out of trouble.

During a drinking bout with several of his assistants, at the Filling Station on Barton Springs Road in March 1977, Bullock ragged his friend and trusted legal aide, Don Ray, for spending too much time trying to collect sales taxes at such events as county fairs, Willie Nelson's Fourth of July Picnic, Trade Days, and the like. The discussion degenerated into an argument, with Bullock telling Ray, "I'm going to whip your ass."

They went into the parking lot and squared off, two drunks probably incapable of inflicting much damage. But, Kuempel, the former reporter and now one of Bullock's press assistants, stepped between them and headed off the fisticuffs.

When Ray didn't show up for work the next morning, Wood called him. "Where are you? You sick?" he asked.

"No, I quit last night," Ray said. "Bullock and I got in a fight, and I quit. I've been thinking for a long time about going into private practice. I want you to think seriously about going in with me."[10]

About the same time, Bullock and Amelia separated, and his depressions appeared to some associates to be deeper and more prolonged. He moved to a small farmhouse on a pond near Creedmoor, where the demons of his soul multiplied. In a sense, the Velcro was becoming frayed, and Bullock was about to slide off the planet. Alone, drunk, and depressed, he later told friends, he contemplated suicide and even played Russian roulette with one of his guns.

CHAPTER 14

NO MORE MISTER NICE GUY

Political adrenaline runs strong when the Legislature is in session, and only partly because of the partisan and ideological sparring over bills. It is just after elections, the point when futures are measured, waters are tested, odds are calculated, and partners are picked for the electoral dance of dreams. Who's in and who's out? Who's plotting which race? Who has the pole position?

Publicly, Bullock spoke little about his plans, but in private it was evident that his gubernatorial ambitions had not deserted him. As the 1977 legislative session got under way, the 1978 elections—the governor's race, chiefly—generated as much buzz as a honey farm. Dolph Briscoe had served one two-year term, was reelected to his first four-year term, and made no secret of his plans to run one more time. But he was vulnerable, especially to a Democratic primary challenge.

As the new session started, Bullock predicted that an additional $3 billion would come into the state's coffers. Competition for it was fierce. Junior colleges, nursing homes, educators looking for a revised school-finance system, property tax reform, county ordinance-making power, agricultural tax relief—all wanted slices of the pie.

Briscoe's ineffectual performance had withered into a blasé detachment from the job, and Bullock wasn't the only Democrat making guarded calculations. The Republican Party was growing in Texas, but still had not commandeered the governor's mansion. Whoever knocked off Briscoe in the primary would likely be the next governor. Even Preston Smith, crushed in the 1972 primary, was fantasizing about a comeback. Lt. Gov. Bill Hobby was an oft-mentioned possibility, but he had not shown robust interest in the job.

The most likely Democrat to test Briscoe was Atty. Gen. John Hill, who had made a failed attempt at the governor's office in 1968 and had been on the Texas political radar screen ever since. Bullock had helped him defeat Atty. Gen. Crawford Martin, but now he was sizing him up anew. According to Bullock's confidants, he was intimidated by the notion of running against Hill. He wanted to know Hill's intentions before making his own decision on the race.

Bullock knew that Carlton Carl, an intern during Preston Smith's governor days who later worked for Bullock briefly in the comptroller's office, had known the attorney general for several years and was on friendly terms with him.

"Get John Hill and bring him over to the Verandah [a bar], and let's have a drink," he told Carl. Hill was not known as a day-drinker, but he accompanied Carl to the meeting.

With few preliminary pleasantries, Bullock asked him, "John, are you going to run for governor?"

"Well . . .," Hill hesitated. "Uh . . ., Bitsy and I are thinking about it."

"If you tell me right now that you're running for governor, I'll bust my butt to get you elected," Bullock said.

Hill hemmed, hawed, muttered, stammered, and was decidedly noncommittal. After Hill left the bar, Bullock turned to Carl and said, "I'll never support that sonofabitch."[1] Bullock wanted information, and Hill wouldn't supply it. Bullock was impatient, and Hill was keeping him waiting. *Sonofabitch.*

It was just after sunrise on a Saturday, and Buck Wood was still sleeping, until the phone rang. It was Bullock, calling from his farmhouse. "I want you to come out here," he said.

Without asking why, Wood got out of bed, dressed, and headed south out of Austin. As chief deputy comptroller, a position Wood had assumed after Ervin Osborn died in December 1975, Wood had several projects in the works and assumed Bullock wanted to discuss one of them. When he arrived, it was seven-thirty, and Bullock was drinking a Budweiser.

"I need to make a change, and you're the change I need to make," Bullock said in the low monotone Wood had come to recognize as a mark of his boss's depressive states. "You've done a good job, and I'm proud of it, but I think you've peaked. I want you to start looking for a job. You don't have to come to work. Take a month or two and find another job."

Bullock had often fired top-level employees in a rage and rehired them the next day. But this was different. This was an icy execution carried out just after sunrise on a weekend. Wood was stunned. He had never been in private law practice, but he made a list and started scheduling appointments with firms that might hire him. Two weeks into his job search, Bullock was making regular visits to his office to talk about state business and, oddly, giving him long-range assignments, acting as though nothing had happened.

It was axiomatic in the comptroller's office that everyone's time comes—the time to walk away from the madness or be pushed from it. Bullock's behavior was growing more erratic and more intense. Like many others who had left the comptroller's office, Wood needed a breather. He expected an amicable parting, since Bullock had already fired him. He decided to join Don Ray in private practice.

On a morning in April, he sauntered into Bullock's office and casually announced his decision. "I'm going to be Don's law partner," he said.

Expecting a handshake, congratulations, best wishes, or some other expression of friendship, Wood was startled by Bullock's response.

"You are the most ungracious sonofabitch I've ever been around," Bullock roared. "After all I've done for you, you leave me in this lurch. Get out of here. I don't want to see you in this office again."

"Bob, I'm not leaving until the first of May."

"You can leave now. I'll pay you until the first of May."[2]

Lurch may have been hyperbole, but not by much. Losing his top deputy during the last few weeks of the legislative session. Revenue estimates necessary at a very busy time. New tax schemes and exemptions being hatched. A full plate for the Legislature. The timing was not good.

Bullock was true to his vow never to support *that sonofabitch* John Hill. Speculation about Hill's candidacy was mounting, and Bullock was convinced he would run. He opted, therefore, to seek another term as comptroller and support Briscoe in the gubernatorial primary—not just support him, but lay waste to his chief opponent. The reasoning wasn't so complex. Briscoe had promised to serve only two four-year terms, meaning that if he were reelected, he would exit in 1982, leaving Bullock the opportunity to run without facing an incumbent. If Hill won in 1978, Bullock might not have an opening for another eight years. In mid-July, with no declaration of intentions from Hill, Bullock addressed the 17th Constitutional Convention of the Texas AFL-CIO and announced that he would run for governor in 1982.

"Surely by then Dolph Briscoe will permanently reside in Uvalde," he said. "And surely John Hill will finish making up his mind what he wants to do."[3] That was a preview of what was to come, the beginning of a stream of vitriolic missives and speeches meant to discredit and humiliate the attorney general.

Bullock wrote, and released to the press, a letter to Hill complaining about the attorney general's lethargic prosecution of the backlog of sales tax delinquencies. "In short, it appears that the quality of tax prosecutions in your office is sadly lacking and that possibly millions of dollars have been lost due to inactive pursuit," Bullock wrote. He personally delivered the letter to Hill, and the meeting was brief and acrimonious.

"Before he got through reading the first page, he [Hill] said, 'You would do anything to me,'" Bullock later told reporters. "I saw real hatred in his eyes. I don't mind telling you I had a very uneasy feeling when I left there."[4] So addled was he that in rushing for an exit, he ended up in the attorney general's executive washroom by mistake. The story got the kind of newspaper play that Bullock expected.

To many of those around him, Bullock's attacks took on tones of eerie incoherence. Until that summer, Hill had not been his enemy, had not wronged him or provoked him. Yet Bullock was waging scorched-earth warfare, as though driven by cackling, dark demons seen and heard only by him. His methods were extreme, but his motives were more likely pedestrian: To bury his rivals, to keep the political prairie clear of large brush that might impede the progress of his own ambitions.

On Thanksgiving Day, he issued a press release calling Hill a turkey and bestowed upon him Bullock's annual Turkey Day Award, complete with a depiction of a Thanksgiving bird wearing a suit with Hill's head on its shoulders. Ostensibly, the reason for the award was Hill's failure to take legal action to help solve the energy crisis Texas and the rest of the nation were facing because of reduced oil prices from the Persian Gulf.

"If he would just allow all of his hot air to be harnessed and piped into homes and offices, there wouldn't be any need to use our oil and gas resources this winter," the press release said.[5]

In another press release, he said Hill could not fulfill all of his promises and should "be honest with the voters of this state and tell them now which promises he intends to welsh on."[6] For months, Bullock's ruthlessness and unflinching language were the sort of farcical theater that amused the citizenry and bemused political writers and political insiders. It was goofy but harmless . . . until it turned goofier. In a speech in San Antonio, he escalated the rhetoric to a level starkly acrimonious, even by the standards of Texas's gun-slinging politics.

"The voters," he said, "will have a clear choice between a proven governor and a sonofabitch."[7]

Texans had become accustomed to Bullock's outbursts, but this was a disturbing strain of political discourse. For good reason, the question was starting to be asked: Is this guy traveling with a full suitcase? The answer was *maybe not*.

He lived alone, drank alone, and nursed the black moods that were becoming deeper and more prolonged. At work he was indefatigable. He continued to transform and modernize the comptroller's office, played the Legislature the way Willie Mays played center field, and waged war on John Hill the way Sherman marched to the sea. He partied with the women who worked for him and still used his state airplane as his personal plaything. All looked normal, but underneath, he was unraveling.

The crash came in November 1977. He and Amelia filed their divorce papers that month and Bullock, gaunt and weary, his mental state deteriorating, found no solace in the farmhouse on the pond, where the nights were brooding and fretful. His physical condition suggested to friends that he may have been suffering from lung cancer, and they persuaded him to check into M. D. Anderson Hospital in Houston. Tests revealed no malignancy—only a precancerous lesion of the mouth and throat—but to no one's surprise, he was diagnosed as manic-depressive, a condition aggravated by excessive drinking. His liver also was damaged by alcohol, and his blood pressure was being pushed off the chart by heavy smoking. The doctors agreed to treat him only if someone stayed with him on an around-the-clock suicide watch. His top aides took turns shuttling from Austin to Houston on a state airplane.

His personal and professional lives were in shambles, and he indicated to his caretakers that he felt incapable of coping with them. Three divorces. Lawsuits for failure to pay his debts. Killer addictions. Periodic estrangement from his son. Accusations of corruption. A political future in peril. Collier was one of the crew that rotated in and out of Houston to keep watch on him. In one period of acute funk, Bullock told him, "I want you to draft a letter of resignation for me." Collier nodded, but sat on the request for a few days until improved spirits pushed thoughts of quitting from Bullock's mind.[8]

He was released after a couple of weeks, but little in his lifestyle or disposition had been altered by the dire warnings of his physicians. He was unable, or unwilling, to stop smoking and drinking. For a few months, he took lithium for the bipolar disorder but discontinued treatment because, he complained, "it took the edge off of my personality."

His personality was clearly edgy entering the election year. He and his staff, working on state time, put together an elaborate reelection strategy in the fall of 1977, mostly at state expense: News releases individually tailored for local newspapers, tapes for local radio stations, color slides for television stations, and extensive use of his card file of local officials and contributors. Collier complained to Bullock about the bank of secretaries outside his office with "Bullock Campaign 1978" stationery in their typewriters. Bullock took swift and efficient action. He put room dividers in front of the secretaries' desks so Collier could not see what they were doing. January proved that it was all a wasted effort. No one, Democrat or Republican, challenged Bullock for the comptroller's office. The absence of opposition may have convinced him that a year of bad press had left him unscathed and bulletproof.

Trolling for a chief of staff to replace Buck Wood, someone with experience and savvy, Bullock asked friends to approach Ralph Wayne, a former legislator from Plainview who owned a chain of radio stations and savings and loans scattered around the state. It appeared to be an awkward choice, since Wayne had worked for Ben Barnes during the Bullock/Barnes war years. In the Bullock scheme, however, it made sense. Hiring former enemies or adversaries—reporters who wrote negative stories about him, lobbyists who had worked to defeat him, political operatives who had worked for his opponents—was a way of filing down their fangs, of getting them off his back and on his side.

After Wayne brushed aside the overtures of three of the comptroller's emissaries, Bullock made the call himself.

"If you don't take the job, I'm going to resign from this office," Bullock threatened.[9] It was persuasive.

Wayne's arrival brought with it an air of hope among Bullock's lieutenants. Maybe Wayne would give ballast to an agency that was still listing from the storm over the airplane flight logs, the allegations of misuse of funds, the churning payroll and lavish office remodeling. Instead, the new chief deputy rekindled the in-house grumbling and press scrutiny.

Wayne routinely spent some time each workday attending to his private business. He also used the comptroller's airplanes to inspect the comptroller's field offices, particularly those in towns where he had business interests. He put his personal secretary, Sherri Revier, on the state payroll, and she and another Wayne hire, Jay Brummett, spent more of their time managing his private business affairs than the state's.

And his presence did nothing to curb Bullock's growing irrationality. Never one to be challenged, he became even more vindictive, and some staffers felt that he had crossed the line into outright abuse of power. One example involved the celebrated raids. Bullock had long since stopped participating in them, but when his gang went after an Austin restaurant owned by Bill English, who had once evicted him for being drunk and obnoxious, Bullock went along and insisted that the press be alerted. It was a routine bust, and English paid his back taxes, but in a television interview, he accused the comptroller and his crew of being a "bunch of drunks."[10]

Upon hearing that, Bullock exploded. He summoned his legal staff to work that night and ordered them to find a way to close English's business. "They can consider themselves fired until they find a way to shut him down." Another meeting was held the next morning, but because English owed the state nothing, no legal reason could be found to padlock his restaurant.[11]

Bullock's enduring obsession, however, was John Hill. He assigned his staff lawyers to scour Hill's legal settlements of non-tax cases; ordered his security officer to look for flaws or illegalities in Hill's Organized Crime Task Force; and had his claims division research all travel vouchers filed by the attorney general's office. Any useful information was turned over to the Briscoe campaign. Other Bullock staffers produced reams of anti-Hill press releases. His fiscal experts drafted spending and tax-cut ideas for Briscoe. Speeches, position papers, anything Briscoe needed, Bullock stood ready to provide.

It was gaudy overkill that eventually led Briscoe's campaign to try to put distance between the governor and the comptroller. Although party insiders felt Briscoe's hold on the office was fragile, the polls made him a favorite in the primary. He needed financial backing, precinct foot soldiers, and influential endorsements. He didn't need a hit man.

Bullock's focus on Hill was distracted only by his two other passions —women and Old Charter. In April, he met and married Diane Burney, a widowed Dallas socialite. Some of his closest friends were surprised. It was such a quick courtship that they had never met her, and Bullock had not even mentioned her. Buck Wood, who hadn't seen Bullock since he'd left his employ a year earlier, bumped into him. "Well, I got married again," Bullock said offhandedly. Bullock was using his state airplane for daily commutes to her home in Dallas.[12]

In the primary election, voters gave Bullock nothing to lift his spirits. The count: John Hill, 932,345; Dolph Briscoe, 753,309. The three also-rans, including Preston Smith, didn't get enough votes to force a runoff; Hill got 51.4 percent. It appeared that Bullock would have to spend the next four years co-existing with a governor he had tried to bump off. A depressing thought.

Two months later, Bullock was driving home with his ex-wife Amelia and another couple from an Austin restaurant, where he had celebrated his 49th birthday. Patrol officers Mark Smith and William Doyle noticed that he was driving suspiciously. First, he stopped for a green light at Burnet Road and Anderson Lane. Then, he proceeded on Anderson, repeatedly bumping his Cadillac into the curb. By the time they stopped him, both tires on the right side of the car were flat. Bullock told them he and his companions had been at the restaurant since nine-thirty that evening and had consumed "a few beers."

"What time is it now?" Smith asked him.

"About eleven," Bullock said.

It was past one-thirty in the morning.

He refused to take an alcohol blood test and was arrested for driving while intoxicated and booked into the city jail.[13]

"A charge is not a conviction," he told his employees when he showed up for work the next day. He left work early in the afternoon, saying, "Believe it or not, I'm going to celebrate another birthday." He spent the rest of the day at the bedside of his son, who was recovering from serious injuries sustained in a motorcycle accident.[14] At his arraignment ten days later, Bullock pleaded guilty to drunk driving and was sentenced to a fine of $222 and one year of probation on the condition that he refrain from drinking.[15]

Meanwhile, Bullock wanted out of the most recent marriage. He asked Wood to get it annulled. "I said, 'Bob, we're going to have to have affidavits,'"

Wood replied. "It can only be done in case of fraud or if you've never had sex. You can't claim you never had sex."

Bullock told him to try it anyway. Wood did, and found a friendly judge in Travis County. Burney wasn't contesting it. "The judge signed it. I filed it. And that was the end of that," Wood said. "He was happy to get out of it, and she was happy to get out of it."[16]

Nothing, it seemed, could curb Bullock's penchant for infractions and recklessness: not public disclosure of his shenanigans, not brittle health or run-ins with the law, not the cautionary counsel of his closest aides.

One who was increasingly troubled by activities in the comptroller's office was Collier. It wasn't just watching Wayne running his private business at state expense, not just the misuse of state airplanes, not just the abuse of authority; it was a torrent of sleaze that threatened to seep into every cubicle and desk drawer. He saw a female employee whom Bullock was dating call the payroll department and order up a raise for herself. He saw the scandalous purchase vouchers for such things as an $11,000 conference table or a $107 set of gold-tipped desk pens for Wayne. He saw competitive bidding requirements circumvented by splitting purchases into several vouchers and the rigging of bids by drawing specifications so narrowly that all but a preferred vendor were eliminated. For example, Wayne wanted to lease space in a vacated building owned by a bank where he had accounts, lines of credit, and friends in the executive suites. In advertising for office space, the comptroller's office specified that it would consider only buildings with a 2,000-square-foot cafeteria, 954 square feet of internal halls and circulation area, and 3,000 square feet of bank vault. That eliminated every building in Austin except the one owned by Wayne's friends.

Collier realized he was working for a state agency that was out of control, a comptroller who was trekking blindfolded and close to quicksand. His frustration and indignation reached critical mass. Like many of the reform-minded idealists who had been drawn to Bullock, he felt betrayed by a boss who had promised so much and delivered so much but tainted it with indiscretion, if not lawlessness. That summer, he gave Bullock a three-page memo reiterating his concerns. Nothing changed.[17]

Throughout the fall, Bullock was mostly silent on the governor's race. He could not endorse Hill, not after the number he had done on him. On the Republican side, William P. Clements, Jr., a wealthy Dallas oil-drilling contractor, had easily won a much smaller primary over state Republican chairman Ray Hutchison (the total vote was only 158,403, and Clements owned 115,345, or 72.8 percent). Bullock was a devout Democrat, and a *public* endorsement of Clements would have been contrary to his nature. But, he could hope.

Clements got 1,183,828 votes to Hill's 1,166,919—a margin of 16,909 votes—to become Texas's first Republican governor since just after the Civil War.[18] Clements's victory portended a smoother second term for Bullock. With a grateful ally in the governor's chair, his own sway with the Legislature and other agencies could be greatly fortified.

There was, however, one glitch. On the eve of the election, Collier and co-worker George Kuempel resigned from Bullock's press office. They took with them documents of political work done by the comptroller's staff and personal business done by Wayne's secretaries. They also took carbon type-writer ribbons, whose imprints would verify some of what they knew.[19]

In a matter of days, they would be talking to a grand jury.

CHAPTER 15

THE GRAND JURY AND THE FBI

R onnie Earle was sworn in as Travis County District Attorney in January 1977. He was 34 years old and had limited courtroom experience. As is customary with a new regime, he was dealing with a large staff turnover and scrambling to get new assistants up to speed on the full plate of pressing cases headed for trial.

The grand jury that was in session had other demands. In one of his first meetings with the panel, word on the street was that Earle was told, "We want to know what's going on with Bob Bullock." It would have been a hefty assignment even for a seasoned prosecutor, but for a raw novice, the prospect of opening an investigation of a man quickly becoming one of the most powerful politicians in the state was daunting.

Inexperienced and short of staff, Earle had to be content to do little more than gather string. That changed during the 1978 governor's race, in the primary between John Hill and Dolph Briscoe. There were allegations that Briscoe's Office of Migrant Affairs was being used mainly as a warehouse for the governor's political hires. Earle agreed to look into the matter if Hill and Briscoe each would provide an investigator to be supervised by an assistant D.A. It was a prototype of a special section in his office that Earle was trying to create with an earlier grant from the governor's office—a Public Integrity Unit to investigate official corruption.

The Bullock probe had been on and off the front burner for nearly two years. Nothing substantial had been passed along to the district attorney's office, so there was little to bite into—just the cotton candy of scuttlebutt, rumor, and speculation.

The Collier and Kuempel resignations brought another flurry of stories as reporters called asking about their reasons. A *matter of conscience*, they said, and released a copy of the resignation letter they had jointly signed.

It referred to "actions that could be considered wrong legally or morally." It continued: "You have shown yourself incapable of correcting these matters more than temporarily or cosmetically. Moreover, your recent actions show that your arrogance toward the law and disrespect for the public trust placed in you is worse than ever." They urged him to fire Wayne and suggested that he resign because of his health.[1]

The stories reignited the grand jury's interest, and Earle's. The governor's grant money for the Public Integrity Unit was running out, and Earle was trying to get long-term funding from the Legislature. Bullock looked like the ideal argument for such a unit. Collier and Kuempel had held key positions on Bullock's staff, and had firsthand information, access to documents, and sufficient indignation to talk about what they knew.

Earle brushed aside some of the allegations—campaign and personal business activities on state time—as "just politics" and focused on the more serious issues involving the misuse of state aircraft. In fact, he was as interested in Ralph Wayne, the deputy chief comptroller, as in Bullock. The grand jury invited Collier and Kuempel for a private chat. They accepted.

Bullock was furious that his ex-employees had talked not only to the press, but also to the grand jury. And he was incensed that Earle would have the temerity to investigate him. Slipping into his standard combat mode, he labeled Collier and Kuempel "traitors" for going public with their accusations and "burglars" for removing files and other material from the comptroller's office. Earle got the John Hill treatment.

The grand jury's term ended at the close of 1978, and the panel wanted to indict Wayne for misappropriation of state funds. Earle, however, counseled against that, arguing that it could hinder the investigation of Bullock, which would be continued when a new grand jury was seated early in 1979. The panel returned no indictments, but issued an unusual report—grand juries are empowered only to return indictments or no-bills—criticizing Bullock for "fiscal irresponsibility" and for hindering its investigation by destroying records and providing inadequate information. The report was briefly made public, but was sealed after Bullock filed a lawsuit to have the report expunged on the grounds that the grand jury did not have the authority to write and publish it.[2]

Bullock was not aware of it, at least in the early stages, but he had potential problems larger than Ronnie Earle. Other dissatisfied employees had left the comptroller's office and took their gripes to the FBI. One of his former auditors told the feds that he had been coerced into aborting an audit of a company whose owner was a friend of Bullock's. Then, other auditors came forward with similar stories, including allegations that some audits were blocked in exchange for payments to Bullock. Another ex-employee alleged that Bullock had expedited a request from Duval County that forgave 75 percent of the delinquent ad valorem taxes owed by a ranch company owned by Bullock's friend Clinton Manges. A bingo club operator told federal investigators that if auditors from a comptroller field office showed up at his business, a call to Austin solved the problem. The auditors left and never returned, he said.

Memos on rumors, suspicions, and tips from informants flitted between the San Antonio FBI office and the Justice Department in Washington, D.C. On the delicate matter of opening an informal investigation, a field agent warned headquarters: "Comptroller Bullock, who has as much political power as anyone in the state of Texas, will likely make a counterattack against [redacted names of informants] and the FBI." The memo noted that he is "crude, cunning, and smart as the proverbial whip; intemperate with a capital 'I,' [and] ambitious as well. Since Bullock aspires to higher political office, this investigation is proceeding as discreetly as possible at this time. Should any evidence develop which indicates a violation of federal statutes, the investigation will be pursued vigorously and without regard to possible public disclosure."[3]

The feds looked into Bullock's campaign finances and researched investments he was rumored to have made in Latin America. They tried to track down a rumored secret tape documenting payoffs to Bullock and the favors they bought. They checked out a Gulf Coast house maintained by lobbyists. It was a wispy trail going nowhere, and eventually the FBI tried to entrap Bullock by offering bribes through third parties. That failing, the investigation slipped below the surface, where it would trail in Bullock's wake for the rest of his political career.

Another politician, having taken the flak that marred the second half of Bullock's first term, might have been tempted to take a lower profile, to tone down the rhetoric and mend mangled fences. Bullock could not have stayed out of the spotlight if he had tried. The grand jury investigation faded from the headlines, and Bullock made nice with the new governor—he described Clements as the best friend he had in state government—but his demons wouldn't let him rest. Fate and his provocative nature ensured that he would never be far from the front page.

On a Monday night late in March, Robert Jones, an attorney, stopped his pickup truck at a traffic light on Lavaca Street in downtown Austin and was slammed from behind by Bullock's car. Police Officer Karen Brune stated in her report that she believed Bullock was under the influence of alcohol, "but not to the point I could put him in jail." She smelled liquor on his breath, but "he was not stumbling."[4] If Bullock had been given a sobriety test and failed, his probation on the DWI nine months earlier could have been revoked.

In April, he checked into a hospital for hemorrhoid surgery and could not let even that occasion pass without mischief. On the day he was to be admitted, he wrote a detailed advisory for the press room denizens who had taken to covering his every move and persistently commenting on his health. "The keen scatological interest of most reporters originally prompted me to schedule the operation in the Capitol press room," the communiqué said. "My doctors, however, advised me to seek more sanitary conditions. To the disappointment of some reporters, the surgical knife will be wielded by licensed medical practitioners, not amateur back-stabbers."[5]

After the surgery, Sam Kinch, who at regular intervals had aroused Bullock's spleen, sent him a get-well card. Bullock responded by having one of his assistants deliver a package to Kinch in the Capitol pressroom. It was labeled a laboratory specimen of Bullock's hemorrhoids. The packaging and contents, Kinch said, appeared to be authentic, at least to the untrained eyes of reporters who didn't know what surgically removed hemorrhoids looked like. Closer inspection revealed that the "specimens" were canned oysters.

Humor aside, questions of health persisted. Stewart Davis, of the *Dallas Morning News*, described him as a man "whose body never has kept up with his spirit."[6] But by summer, Bullock was looking and sounding more frazzled. He was beginning to part company with Gov. Clements over taxes and spending, was still battling Ronnie Earle and the grand jury, and was still drinking heavily and smoking three packs of cigarettes a day. He had just turned 50 and, at last, the spirit seemed to be going the way of the body. Looking and sounding weary and forsaken that summer, he announced that he might retire from politics when his term ended in 1982 and open a car dealership. *Might* retire. It was typical of Bullock never to close the lid completely.

In October, though, it appeared to reporters that, indeed, they would soon be writing his political obituary—or worse.

As usual, Bullock arose early that midweek morning, but he was not at his desk when his colleagues filed into the office. Sometime after eight o'clock, executive assistant Jack Roberts received a call from Bullock. He was having chest pains, he said. "I'd like for you to come over here." Roberts arrived at the residence, took only a brief look at his boss, and called for an ambulance. Doctors at Seton Hospital determined that he had suffered a heart attack but, once again, the spirit trumped the body. His publicists prepared a press release about his condition, but Bullock insisted on reviewing and editing it from his bed in the intensive care unit.

Later, he remarked that "a lot of people were probably surprised that I had a heart attack because they didn't think I had one."[7]

It seemed that he left the hospital hell-bent on proving them right.

"He bought him an office, but he can't keep it. He's long gone. Send him some roses. At this rate, I don't think even the people of Dallas will talk to him."[8]

That was Bullock four months after his heart attack, talking about Gov. Bill Clements, who had been his "best friend in state government" less than a year earlier.

"Bill Clements has got six barrels, and he speaks out of all six," he continued. "I can't figure him out. It would take Houdini. He's like Alice in Wonderland or Mary Had a Little Lamb."[9]

The governor had offended him on several fronts. Clements persisted in wanting to declare a $1 billion budget surplus, instead of the $300 million Bullock was projecting, to fund a tax rebate in 1981. *Rebate?* A tax *increase* was more likely. Clements had vowed to raise $50,000 to defeat President Jimmy Carter in Texas in 1980. Clements had spent $6 million to finance his 1978 campaign. Clements had politically blackmailed some of his appointees by forcing them to switch to the Republican Party before he named them to state positions. Shades of Watergate and the Nixon administration, in which Clements had served as Deputy Secretary of Defense.

As it had been with John Hill, Bullock's assailment of Clements was stunning in its ferocity and senselessness. The comptroller didn't have to spar with

the governor over projections of budget surpluses and shortfalls; the constitution gave him the final word. For a Republican governor to raise money to
defeat a Democratic president was known in the political vernacular as . . .
partisanship, something widely practiced in election years. Six million for the
governor's office? John Connally had spent $11 million to win one delegate
in his futile bid for the Republican presidential nomination. *Blackmailing*
appointees? Before and after Clements's election, conservatives were drifting
in droves to the Republican Party, and for Clements to persuade his buddies
to make the leap so he could appoint them to powerful positions probably
required little more than a wink or a nod—something less than a twisted arm.
But, the broadside proved that Bullock was back. He had dodged the reaper
once again and had regained his footing and his cruising speed.

That spring, the San Francisco-based *Inquiry* magazine published a long
article by Bill Collier, whose raucous resignation and grand jury testimony had
given Ronnie Earle fodder for his investigation, and it was reprinted by *Texas
Monthly*, resurrecting the tales of decadence and disorder in the comptroller's
office.

"Damn lies," Bullock growled, as he distributed to the press a seven-page
rebuttal to the article. At the same time, he admitted, with no hint of apology, that he drank on the job ("I work 24 hours a day"), became romantically
involved with women on the staff ("Yeah, I'm single; just because somebody
works for me doesn't mean I can't date them"), and provided jobs to the
friends of politicians to whom he owed favors or from whom he was courting
favors ("I don't hire plugs; I let them know they will have to prove their
worth").[10]

He took special exception to Collier's revelation that before being diagnosed with bipolar disorder he had contemplated suicide. "Wrong," he said. "I
contemplated murder—Collier's."[11]

Throughout the spring, Bullock fed his hunger for verbal combat. Two
years had passed since the Travis County grand jury had adjourned without
indicting him or anyone on his staff, but the battle with Ronnie Earle was
not over. Earle had presented evidence to subsequent grand juries, but no
indictments were handed down, and it appeared that none would be. Bullock
obviously wanted the chapter to end, but he chose an odd path to closure—
antagonizing the district attorney who could still be a problem for him. The
feud flared back into public view in July 1980, when Bullock accused Earle of
lying about when he received FBI transcripts of typewriter ribbons used by

Ralph Wayne's secretary in 1978—ostensible evidence that private business had been conducted on state time. Bullock wanted to challenge the transcripts, or attempt to explain them, but did not know until the FBI informed him that Earle had received them ten months earlier.

"Pretty boy Ronnie is caught with his pants down and his rear showing," he said in a press release. "It's long past time for little Ronnie to put up or shut up. His abuse of his law license is unforgivable."[12]

Eight months after Bullock's heart attack, Capitol correspondents were no longer pondering his obituary—political or otherwise. He had returned to such fine form that the Headliners Club of Austin created a special commendation for him—the Bite Your Tongue Award. Bullock accepted it graciously. "By God, I deserve it," he said.[13]

Three packs of cigarettes a day sucked into one lung. A river of booze poured over an ailing liver. Four hours of sleep a night for a damaged heart that had seen its vintage years. What he had contemplated doing with a pistol in the farmhouse by Creedmoor, Bullock now was doing with his lifestyle. His friends dropped hints, and his doctors offered frightful prognoses; Bullock ignored them. But the summer of 1980 was a minor turning point, or the first stirrings of one.

Ann Richards, a Travis County commissioner and comer in Democratic politics, was a friend and drinking buddy of Bullock's. Unlike Bullock, though, she was beginning to recognize the erosive consequences of alcohol. That summer, they traveled together to New York to attend the Democratic National Convention and the re-nomination of President Carter. For an inebriated week, they prowled the bars of the Big Apple and never once set foot inside the convention hall. Once back in Austin, Richards—with the help of an intervention involving several family members and friends—decided that the hangover would be her last. She entered a month-long rehab and made a complete and lasting withdrawal.

After she quit the booze, she encouraged Bullock to do the same, but he was disinclined. He had transformed an antediluvian state agency into a model of efficiency and had made himself a household name and one of the most powerful figures in Texas government—all while rummaging around the bottom of a bottle. In his depressive states, he could be a daring, creative genius, attacking problems other politicians didn't even know existed. In his manic periods, though, he loved nothing more than a good party. In neither state did he comprehend the caricature of himself that he was becoming.

As the Legislature returned to Austin in January 1981, Bullock was in a position to make nearly everyone happy. The decade of the 1970s had been volatile for world oil markets, and oil producers in Texas had been substantial beneficiaries. An embargo of OPEC oil in October 1973 had driven prices from about $2 a barrel to more than $12 within a few months, causing mandatory oil allocations in the United States. For the next six years, prices fluctuated in the $14 to $16 range, until the 1979 revolution in Iran drove production there to a 27-year low. In little more than a year, oil prices soared to nearly $40 a barrel, and drilling rigs were sprouting like dandelions on the oilfields of Texas and other producing states. Consumers were battered by the double-digit inflation spawned by the upheaval—inflation also ate into the value of state revenues—but the oil business roared for most of the decade and spun off sequels in real estate and finance. Bullock wasn't willing to give Gov. Clements the $1 billion surplus projection to pay for a tax rebate, but he had plenty of coins to jingle before the Legislature to barter for his own pet projects.

Bullock had become adroit at using his revenue-estimating authority to gain sway with the Legislature in matters that did not concern the comptroller, and the 1981 session brought to the forefront another peg in his power grid.

That session, the first after the 1980 census, was dominated by redistricting—congressional and legislative. Bullock could play no role in the former, but if the state House and Senate did not redistrict themselves, Bullock would be among five state officials who would do it for them. That is precisely what happened. The Texas Supreme Court ruled a House plan unconstitutional, and Gov. Clements vetoed a Senate plan. That sent the fate of members of both chambers to the Legislative Redistricting Board, made up of House Speaker Billy Clayton, Lt. Gov. Bill Hobby, Atty. Gen. Mark White, Land Commissioner Bob Armstrong, and Comptroller Bob Bullock.

That panel would not meet for its final deliberation until the fall, months after the Legislature adjourned. In the interim, Bullock was steadily in the news for somewhat less august activities.

After news stories reported that the comptroller's office had purchased an $11,000 truck with such luxury extras as mag wheels, tilt steering wheel, AM-FM radio, and an eight-track tape player, Bullock mailed boxes of cow manure to the Austin bureau of the *Dallas Morning News* and the *Mount Pleasant Daily Tribune*. To head off criticism, his spokesman, Tony Proffitt, declared, "He did it on his own time, on his own money."[14]

Then Bullock picked a clearly premature fight with fellow Democrat Grant Jones, a nine-year senator from Abilene and chairman of the Senate

Finance Committee, who had let it be known that "some folks" had approached him about running against Bullock in 1982. Bullock accused him of "political blackmail" to exact a better district for himself from the Legislative Redistricting Board. Bullock said Jones, a curmudgeonly figure who kept a pipe clamped between his teeth for most of his waking hours, had a "negative record" in the Senate and had "damaged the economic health of Texas." Then he added the most stinging affront: "He doesn't know how to fish or smoke a pipe."[15]

A couple of weeks later, Bullock held the spotlight at the annual Boneheadliners show in Austin, where he received the Friendship Award in recognition of his serial assaults on fellow officeholders and Capitol reporters.

Accepting the satirical honor, Bullock disputed the suggestion that he was friendless. He was on good terms with a number of bartenders, he said, and added, "Winchester is my friend. So is Remington . . . Colt . . . Smith and Wesson."[16]

Just a few hours after that ceremony, Bullock made news in a way that no one outside his inner circle had anticipated. He boarded a plane for Orange, California, checked into Care Manor Hospital, and placed himself in the hands of Dr. Joseph Pursch, who had treated former First Lady Betty Ford for alcoholism.

Proffitt was asked what triggered the sudden urge for rehabilitation. He shrugged and said, "Maybe he just got tired of waking up with hangovers."[17]

There was more to it than that. In 1998, as he was about to make his exit from politics, Bullock reflected on his drinking life in a long conversation with Pat Beach, a reporter for the *Austin American-Statesman*.

"I was drunk a lot. Drunk in the office. It got to where I was drinking morning, afternoon, and night. I was fortunate enough to have a staff that picked up and did a lot of work for me. Molly Ivins paid me a compliment once when she said Bob Bullock did more drunk than most people can sober."[18]

Carlton Carl, after leaving the comptroller's office, taught a course for Southwestern University in Georgetown that met at the Capitol. Bullock rearranged his schedule to meet with the class at 10 a.m. in his office. "I can't tell you how embarrassed I was for him," Carl recalled. "He was just knee-walking drunk. He smelled like bourbon, slurred his words."[19]

Bullock recalled being dumbfounded when a doctor at M. D. Anderson Hospital told him, "You drink too much."

"Drink too much?" he said. "I knew deep down I did, but no one had told me that. That's the problem with a lot of your friends. They don't tell you these things."[20]

Close friends may not have been as frank as the doctor, but they had dropped strong hints. Like many alcoholics, Bullock did not want to hear the pious counsel of reformed boozers and do-gooders. Former drinking buddies such as Ann Richards, and other friends of moderate consumption, no longer interested him. "I had stopped visiting with my close friends. I was ashamed of my condition, and I'd kind of cut off my relationship with my family."[21]

Perhaps a final indicator that he was out of control came in an incident involving his son Bobby, who also was swimming in a turbulent wake—run-ins with the cops, hanging out with a drug-using crowd, and, like his father, dueling with the demons in his head. Sometime earlier, Bobby appeared one day in the comptroller's office, and after an exchange of words with his father, he went into the auditorium and refused to leave. Bullock called the Capitol police and had his son removed and taken to jail. He fretted over Bobby, but was powerless to control him. He often called Sam Kinch, his friend/nemesis of the press, who lived three doors down the street from Bobby. He asked if Kinch knew what was going on at the house, if strange-looking characters visited there, what kinds of cars were parked there.

Early one evening, after not hearing from Bobby for a long time and not knowing where he was, Bullock got a tip that his son was spending time with one of Bullock's enforcement officers—who had recently been suspended from the comptroller's office because he had been charged with possession of hashish and marijuana. Bullock called one of his assistants and said, "Go get me a gun. We're going to this crack house, and I'm going to get Bobby out of this mess."[22]

A neighbor saw a man approach Burn's house with a large pistol and called the police. When the police arrived, the neighbor told them that the man, with the pistol in his back pocket, had followed Burns and his wife to their car and then had ridden away in a taxicab. When police stopped the cab that had answered the call to the house downtown, and surrounded it, they discovered its occupant was Bullock. They frisked him, but couldn't find a gun, and escorted him to his destination—the Quorum Club. Bullock issued a statement the next day saying he'd confronted the suspended worker about "a not-so-happy situation that I felt might involve my son, Bobby."[23]

One of his friends recognized that an intervention was required. Roy Minton, his lawyer, had bailed him out of enough tight spots and bad marriages to speak to him with candor and authority: "Roy and his partner sat me down and told me how sorry I was and that if I didn't do something I was gonna kill somebody or kill myself."[24]

For once, he took the advice to heart. Within a week after the gun incident, with Minton's help, he contacted Care Manor Hospital and arranged to check into the $285-a-day facility on September 14.

"The last day I drank was when I went into that treatment center," Bullock told Beach. "They told Minton, 'He can drink all he wants until he gets here.' Sure enough, I did just that. The first time I ever had the DTs was when I landed in Orange, California. I felt like I had snakes all over me. It was a miserable experience."[25]

Bob Bullock and legendary University of Texas Regent Frank Erwin swap stories at a Democratic Party unity barbecue at John Hill's Dripping Springs ranch. Dave McNeely, 1974.

Bullock gives sagging budget projections to Senate members. Behind him are Lt. Gov. Bill Hobby, left, and Finance Committee Chairman Grant Jones. *Austin American-Statesman*/Bob Daemmrich, Mar. 10, 1983.

Tax collector and revenue estimator Bullock, glaring over half glasses. *Austin American-Statesman*/Ralph Barrera, Dec. 19, 1986.

Bullock talks to Bob Johnson on Senate lectern while Paul
Hobby talks on phone. *Austin American-Statesman*/Larry
Kolvoord, Aug. 25, 1991.

Nationally syndicated columnist and former *Texas Observer* editor Molly Ivins chats with Bullock on Senate floor. Senate Media.

The relationship between the two former drinking buddies in the 1970s became much frostier as governor and lieutenant governor in the 1990s. Senate Media.

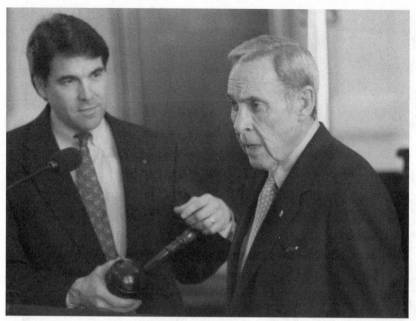

Rick Perry, visiting Senate chamber with Bullock on Nov. 17, 1998. Perry had won the election to succeed Bullock as lieutenant governor on Nov. 3. Bullock is responding to questions from reporters. *Austin American-Statesman*/Tom Lankes.

Bob Bullock, Nov. 24, 1998. He never was able to quit smoking. *Austin American-Statesman*/Tom Lankes.

Bullock and Bush share a laugh at the dais of the Texas Senate on Jan. 12, 1999, the opening day of the 76th legislative session. Bullock has just introduced Bush as the next president of the United States. *Austin American-Statesman*/Ralph Barrera.

Woman laying flowers on Bullock's grave, June 22, 1999. Sargent © 1999, *Austin American-Statesman*. Reprinted with permission of Universal Press Syndicate. All rights reserved.

Gov. Bush, Bullock, Jan Bullock, House Speaker Pete Laney, and State Preservation Board Chairman Dealey Decherd Herndon at the groundbreaking for the Bob Bullock Texas State History Museum, Apr. 18, 1999. Senate Media.

Bullock's statue being replaced by Tom DeLay's, Oct. 10, 2003. Sargent © 2003, *Austin American-Statesman*. Reprinted with permission of Universal Press Syndicate. All rights reserved.

CHAPTER 16

DRUNK SCHOOL AND BEYOND

What began as a three- or four-week tour of rehab turned into nearly two months of intense counseling, reconditioning, deprogramming, attitude adjustment, and physical exercise. His doctor had treated former First Lady Betty Ford, astronaut Buzz Aldrin, actors John Wayne and Dick Van Dyke, presidential brother Billy Carter, and other celebrity clients, but there were no stars in Bullock's class. He was thrown in with affluent but no-name teenage addicts, octogenarian lushes, executives, professionals, and others with snakes in their heads. He was kept under close supervision and, as a precaution, his razor and other hazardous belongings were taken from him. It was humbling, he said. He prayed, talked to friends and family daily by telephone, and took medication—Persantin to thin his blood, Enderol to lower his blood pressure, and aspirin to ease discomfort. He was introduced to the 12 steps to recovery and was told he likely would have to practice those steps each day for the rest of his life.

When the doctors felt their mission was accomplished, a private plane arrived from Texas, compliments of Clinton Manges, to return Bullock to Austin. *Who would be aboard?* his friends silently wondered. *Would sobriety be a mellowing agent, or would a clear head sharpen his tongue and his temper?* Long considered a man with an evil twin, the duality of his personality was summed up in a popular saying around the comptroller's office: "Bob is as noble as John Kennedy and as barbaric as Idi Amin, and always at the same time."[1] The Idi Amin side generally was chalked up to booze. Was it possible that the bad Bullock had been exorcised?

The tales Austin's bureaucrats and politicos reveled in telling about him were more likely to involve savagery than benevolence, but his close friends swore that he was not without feeling and sentimentality. Somewhere, wrapped up in that spring-loaded bundle of implacability, they said, was a tender heart. Claudia Stravato, who worked for Bullock and became his friend, told *Texas Monthly*, "He had to put on such a brusque exterior, but he was soft as mud inside. He could cry at the drop of a hat."[2]

And here are Bill Collier's words, written about the Bullock he knew in better times, in better moods, before things went wrong and the *other* Bob Bullock threatened to take over completely:

> Christmas Day, 1976. I was spending the day alone at a rented farmhouse, broke, broken by a nasty divorce, trying not to be miserable, concentrating on cleaning the wild duck I had shot that morning on the pond out back. The crunch of tires on gravel, sound of the door opening: In walked my employer and friend Bob Bullock . . . and his constant companion, a bottle of Old Charter.
>
> "I knew I would find you out here cryin'," Bullock said.
>
> "I wasn't crying," I protested.
>
> We had drinks. Bullock told of a horrible Christmas he spent alone and sick in a run-down hotel room after one of his divorces. Then about another Christmas when he and other misfits got together to cheer each other up but he wound up hiding in a back room so he could cry unnoticed.
>
> We both cried. We had more drinks.
>
> "I love you like a brother," Bullock said.
>
> He gave me the bottle and fifty dollars and saw me off to San Angelo, where, he reminded me, a woman who cared about me was waiting. He was right, and it was a good Christmas after all.[3]

There were about 3,000 employees in the comptroller's office in 1977, and it would have been nearly impossible for Bullock to know all of them. But, like a politician running for mayor of a small town, he was intent on knowing at least something about each one, or as many as a cranial database could absorb. He sat for hours in his rocking chair, reading personnel files and tucking away tidbits for future use. Then, in a conversation with a staff member, he would mention an item of personal information he had gleaned from the files—alma mater, birth date, number of children. Was it to let them know he was interested in them or to let them know that he knew things? Was he Kennedy or Amin at that moment? No one could be certain. The employee might be pleased that the boss was interested in him or her. More often, he or she was nagged by the questions *Has he been checking up on me? Why?* Now and then, they found that he used that information about them in ways that were contradictory to his public persona of a politician given to wrathful rampages and vengeful plots.

A few months after he became Bullock's chief of staff, Ralph Wayne's 14-year-old daughter was killed in an automobile accident in Brownwood. After attending his daughter's funeral, Wayne returned to the Austin townhouse he had rented but had not taken the time to furnish with a television. In his bedroom, he found a large Sony Trinitron and a note from Bullock: "I know you won't be sleeping much, so I thought this would help."

A couple of days later, Wayne flew his private plane to South Padre Island, rented a condo, and planned to spend some time working through his grief by reading and walking the beaches and jetties in solitude. He spent a day on the sand under a gloomy overcast and returned to shelter before the rain came. He stayed up all night, finally fell asleep at six o'clock in the morning, and was awakened by a knock on the door at ten-thirty.

Wayne, telling the story to *Texas Monthly*:

> I opened the door and it's Bullock. He said, "You all right? Family's looking for you. Hell, everybody's looking for you."
>
> I said, "Yeah, I'm all right."
>
> He got up and left. He knew the numbers on my airplane and tracked me down. Found it at the Cameron County airport.[4]

Even Ben Barnes, an old nemesis about whom Bullock had once vowed to "tell a lie a day" for the rest of his life, got an unanticipated glimpse of a curiously conciliatory comptroller. After losing his race for governor in 1972, Barnes returned to Brownwood to work for his friend and benefactor Herman Bennett. For nearly a decade he had no contact with Bullock. One day, out of the blue, he received a phone call: Bullock was flying into town and wanted to meet at the Brownwood airport. Not knowing what to expect, Barnes agreed, and the two met in a hangar where Bullock's plane was being serviced. It was a short but memorable encounter.

"We've hated one another long enough," Bullock said. "We ought to be friends."

They shook hands, and Bullock departed. A few months after that meeting, Barnes moved back to Austin to join with John Connally in a commercial real estate development business. They had been masterful politicians but, at least in this instance, were hapless businessmen. Their development company began at a time when the Texas real estate market was in a silent decline that was about to become a thunderous collapse. The day after they filed for bankruptcy protection, Bullock showed up at Barnes's office, handed him $10,000, and said, "Just pay me back when you can."[5]

Employees told of thank-you letters coming to his office from people they had no idea he had helped. At Christmastime, he received cards of thanks for favors he had rendered but had not discussed with anyone.

"He helped hundreds of people," said Nick Kralj, the Quorum Club owner and sometime political operative. "He would help people who were not capable of reciprocating in any manner."[6]

That was the Bob Bullock everyone hoped would come back from rehab, and there were hopeful signs in the early days. He arrived in Austin on a Friday, and after a meeting of the Legislative Redistricting Board on Sunday, he met with Capitol reporters. Tanned and trim, without the puffy bloat of booze, he sounded humbler and gentler, almost self-effacing.

"It's not particularly easy for me to sit here before you and admit I'm an alcoholic," he said. "But I am an alcoholic. I feel very good. I feel good inside. I'm not so sure it's important that you understand me as that I understand myself. Alcoholism is an incurable disease, but it's a proven fact that one can be completely whole again if he doesn't take alcohol into his system again. Of course, that is my hope and prayer—that I do not."[7]

He talked about becoming a slave to alcohol and his inability to fight it alone. He owned up to the "alibis" and denials. He expected his alcoholism to be an issue in his reelection bid, and he invited his opponents "to say anything they want about me," but he hoped the public would "gauge me by my conduct in office and the job I'm doing."

He told of going to a restaurant the night before with a young woman, and after they were seated, the waitress asked if they wanted to order a drink. "Thank you, I've already had too much," Bullock said.

"I'll tell you [reporters] the same thing today. I've had too much," he said, ending the press conference on that note.[8]

Dozens of friends and colleagues had crowded into the room. They applauded as Bullock finished his remarks and walked toward the door without taking questions. One reporter described him as "less caustic than before," perhaps signaling optimism that the good Bob Bullock was now in control. That was before contradictory signals were received.

At a fund-raiser in Houston a couple of weeks later, Bullock thanked a hundred or so high rollers for showing up and said, "I probably gave some of y'all hell when I was drunk. I'm probably going to give you hell when I'm sober. But I'm gonna stay sober so you might as well count on hell again."[9]

"If I told you some of the things I think Texas can do, you'd think I'd gone back to drinking," Bullock told a reporter as 1981 drew to a close. Six weeks out of the hospital, he was brimming with ideas and eager to talk about them.

"I like to think I'm an idea person," he said, offering as evidence a tax form slightly larger than a credit-card receipt, a simplified replacement for the old forms that were printed on legal-size paper. "I got the idea from MasterCharge and Visa. If they can do it [track receivables on a wallet-size receipt], I figured we could too."[10]

Another innovation: Bullock ordered each of his auditors, when they had finished going over a business's books, to leave with the taxpayer a form asking for an evaluation of the auditor's performance in such areas as courtesy, thoroughness, and convenience. That was an extension of earlier customer-service initiatives, such as establishing independent hearing examiners to arbitrate taxpayer complaints and installing a toll-free WATS line for taxpayers to call to get tax information.[11]

Besides continuing to fine-tune the comptroller's office, Bullock was surveying a larger horizon. "When he came back, there was renewed energy, increased focus—truly a rededication to Texas," said Jack Roberts. "He made up his mind that he was going to rededicate his life to the betterment of Texas."[12]

That rededication included a restlessness to swim in a bigger pond, politically speaking. He was paid $56,200 a year to preside over the largest agency in state government, whose budget he had pumped up to $82.7 million biennially and whose payroll he had expanded to 2,505. But like most career politicians, marching in place was a distasteful option. He had wanted to be governor all of his adult life, but the time was never right. Now he was 52 years old and wondering if the time would ever be right. He had committed to another term as comptroller, and 1982 posed few obstacles to that. Beyond the next four years, however, the stream was murky. New Democratic faces were smiling in the wings, and the tremors of an accelerating Republican progression, in Texas and elsewhere, were ominous.

As Bullock contemplated his prospects, the Texas Democratic Party did the same. Bill Clements's upset victory over John Hill in the 1978 gubernatorial race and Sen. John Tower's narrow reelection were followed by Ronald Reagan's rout of President Jimmy Carter in 1980—an election that saw large numbers of down-ballot Republicans ride Reagan's wake into office. Democrats were worried. Among them was Sen. Lloyd Bentsen, who had seen some of his most prominent Democratic colleagues—Frank Church of Idaho and Birch Bayh of Indiana—knocked off in 1978 and 1980. Bentsen resolved that the same fate would not visit him. Lt. Gov. Bill Hobby agreed, and they teamed up to put together a Democratic strategy that was a first in Texas: coordinating the campaigns of all statewide candidates. Essentially, it was an effort to make the best use of talent and money for common causes, such as get-out-the-vote efforts—targeting swing voters as well as the party faithful.

Before the Republican awakening, such a coordinated campaign was unnecessary. Most Texas politicians were Democrats, and the ideological battles were fought in the party's primaries, where coordination was not possible. The primary winners went their independent ways as they usually coasted to general election victories—if, in fact, they were even opposed by Republicans. Things had changed. Not only were Republicans fielding more players, they were getting generous help from special-interest political action committees with deep pockets and a zealotry for dominance. For Democrats, fund-raising alone was thin life support. They needed teamwork.

Bentsen recruited Jack Martin, a talented young political operative who had worked in his campaigns in the 1970s and had co-managed, with John Rogers, John Hill's near-miss run for governor in 1978. Martin then drafted Dan McClung, a political consultant from New Orleans, who had experience in several Texas races. Late in 1981, they met in the coffee shop at the Driskill Hotel and sketched out their plan on a cocktail napkin. Clements employed costly, high-tech methods in his 1978 win, and the Democrats figured he would do it again, making him hard to unseat. Martin and McClung reasoned that they would have to match Clements's strategy by spending $1.2 million on voter registration, phone banks, door-knocking, direct mail, absentee-ballot distribution, rides to the polls, and other mechanisms to maximize the vote. Bentsen and Hobby, prodigious fund-raisers, would put up half the money for the coordinated effort; the other candidates would supply the other half. At the time the plan was drafted, they didn't even know who all the down-ballot candidates would be, but the assumption was that they would participate.

Most reluctant of them was Bullock. He still believed more in personal political organizations than in partisan ones and, perhaps as important, uniting with Democrats he had slapped around in the past, and those he would likely slap around in the future, was a disquieting incongruity. Moreover, emerging from the Democratic primaries, along with such fixtures as Bentsen and Hobby, was a potentially potent lineup of future political stars:

- Mark White, a young Houston lawyer who had been Gov. Dolph Briscoe's secretary of state before being elected attorney general in 1978. Like Hobby and Bentsen, he was a moderate-to-conservative Democrat with little baggage to inflame opposition among businessmen and other Republican-leaning voters. He also had been aided in his attorney general's race against Price Daniel, Jr., by the fact that organized labor hated Daniel for allowing a right-to-work law to be included in a proposed revised constitution. It failed, but the laborites didn't forget. As attorney general, White had been incessantly traveling the state, and he was a high-profile critic of Republican Gov. Clements. With 592,658 gubernatorial primary votes, or 42.7 percent, he led five opponents, including second-place finisher Buddy Temple with 409,693 votes, and third-place finisher Bob Armstrong with 252,189, or 19.1 percent. White's total was not enough to avoid a runoff. But after Temple studied the results, he realized that White had led in virtually all demographic groups, and his own polling convinced him that he could not win. He withdrew from the race, and White was declared the winner.

- Ann Richards, the upstart Travis County commissioner who had never run a statewide race, took advantage of a mini-scandal involving State Treasurer Warren G. Harding, and unseated him in the Democratic primary. Like the other down-ballot candidates, she was perceived as more liberal than those at the top of the ticket, but she had savvy and an engaging wit, which spilled out in a drawl as smooth as cream gravy. She represented change, particularly for women. If women could keep the checkbook at home, why not do so for the state?

- Jim Mattox, a former congressman, was nominated for attorney general. A veteran of four years in the Texas House followed by six in the U.S. House of Representatives, Mattox was drawn out of his congressional seat by Clements's veto threats. By the time a federal court undid that redistricting, Mattox was so involved in the attorney general's race that he kept on with that effort. Mattox and John Hannah, a popular former state representative from Lufkin, beat out former state Sen. Max Sherman of Amarillo and state Sen. Jack Ogg of Houston to get in a runoff. Mattox, who charged that Hannah had exaggerated his legal credentials, won the nasty runoff and an unlikely promotion toward being what he called "The People's Lawyer."

- Garry Mauro, Bullock's friend and former aide, had the nomination for land commissioner. Mauro had managed statewide campaigns for Ralph Yarborough and Bob Krueger, and had spent more than a year as executive director of the Texas Democratic Party. He knew where the troops were. Mauro was a close friend and former political-management partner from those earlier races with Roy Spence, a co-founder of the GSD&M advertising firm, and got top-notch TV ads as a result. Mauro ran ads attacking his primary runoff opponent, state Sen. Pete Snelson of Midland, for sponsoring a statewide property tax.

- Jim Hightower, a populist running for agriculture commissioner, was the most unabashedly liberal of the crop. A former journalist who had been editor of the *Texas Observer*, Hightower had a wit to match Ann Richards's, and had come within a couple percentage points of unseating Railroad Commission member Jim Nugent in the Democratic primary two years earlier. Hightower got unwitting help from Reagan Brown, the sitting agriculture commissioner. Brown, a conservative Democrat, melodramatically stuck his hand in a fire-ant mound in front of reporters to garner publicity, only to be stung dozens of times. And in a huge slip of the tongue, in a speech being captured for TV, Brown referred to George Washington Carver as "that great black nigger—uh, educator."[13] Brown never recovered from the double gaffes.

All were considered attractive, ambitious candidates with promising futures in Texas politics. With Bullock's history of slicing up his competitors, it is not unreasonable to imagine that he saw the 1982 slate as worrisome to his own ambitions. The other nominees embraced the "Coordinated Campaign" idea so, like it or not, Bullock was compelled to go along. Money was not a problem: He had only token opposition that year, from outgoing Republican state Sen. Mike Richards of Houston, who had been drawn out of his Senate district and was not expected to have much chance to upset Bullock.

Besides the coordinated effort, the Democrats had a few other things going for them in the election year of 1982. The nation was limping through the second of back-to-back recessions that followed Ronald Reagan's election. Economists generally credited the downturn to Federal Reserve Chairman Paul Volcker rather than to Reagan. Arab oil embargoes of the 1970s and the resulting spiral of double-digit inflation and eroding value of the dollar had pushed the Fed to tighten monetary policy in an attempt to purge America of its inflation psychology. It was a painful remedy. Factories and businesses shut down; millions of workers lost their jobs and their homes. One of the early indications of how severely the recession was affecting ordinary citizens was a *Wall Street Journal* account of formerly middle-class citizens living under a viaduct near downtown Houston.

Reagan may not have been responsible for that, but his administration, which went to Washington pledging to shrink the size of government, was making the lower and middle classes edgy with talk of cutting Social Security and other social-service programs. Because of its oil production and robust commercial real estate development, Texas suffered less than the Rust Belt states, but there was enough pain and apprehension to give impetus to the Democrats as the election approached.

A few days before the election, Sen. Bentsen asked Martin how things were shaping up.

"Senator," Martin said, "you're going to win by a substantial margin. As a matter of fact, every statewide Democrat is going to win."

Everyone? Bentsen was surprised. "Does that include Mark White?" he asked. Of all the state races, that one had appeared the most likely to be retained by a well-heeled incumbent.

"Yessir, him too."

"Ooooh," Bentsen flinched. "Bill [Clements] isn't going to appreciate that."[14]

Indeed, the coordinated campaign was more successful than anyone expected. On election day in Houston, long lines of African American voters waited in the pouring rain to vote before the polls closed at seven o'clock. They had been contacted at least half a dozen times, and monitors kept tabs on how many had voted in each precinct. In those where turnout lagged, "flush teams" were dispatched to find voters and prod them into the booths.

By the time it was over, turnout exceeded what the Republican prognosticators had forecast by half a million. Clements got nearly 300,000 more votes than he had in 1978, but lost to White by about 232,000. Bentsen and Hobby skated to reelection, and every statewide Democrat further down the ballot also won.

Unity. Party cooperation. Common cause. Those things had put the Democrats, at least for a while, back on solid footing. All was blissful for a few weeks. However, on January 7, even before Mark White was sworn in as governor, Bullock announced that he would run against the new governor four years hence.

"The day after the election, I filed with the secretary of state a statement saying I would be a candidate [in 1986]," Bullock said. The statement didn't specify which office he would seek—there were consequences to formally declaring one's candidacy too soon—but Bullock made his intentions clear. "It's something I've wanted to do since the day I was born. I'm going to run . . . you bet."[15]

Sobriety may have mellowed him in some ways, but it did not sap his appetite for brawling. "I think he [White] ought to be inaugurated," he said. "That's fine. He can have four years, then I'll have four."[16]

A week later, preparing to check into Brackenridge Hospital for spinal disk surgery, Bullock used the medical condition to take another half-joking swipe at the new governor. "Keeping up with all the backsliding, flip-flopping, and broken promises in this change of state administrations has caused me a serious pain in the neck," Bullock said. The disk may have been ruptured, he said, when he "bowed his neck" the week before and revised his estimate of state revenue downward by $956 million—a forecast certain to inflict pain on the new governor, who was elected on promises to raise teachers' salaries and not raise taxes.[17]

CHAPTER 17

THE TAX MAN COMETH

"**S**omething funny is going on between the comptroller and the governor," said Sen. Bill Sims, a San Angelo Democrat serving his first term in the Legislature.[1]

Funny, maybe, but no one was laughing. No chicanery was necessary that year to make politicians rethink their campaign promises. Although it was not starkly evident out in the precincts, Texas had slipped into a period of economic decline that would be long, slow, and devastating. The seeds for that grim epoch were sown in Washington, D.C., in the Persian Gulf and in the exuberant cubicles of the banking and thrift industries.

Forty-dollar-a-barrel oil had been very good to the state by sparking tremendous increases in exploration and production in the 1970s. That drove up tax collections, drove down unemployment, and set off a commercial-development orgy of such magnitude that the construction crane was labeled "the national bird of Texas." But in 1980, the good times hit a wall. The feverish oil-patch activity at home and abroad had piled up surpluses that made it seem that the world was awash in crude. Prices began a long, steep slide. At first, the impact was almost imperceptible. Thirty-eight-dollar-a-barrel oil still looked fat, considering that in 1979 the price was closer to $15.

In the larger economy, some of the price decline was masked by the building expansion that had acquired its own momentum, thanks partly to another development in the 1980s. Ronald Reagan's election to the presidency promised—and delivered—an aversion to regulation. Nowhere was that attitude more ruinously reflected than in the supervision of banks and thrifts, which bankrolled much of the construction explosion. While the regulators took naps or played golf, financial institutions were free to engage in immoderate—and often fraudulent, it turned out—lending practices that hinged on the assumption that the good times would roll on forever. But construction's fate was tied to oil's, and the two were riding in tandem toward a rocky precipice.

In 1982, while Texas was sucking what seemed to be the last of its oil from the ground and OPEC nations lowered prices as they stepped up production, the long-range prospects still were not so obvious that candidate Mark White could perceive the hardship that awaited him. Oil, by then, was just over $30 a barrel, but the Texas boom appeared to still have steam. As the gubernatorial race entered the stretch, he continued to pledge to raise teachers' pay without raising taxes. Bullock's early warning radar gave him a different picture. In September 1982, less than two months before the election, crude dipped toward $30 a barrel, and depressed prices were certain to ripple through other segments of the economy. Bullock realized that he would have to rework the revenue estimate he was preparing for the new governor and legislative session.

Billy Hamilton became revenue estimator on December 6 that year, which he described as "the worst time in history." His first task was to slash the estimate. "Our consensus was it should have been $1.4 billion," he said, "but I didn't have the nerve to say *over a billion dollars*. So I said *$956 million*. And so, he [Bullock] went with that."

Things only got worse. Exploration slowed, low-producing wells were capped, unemployment crept up, and bankruptcies and foreclosures loomed for the former wheelers and dealers in oil, real estate, and finance. How long it would last and how bad it would be was a mystery. Bullock had a crew of Ph.D. economists responsible for revenue estimating. He had an economic advisory board. He incessantly read and culled from economic reports. There was, however, little expertise on the future of oil prices, few reliable compilations of data. He was frustrated that his staff of experts and analysts could not give him a reliable forecast.

"When you've had an upward trend, your models are reflecting that trend, and it's hard to get them to change reality," said Hamilton.[2] The comptroller's aces were not alone in their befuddlement. Only a few years earlier, publishers were churning out books by experts on the "new age of shortage"; now the world was drowning in abundance. After that initial $956 million reduction in the revenue estimate that greeted legislators at the beginning of the session, Bullock continued to warn that further declines were likely, leading to suspicion, particularly among freshman legislators, that he was playing politics with revenue to force White to break one of his campaign promises—the one to teachers or the one to taxpayers. That would have been no news flash to the veterans, who knew Bullock as a master of horse-trading with the revenue estimates. But this time, he was dealing real cards. For the first time in decades, a governor took office amid declining revenues, and the comptroller had less latitude to punish and reward. Lt. Gov. Hobby, a veteran of budget writing, gave credence to Bullock's gloomy forecasts by declaring early in the session that teachers' salaries could not be raised without a corresponding increase in taxes. But, by declaring so early that he was gunning for White's job, Bullock invited suspicions about all of his actions that even remotely affected the governor. What better way to stiff White than to issue punitive revenue forecasts?

Adding to the perception of artifice was the scantily concealed antagonism between the two men. For public consumption, they professed mutual admiration ("He's my governor," Bullock told reporters; "We've been close friends for many years," White said), but it didn't take a clairvoyant to see through the façade.[3]

"When you get two big egos like those guys walking around, somebody is bound to get into a conflict," Rep. Paul Ragsdale, a Dallas Democrat, told Richard Dunham, of the Dallas Times Herald, two months into the legislative session. An anonymous official from the recently departed Clements administration allowed: "It's kind of interesting to sit back and watch them sharpen their knives because the carving is inevitable."[4]

The friction went at least as far back as White's election as attorney general, where he was, in essence, Bullock's lawyer. The client recurrently expressed displeasure at the way he was being represented. As he had done with Atty. Gen. John Hill, Bullock groused about what he considered White's lethargic enforcement of tax delinquency cases or his opinions on legal questions involving the comptroller's office. In response to one of White's opinions in 1980, Bullock called him "dumb" and said the opinion "makes about as much sense as a square bowling ball."[5]

The enmity also flared when the two men were thrown together on the Legislative Redistricting Board, while White was attorney general. They exchanged insults during the panel's first meeting, clashing over the redrawing of the West Texas district represented by Rep. Bill Heatly, the dean of the House and a Bullock friend. At one point, Bullock said the haggling was making the board look like "buffoons."

"Speak for yourself," White said.[6]

Bullock sometimes used unorthodox methods to find the pulse of the economy. He would sound out small businesses—Melba's Boutique or Tarrytown Texaco, for instance—as well as the Texas Automobile Dealers Association or Texas Industries for anecdotal clues. Bewildered by the oil patch, he resorted again to the unconventional. He insisted that Hamilton accompany him to Houston, where he was confident he could get answers. They called on Dr. John Boatwright, the chief economist for Exxon Oil Co. and a man Bullock greatly respected.

"Tell me what oil prices are going to be for the next three or four years," Bullock demanded.

"Bob, we have no idea what they're going to be," Boatwright said.

Thank God, Hamilton thought. If Boatwright had suggested a target price, Bullock would have been disdainful of his own estimators and, worse, it potentially would have formed the basis of skewed revenue forecasts.[7]

It turned out that the revenue estimate would have to be slashed again. White delayed releasing his proposed budget while Bullock worked on the revisions. Then, it appeared, politics crept back into the process. Bullock waited until White scheduled his budget message to a joint session of the Legislature for March 9. On March 8, the comptroller issued new numbers, slicing another $500 million from the estimate—putting it close to the $1.4 billion Hamilton had been afraid to utter three months earlier. More striking than the amount was the timing. The governor had no more than 24 hours to adjust his budget proposals downward by half a billion dollars.

Not everyone around him was convinced that Bullock's alcohol rehab had stuck, and his war on Mark White smacked of the pre-sober idiosyncrasies everyone generally attributed to the influence of liquor. The ubiquitous bearded man was a classic example. He tagged along in February when Gov. White invited reporters on a tour of Austin's tent cities of jobless people. He was at the Capitol when U.S. Sen. John Tower announced he would not run for reelection. He was there when Bob Krueger, Kent Hance, and Phil Gramm announced their candidacies for Tower's seat. He was at the courthouse when Atty. Gen. Jim Mattox was arraigned on a commercial bribery charge. Above all, he was always present for White's weekly news conferences. Shortly, his identity was revealed: John Moore, the comptroller's $54,000-a-year "director of tax information." His actual assignment: Bullock's eyes and ears on state politics—chiefly the governor's office.

"My job is not political," Moore protested to reporters. "It's my job to stay informed of what's going on. There are very few issues in this state government and in this capital that do not sooner or later touch the comptroller's office, and we need to be independently informed of what's going on."[8]

Bullock refused to discuss the matter, resurrecting old questions about the misdemeanor offense of using state employees for political activities, the same activity that had attracted the attention of grand juries a few years earlier. Did this hint at the return of the imprudent, inebriated Bob Bullock?

Some employees believed he furtively drank vodka from a coffee mug in his office. Others were convinced that in social settings—a backyard barbecue or hunting trip—he drank rum from a Coke can. Claudia Stravato, who often helped Bullock with the 12-step exercise that was part of his ongoing treatment, observed that he could never get past the fourth step. "He worked so hard . . . but when he got to the fourth step—make a searching and fearless moral inventory of yourself—he couldn't think of anything good," she was quoted in *Texas Monthly* after his death. "You're supposed to think of your good points and your bad points and it used to break my heart that he never could think of anything good about himself. He would jump and do the twelfth step all the time, which is saving people."[9]

Questions about his rehabilitation gained some validity on the afternoon of March 21 on a stretch of Interstate Highway 35 in Georgetown, north of Austin. State trooper Ruben Duran, driving north, aimed his radar at a southbound 1983 BMW. *One hundred six miles an hour.* He zapped the oncoming car again. Same reading. Again. Same reading. He crossed the median and gave chase. The BMW pulled to the side, and Duran approached and smelled alcohol on the driver's breath. He also saw three empty Budweiser cans on the floorboard.

He looked at the driver's license: Robert Douglas Bullock. The name meant nothing to the trooper. He invited the driver to sit in his patrol car while he ran a check on his driver's license and auto tag number.

"How much have you had to drink?" Duran asked.

"Only two beers," Bullock said. He explained that he was trying out his new car and realized what he was doing was dangerous. "I'll be more careful," he said.

Duran talked to Bullock for a while "to ascertain whether or not he was intoxicated." Satisfied that he was not, he wrote a ticket for speeding and sent Bullock on his way.[10] A week passed before the press got wind of the incident, and Bullock, vacationing in Colorado, was not available to reporters. It fell to his aide John Moore, the ubiquitous bearded man, to put out his version of the story.

He was speeding, Moore agreed, but he disputed the rest of the story. *He did not tell the trooper he had been drinking. The beer cans were not his. Friends left them in his car.*

"It is heartbreaking to me that the story is being told this way," Moore said. "It is not there. It did not happen."[11]

Back in Austin, where speed was now the imperative, everyone had geared down and the legislative session was in slow motion. Less than two months remained before adjournment, and no solution to the budget conundrum was in sight. Hobby's early session prediction that new taxes would be needed was correct, and he probably would not have raised the subject if he did not have the votes in the Senate to pass a tax bill. By constitutional mandate, however, tax bills must originate in the House, and there was little enthusiasm there, particularly with the governor also waffling on the issue.

A third revised revenue forecast later in the session meant that the Legislature would have $3 billion less over the next two years than had been thought a year earlier. That was not enough tarp to cover the government's whole wagon train. In mid-May, House Speaker Gib Lewis called Bullock and wanted another $100 million to fund a teacher pay raise. Three days later, Lt. Gov. Hobby called with a request for another $90 million. White was pleading for taxes to be raised, but declined to specify which ones. That angered legislators, who felt they would have to take more than their share of the heat back home if the governor sat on the sidelines. House Speaker Gib Lewis gave the governor an ultimatum: Unless he became involved in the matter, there would be no tax bill.

Bullock used the turmoil to bear down on White. "He's a P.R. man. Hell, he's not a governor," he told Saralee Tiede, of the *Fort Worth Star-Telegram*. "I've seen his schedule; he's so busy running around Texas, running for vice president or for governor, one of the two, that he's not in Austin. During a session of the Legislature, the governor's got to stay here, got to be on top of what's happening."[12]

While trashing the governor, Bullock also was emerging as the steadiest ship in the fiscal storm. He recommended a law that could raise $500 million by speeding tax collection, and the Legislature jumped at the idea. He suggested a study of school finance, and Lewis announced the next day that the House would undertake one. And, while nearly everyone balked at revenue-raising specifics, Bullock did not. "I'll tell you where they can raise more money than they can say grace over," he told Tiede. "Raise the sales tax half a cent and put a one percent increase on oil and gas severance. The oil companies couldn't complain too much. They could [raise teacher pay] with no problem if they'd go gasoline tax. Even two cents."

He found no takers in the Capitol. In response to Lewis's prodding, White offered one revenue proposal that went nowhere, except into Bullock's gun sights. "White, the crazy thing, proposes a five-cent sales tax in unincorporated areas," he told Tiede. Mangling a simile, he added, "It's as unconstitutional as the rear end of a goat."[13]

Time ran out for White. What had been a lackluster session for him on several fronts expired without a tax bill or an adjustment in teachers' salaries. He needed a solid score on the education issue to give his administration—and his political aspirations—momentum. He vowed to call a special session the next year to deal with that issue—after a study. Dodging an insurmountable problem by entombing it in an interminable legislative committee boondoggle was a time-honored political feint, but White had grand plans. Working with legislative leaders, he established a 16-member panel, the Select Committee on Public Education, also called the Perot Commission because it was headed by Ross Perot, the Dallas multimillionaire and political dabbler best known for founding Electronic Data Systems, Inc., and for sending a private army to rescue his employees who were imprisoned in Iran when the shah was overthrown. White selected the chairman and five members; Hobby and Lewis named five members each. Drawn from academia, politics, and business, they were given an ambitious charge, potentially as controversial as it was comprehensive.

A serious review and reform of public education in Texas were long overdue, and White went far beyond the study of school finance suggested by Bullock and embraced by Lewis. The committee was instructed to review the salaries of teachers and determine if they were sufficient to attract and retain good instructors; develop an equitable method of merit pay and a package of fringe benefits; recommend ways to ensure that teachers are competent and the curriculum is the best; review the Foundation School

Program—the minimum each school must provide—and its relationship to the true cost of educating students; review the school equalization and ensure that any changes do not increase total taxes; propose new revenue sources or tax reform for education; bring the educational system in line with the high technology demands of the future; recommend ways to better maintain discipline in the classroom; determine the cause of school dropouts and recommend ways to stop the trend; study the needs of children of legal and illegal aliens and migrant workers; review the role of regional education service centers; and study the effects of recent court decisions on the public schools.

There were contentious nuggets in White's design. Merit pay for teachers was certain to draw fire, as was subjecting teachers to testing for competence. The emphasis on the needs of poor and minority students was another. White predicted, in fact, that the school equalization issue would be the most troublesome because of the "hard political and practical elements." Because schools were financed largely by local property taxes, the resource gap between rich and impoverished districts was stark and often starkly grotesque. Taxable property in the Edgewood school district, for example, totaled $22,366 per child, while it was more than $1 million per child in the small Kenedy County district. The state, which contributed to school aid mainly by paying teachers' salaries, had never found a way to equalize school financing, given the disparities in local property values.

Bullock was one of Hobby's appointees—chairman of the subcommittee on school finance—and the assignment energized him. He had modernized and revolutionized the comptroller's office, but this was different, bigger. It was an opportunity for hands-on participation in molding something important for the state, a chance to establish a lasting legacy. He wasted no time.

"You're going to learn everything there is to know about school finance," he told his aide, Jim Shear, "and you're going to do it in nothing flat. I want to know how the schools work in Japan. I want to know how they work in Germany. I want to know how they work all over the world."[14]

Shear's colleagues considered him "extremely smart, extremely creative," even though he never earned a college degree. Within six months, he had become one of a handful of experts on the subject in Texas.

Under normal circumstances, the deceased would be the reigning topic of conversation at the funeral. But, on that Thursday in October when Rep. Matt Garcia was laid to rest, Bullock was running for governor, and he was impossible to ignore. As most of the State Capitol pols were donning their jackets for Garcia's rites, Bullock made what news reports described as a "sur-prise" incursion into the talk of the day. The *surprise* probably was reserved for those who did not know him well. Everyone else had long ceased to be shocked by anything he did.

Why he picked that hour on that day was never clear, but a prepared statement—a rehash of his previous criticisms of the governor—"provoked astonished whistles, grins, and head-shaking among lawmakers who read it as they left a memorial service for Garcia," wrote Bruce Hight, in the *Austin American-Statesman*.

"Gov. Mark White ought to pay more attention to state business and spend less time playing with his new yacht, vacationing in New England, and running for vice president," Bullock's statement said in part. "In a way, I hope he's elected vice president. I can't think of anybody better qualified to hold an office without any official duties than Mark White."[15]

Yes, White owned a sailboat, anchored on Lake Travis, in partnership with two friends, but at 31 feet in length, it was hardly in the *yacht* class. Yes, White had vacationed in New England recently, taking his family to Providence, Rhode Island, to watch the America's Cup races. Vice president? White's name was being passed around in Democratic Party circles as a poten-tial candidate, but the governor denied he was courting a spot on the nation-al ticket, and there was no evidence to the contrary—but there was serious speculation over the airplane. Did White purchase a jet for the governor's office just to travel around Texas, where some airport runways were too short for a jet to land?

Even for a declared candidate, Bullock's onslaught seemed like overkill. Political jockeying three or four years before the next election is not unheard of, but normally it is carried out with tact, subtlety, and finesse, saving the long knives for the end game. It is plausible to assume that Bullock was driv-en by the drums of time. For more than a decade, he had lingered in the wings, an understudy waiting for the opportunity that never knocked. Now the clock ticked louder. He was only 53 years old, but his health was so wracked that delaying his ambitions might be to deny them. Too, the crop of promising new faces coming off the assembly line complicated the distant future, as did the emerging Republican threat. In his mind, 1986 could have looked like the last train to glory.

The incessant flak didn't play well around the state. "What does Bullock think he is doing?" asked an editorial in the *Abilene Reporter-News*. "It is ironic that he sees fit to accuse White of 'reaching for the next rung on the political ladder' when he himself is reaching for the rung marked 'governor's mansion.' Perhaps it would be better for the state if both White and Bullock ignored the political ladder for the time being and concentrated on the pressing matters at hand."[16]

There certainly were *pressing matters* to contemplate, not the least of which was the quickening pace of the oncoming economic calamity. OPEC cut its oil prices by $5 a barrel, further depressing the price of Texas crude to less than $28 a barrel. In four years, oil had lost nearly a third of its value, and the only coherent trend that could be discerned was continued volatility and uncertainty. Still hanging, and still pressing, was the matter of education reform.

The Perot Commission proceeded swiftly and efficiently. Split into subcommittees, the members held hearings around the state and invited input from teachers, administrators, parents—anyone with an opinion, idea, or gripe about public schools. A few revolutionary notions began to evolve, and Perot, a master salesman, kept the issue before the public, touting the commission's importance to the future of Texas and drumming up a grassroots fervor to prevent this study from being just another academic exercise consigned to an archive and forgotten.

As the work progressed, however, economic realities shadowed it. To implement anything the commission recommended would take money, and there was little optimism among the legislative leadership that a 30-day special session—just months before the general election—could produce a tax bill. Hobby was especially pessimistic. Why look at the Perot Commission's report if there were no chance of funding it?

On December 6, in what may have been a studied assessment of the political and economic realities but also another jab at White, Bullock predicted to reporters that there would not be a special session to study school finance, "so the schoolteachers are going to get it in the neck."[17]

CHAPTER 18

NO GROUNDSWELL FOR
"GOVERNOR" BULLOCK

I t was a hefty political wager but, as promised, Gov. White summoned the
Legislature back to Austin for a special session early in June 1984. "His
neck is out about 900 yards on this one," said Sen. Oscar Mauzy, a Dallas
Democrat and veteran advocate of education improvements. Another
legislator concurred: "I really believe if he doesn't get anything, he's gone.
I don't even believe the teachers would stick with him."[1]

In his first year as governor, White's relations with the Legislature were
strained. He tried to push his programs through with intimidation and saber-
rattling, using paid advertising to bring public pressure to bear on recalcitrant
lawmakers and stumping in the districts of key members. He drew a line in
the sand and got walked on, an experience that mellowed, if not humbled,
him. Asked at the end of that first session if he had learned anything, he half-
jokingly noted that he had reread the separation of powers clause in the state
constitution. Thereafter, he became a model of temperance and congenial-
ity, mannerisms that would be requisite now more than ever.

He was prepared to ask for new highways as well as education reform, and
the largest tax increase in Texas history to pay for them. If the Legislature
went along, he would be the first governor in more than a decade not only to
preside over a tax increase, but to also request it. If the Legislature balked, he
would be viewed as ineffective. Either way, his political fortunes were at risk.
Either way, Bullock would have a full ammo belt to fire at him. White was
gambling that improving education would enhance his stature enough to
withstand any flack over higher taxes. Too, it would be two years before he
would have to face voters again. The unknown was whether legislators were

willing to take the same gamble. Most of them would face voters before the dust settled.

On June 4, White addressed a joint session of the House and Senate and made his pitch. If they would pass new taxes for the first time in 13 years, he said, "You can be assured of my commitment to avoid additional taxes in the regular session in 1985."[2] Adopting Bullock's recommendation, he proposed raising the sales tax by a penny and doubling the gasoline tax to 10 cents a gallon. By also upping the taxes on tobacco and alcohol, the state would have an additional $4.8 billion over the next three years.

Only one legislator applauded: Rep. Stan Schlueter, a conservative Democrat from Killeen who chaired the tax-writing House Ways and Means Committee. His enthusiasm was not for new taxes, but for settling the issue immediately rather than postponing it until 1985. "I don't think anybody thinks we can do it without a tax bill next session," he said. "We might be willing to do this once, but we don't want to do this two times."[3]

That same day, Bullock—as if to raise the political stakes for the governor—told a group of public employees that they deserved a pay raise, and blasted White for not including one in his tax package. White proposed more money for teachers and highways, Bullock said, but "there's not one dime in there for the state employees who are going to administer it or the comptroller's staff to collect it."[4]

The next day, the Legislature met in joint session again to hear from their banker.

"When [Lt.] Gov. Hobby and Speaker Lewis invited me over here, they asked me to talk about money," Bullock began. "That being the case, I could make the shortest talk in legislative history: You don't have any. It is as simple as this: If you spend any additional money on any new or any existing program, then you must find a way to pay for it."

He noted a recent London meeting of OPEC ministers, who "dropped the bottom out of world oil prices," leaving Texas to sit "helplessly by as . . . the drop in value of Texas oil prices sent shock waves throughout our economy. We not only lost millions in severance tax money, but the oil and gas industry accounts—directly or indirectly—for 30 percent of our sales tax. Consequently, in 1983 our sales tax failed to grow for the first time in its history." He touched on the "devastating blow" of Mexico's devaluation of the peso, on the national recession, and on the previous summer's drought followed by a winter freeze that played havoc with crop production. He predicted that the Legislature would have $33.1 billion for the budget period of

September 1, 1985, through August 31, 1987. That would be a mere $1.3 billion more than the previous budget period.

"Just in the few hours you have been in session, I have already been asked one question repeatedly: 'Bullock, is there a chance the revenue picture will get better?' My answer is simple. No, I don't anticipate any great change."[5]

What the Perot Commission proposed was nothing short of a profound revision in school financing and accountability, which meant that passage was not a slam-dunk. In some ways, it was viewed as a continuation of the historic struggle between rural and urban areas. A coalition of big-city school districts and poor districts united behind the new system of financing, which was designed primarily by Bullock. The Mexican American Legal Defense and Educational Fund filed a lawsuit challenging the existing system as unconstitutionally inequitable. On the other side, the Texas Association of School Administrators opposed any changes to the financing method.

Urban districts stood to benefit because the new plan recognized, for the first time, the cost of educating the disproportionate number of hard-to-educate children (non-English speaking, handicapped, disadvantaged) in urban districts. Those schools would receive extra money, both for special education programs and to pay the higher salaries to lure teachers from suburban districts. Working with Bullock, school officials in the urban and poor coalition designed a basic grant of $1,715 per student for 1984–1985. The state would pay 60 percent. But, the actual size of the grant would be determined by a district's wealth, with more money going to poor districts and less to wealthy ones. Moreover, poor districts would receive additional equalization aid to add programs that rich districts routinely provided. To ease the transition for districts that would lose state funding under the plan, the state would pay half of the losses that local districts recouped by raising local taxes.

"The formula we worked on with Bob Bullock had built-in equalization in the purest sense," said Gene Gutierrez, an associate superintendent of Fort Worth schools. "This guarantees a basic amount to educate each student no matter where he lives."

Fairness aside, there were political realities to consider. "It will not pass the Legislature," said state Education Commissioner Raymon Bynum, who was trying to work out his own financing formula. "It causes more than 200 districts to lose money, and that's always a political problem."[6]

He joined with Rep. Bill Haley, the chairman of the House Education Committee, to offer an alternative plan that increased aid to poor districts from $362 to $500 per child. Bynum told legislators that the plan would result in losses to only 10 percent of the school districts. It also did little to equalize school financing. Bullock said the plan, in fact, only aggravated the inequities. If it, or some other ineffective plan, passed the Legislature, he said, he would join the Mexican American Legal Defense and Educational Fund's lawsuit against the state.

Meanwhile, a lobbying team headed by Tom Luce, Rusty Kelley, and Jack Gullahorn—financed by Perot—mounted an adroit campaign to steer the reform bill through the Legislature. White launched his own offensive, recruiting his own lobbying team and inviting legislators in small groups to the mansion to discuss school reform. He produced television commercials, but unlike the unilateral, heavy-handed efforts of 1983, he included Lt. Gov. Hobby, House Speaker Gib Lewis, and House Ways and Means Committee Chairman Stan Schlueter in them. He met with lobbyists and vowed to hold down spending in other areas to allow improvements in education and highways. He was unfazed when Republican state Chairman George Strake unveiled a billboard in Austin criticizing White for having campaigned against new taxes and now calling a special session to raise them. "Is Strake opposed to better education and highways?" White scoffed.[7]

The salesmanship was winning. Speaking to the House Appropriations Committee, White laid out areas in which he believed expenses could be trimmed so that there would be no need for another tax increase in the 1985 regular session. "He's got a good program," said former House Speaker Billy Clayton. "If we could stick with it, I think it would work."[8]

Skillful management would be required to get the package through both houses. Hobby, after a decade as lieutenant governor, had no shortage of the necessary deftness. He had mastery of the state funding structure, of the sprawling bureaucracy, and of the Senate's political undertow. He was dispassionate—stoic, some would say—and persuasive. The son of a former lieutenant governor and governor, for whom Hobby Airport in Houston was named, Hobby also was a multimillionaire, with a sense of *noblesse oblige*. Lewis, by contrast, was down-home and laid back. A native of Mexia, who owned a label and printing company in Fort Worth, he gave the impression of being interested in being speaker because it was the political equivalent of being elected Prom King, and it provided perks and leverage that led to lots of other things. While Hobby still dealt with a stammer from his childhood, Lewis was more noted for mangling the language—to the point that some reporters collected "Gib-isms." Lewis, to a large extent, was an uncertainty. His first session as speaker had been marred by conflict-of-interest accusations, and he was generally regarded as more of a "good ol' boy" than a heavyweight dealmaker, an assessment he did not dispute. He preferred to be a "member speaker" rather than a trail boss. Saralee Tiede, of the *Fort Worth Star-Telegram*, described his style as "hesitant, laissez-faire."[9] Although the House speaker has an ample toolkit for shaping and moving bills, the larger chamber is often more rebellious and rambunctious than the Senate. Something as monumental and quarrelsome as an unprecedented tax increase would be a revealing test for Lewis.

As bills were drafted to enact the Perot Commission's recommendations, Lewis stayed in the background. But, as it became apparent that the package was in trouble, he became more assertive, drafting compromise proposals and using the powers of his position to push them. When four rival education groups protested a provision for testing teachers for competency, Lewis told them that if they did not support the bill, merit pay would be rammed down their throats. That was something they loathed more than testing. All four groups signed a letter endorsing Lewis's compromise bill. When a revolt simmered in the House—his own education committee rejected Lewis's plan—he rewrote it and invited all the chairmen to lunch to "explain some things to them." The speaker controls who serves on the House committees and who chairs them. Rumors circulated that he had threatened some chairmen with their jobs. On Thursday, the day before the bill came up for a final vote, he presided over a 14-hour session, repelling dozens of amendments that would have crippled the measure. On Friday, the bill sailed through the House.

"Gib Lewis is the speaker, and what you saw was the power of the speaker," Mike Morrow, executive director of the Association of Texas Professional Educators, told the *Dallas Morning News*.

"It was very, very clear that he understands and can use the power of the speaker," observed June L. Karp, a lobbyist for the Texas Federation of Teachers.[10]

Across the rotunda, Hobby's mettle also was being tested. While a conference committee was reconciling House and Senate versions of the bill, three of the four teacher groups withdrew their support. Becky Brooks, president-elect of the Texas State Teachers Association, held a press conference to complain that the career ladder established by the bill was not adequately funded, meaning that some teachers would get no pay raise. Also, she said, the salary supplements provided by the bill could be handed out arbitrarily, resulting in the equivalent of merit pay. "Even a dog knows the difference between being stumbled over and being kicked," she said.

Hobby was infuriated. He summoned the teacher representatives to his office for a meeting with more than a dozen senators. He strongly suggested that they apologize, issue a retraction of their statement, and return to supporting the bill. They declined.

"Leave my office and don't come back—ever," Hobby told them.

Senators who watched were dumbfounded by the lieutenant governor's rare display of anger. Sen. John Montford, of Lubbock, described the confrontation as being "like the Alamo, without the blood."

Later that day, Hobby was unrepentant. "I'll never see that bunch again," he said. "TSTA has been declining in credibility for a number of years, and that's about the tombstone for them as an effective force."

As chairman of the Legislative Budget Board, Hobby was the most powerful budgetary force in state government, and educators were aware that their low standing with him could have serious consequences. Said John McDonald, one of two TSTA officials at the meeting: "We're walking on our knees today, but we've got our head held high."

Annell McCorkle, of the Association of Texas Professional Educators, added, "We just hope the leadership won't be vindictive."[11]

Enacting school reform was the easy part, relatively. Teacher salaries were raised, the State Board of Education was revamped, and stricter standards for teachers and students were mandated—including the controversial teacher-testing provision and a no-pass, no-play rule applied to extracurricular activities for students. The tax bill to pay for it was another matter. Despite forceful legislative stewardship, gubernatorial diplomacy, and capable pro-reform lobbying, it remained endangered to the end. Both houses agreed to double the gasoline tax; raise taxes on liquor, beer, wine, hotel rooms, motor vehicles, and corporate assets; and extend the sales tax to cover tobacco products, some computer software, cable television, automobile parking, and laundry and dry cleaning. But the bill hit a major snag, potentially a fatal one. With the special session slipping toward an adjournment deadline, the House unanimously rejected the Senate's tax bill because, as Rep. Stan Schlueter described it, "They took a tax off business and put it back on the general public."[12]

What the Senate bill did was raise the sales tax by a quarter of a penny and reject the House bill's sales taxes on advertising, repairs, amusement admissions, and mixed drinks. Schlueter's colleagues applauded when he moved to reject the Senate bill and refused to appoint House members to a conference committee to hash out the differences. That began a marathon session that lasted through the night. Early the next morning, legislative leaders met with White and emerged at 9:15 to announce that a compromise had been reached.

Still, it wasn't over. At mid-morning, Sen. John Leedom, a Dallas Republican, told reporters: "The idea of increasing taxes by $4.8 billion with the Senate having only three days to consider it is unconscionable." He said he intended to kill the bill by filibustering until the midnight adjournment deadline. Even a plea from White did not dissuade him.

At 11 o'clock, Bullock and Legislative Budget Board director Jim Oliver summoned Leedom to the Senate members' lounge and told him that his tactic would cost the state $100 million by delaying the collection of new taxes. Thirty minutes later, Leedom came out of the meeting and told reporters he was abandoning his filibuster.[13]

Finally, the deal was done. The Senate passed the bill first, by a vote of 22–9, and then Hobby and White strode into the House chamber to announce the result. The House passed it 81–65 and erupted in applause. "I never thought I'd see the day they'd clap for a tax bill," said speaker-turned-lobbyist Billy Clayton.

Euphoria skittered like dust devils around the Capitol.

"This has got to be one of the best days in the history of Texas," beamed White, who was praised by legislators for his role in the success.[14]

"The governor has done all he was asked to do, and he stayed out of it until he was asked," said Rep. Bill Messer.

"Mark has really learned how," Rep. Wayne Peveto agreed.

"The leadership was together and dedicated in a singular way," observed Sen. Ray Farabee, a Wichita Falls Democrat, who served on the Legislative Budget Board and was chairman of the State Affairs Committee. "For the first time, Gib Lewis . . . is being recognized for the leadership capability a few people always said was there."[15]

"Everybody pulled together for a much brighter future for the children of Texas," said Ross Perot.[16] "The governor, lieutenant governor, and speaker of the House have done a five-star job."[17]

Perot also gave Bullock credit for devising a finance system that would eventually narrow the gap between rich and poor districts, but the session clearly had been White's moment, and Lewis's and Hobby's.

"This is the most remarkable special session I have ever seen," said George Christian, of the Texas Association of Taxpayers.[18]

Apart from putting together a plan for paying for the education and high-way packages and persuading Sen. Leedom to forsake his filibuster, Bullock was not in the news often during the session. He suspended his public flogging of White but occasionally spoke about his undiminished lust for White's job. But the success of the special session had an effect on him. The sight of White emerging as a courageous knight tilting at inferior public schools led him to a sober reassessment of, and possibly an irreconcilable decision about, his own political future.

Two weeks after the session closed, Bullock approached White at the Democratic National Convention in San Francisco and informed him they would not be opponents for the gubernatorial nomination in 1986. A week later, he told reporters, "It's something I've always wanted, [but] there just wasn't any clamor for my services, frankly. There wasn't any great groundswell. That was one of the main considerations—the fact I just could-n't win it. I thought Gov. White exhibited a great deal of leadership in the special session that he did not necessarily exhibit a year earlier. I thought a year ago that we had a governor's office of trial and error."[19]

In an interview with *Associated Press* reporter Jack Keever, Bullock talked about what he would have done if he had stayed in the race. On his desk, he spread old highway maps marked with the political trips he had taken while running for comptroller in 1974 and 1978. "I visited every county twice," he said. "I drove over 100,000 miles by myself."

Keever suggested that now, 10 years later, he might not be able to repeat that ordeal. "Hell I can't," Bullock said. "If you want it bad enough, you can do anything."

Those plans were gone now, and in a bit of self-aggrandizing torque, he blamed himself for vanquishing them. "From what I read in the paper, yes, Mark White appears to be in pretty good shape right now," he said. "He's gotten better. You want to know something? I'm responsible for that. When I announced [for governor], I made Mark White a better governor for Texas. I really firmly believe that that's true. I think I've made him a better governor."[20]

In other interviews, he revealed additional factors in his decision, most of which centered on his own past conduct and lifestyle. In an interview with

Raul Reyes, of the *Houston Chronicle*, Bullock described himself as a "scarred personality" that Texans would not want to be their governor.

"Here's a guy who's an alcoholic," he said. "He's been a lobbyist. Divorced. The subject of a grand jury investigation that was crippling . . . hurt me bad. A man who has had [civil] judgments outstanding against him, which I did. Would they want that type of individual in the governor's office? It hurts me to think that was the case, and each one of those things, none were imposed on me. No one ever made me want to drink. The governor, that's the number-one man in the state, and that's somebody to be looked up to and, hopefully they can be proud of."

His words were of resignation rather than rancor and contained a rare wisp of self-pity. "No one really gave a doggone whether I ran or not," he said.[21]

CHAPTER 19

THE OIL BUST

T wo moods filled the Capitol as legislators slogged back to their offices for the 1985 session—gloom and doom. Since they last met and enacted the largest tax increase in Texas history, oil prices had remained on a southbound trajectory, and the unthinkable was being thought. Another tax increase or draconian cuts in vital state programs.

"If the price of oil slips some more, then we're really in hot water," said Sen. Farabee.[1]

At the end of the previous summer's special session, Bullock once again raised the specter of the most dreaded tax of all. "There are only certain taxes known to civilized man, and Texas has nearly all of them, except the income tax," he said in an interview with Henry Bryan, a political writer for the *Dallas Times Herald*.[2] He predicted that a personal or corporate income tax was less than 10 years away. Then, in December, when members of the Legislative Budget Board held their final meeting before the new session, Bullock informed them that they would have $900 million less than they were budgeting for the next two years. He reminded them that every $1 drop in the price of oil removed $40 million in severance taxes from state revenue—not to mention the negative effect on sales and franchise tax revenue—and prices had skidded by another $5 a barrel in the past year.

All signs pointed to prices falling in the near future to levels not seen in a decade or more. The knives were brought out, but sometimes the legislators brandished them at each other as well as at the budget. Tempers flared over such things as postponing the $100 million pre-kindergarten program—a cornerstone of the education reforms of the 1984 special session—cutting health care for cancer patients, indigents, and children; and higher education. Some sacrifices, however, were inevitable, and Gov. White, Lt. Gov. Hobby, and House Speaker Lewis personally called the presidents of colleges and universities to tell them how hard they would have to bite the bullet: Perhaps as much as 25 percent. The next day, Bullock dropped the revenue estimate by another $129 million.

No one accused him of playing politics with the revenue estimates this time around. Not only had his previous forecasts proved to be deadly accurate, he seemed to have no political horse in the stable now. Next year, he would run for reelection, not for governor, and so his motives were not suspect.

To set an example for other agencies, Bullock laid off four percent of his staff—149 workers—and closed several of his field offices. "I think the oil thing is going to get worse," he said.[3] His actions saved only $6 million, but he said he hoped it would encourage other agencies to look beyond some of his nickel-and-dime suggestions, such as switching from paper towels to electric hand dryers, and go for the big item: Cut the number of people on the state payroll. At the same time, however, Bullock told House and Senate budget committees that the state would net $1 million every two years for each extra auditor he hired—an alluring inducement for them to increase his budget. He was pinched, but he wasn't a fool.

Beyond periodic updates of bad economic news, Bullock turned his attention to other matters, personal and political. He was 55 years old and frustrated. His 1986 reelection looked like a done deal (Republican Chairman George Strake acknowledged that the GOP would not target Bullock for a serious challenge), and it appeared that the job was his for a lifetime if he wanted it. He would remain in a position to influence the Legislature and the lives of every Texan, but he was weary of sending in plays from the sidelines, many of which were ignored. He was looking at the Capitol from three blocks away and wanted to get back inside it. How?

He was well outside the dominant political story that winter and spring. The impending rematch between Mark White and Bill Clements, which promised to be as acrimonious as their first meeting, preoccupied political writers and the Capitol grapevine, but Bullock occasionally made news with scary tax palmistry. "I see the possibility of an income tax, corporate and individual, as becoming imminent in Texas in five or six years," he said in an interview with *Quorum Report*, a political newsletter. That moved the horizon closer by five years than his prediction of the previous summer. "I sure hate to see it happen, but I have little doubt that it will."[4]

Appearing with House Speaker Lewis on a panel before the Texas Associated Press Managing Editors Association in Galveston, he reiterated the looming eventuality, to which Lewis took exception. "In 10, 15, 20 years, we may have to explore the possibility of corporate [income] taxes, but I hope we never have to while I'm in the Legislature," Lewis said.[5]

For reasons unknown, Bullock's tax talk caused few ripples, other than scattered editorials railing against the idea and a few legislative leaders assuring audiences that it would not happen. He was, after all, the tax collector, not the tax leveler. His ruminations about the fiscal future may have seemed innocuous to audiences preoccupied with the economically pernicious present.

In fact, Bullock's personal life received nearly as much ink as his fiscal rhetoric. On April 19, the *Austin American-Statesman* reported, under a three-column headline:

> Comptroller Bob Bullock and Jan Felts Teague, an executive for *Ultra* magazine, are honeymooning in New York. Bullock 55, and Teague, 35, a former employee at the comptroller's office, were married Wednesday night at Green Pastures restaurant in Austin. The couple were joined by friends and family members inside the restaurant for the wedding ceremony and reception, which lasted about two hours. The marriage was performed by Joe Reynolds, a Presbyterian minister who is a member of the comptroller's staff. It is Bullock's fifth marriage.[6]

From all appearances, that ceremony seemed to usher in a calmer, happier era in Bullock's life. His health appeared to be better, and some of the flamboyance of his earlier years—the hair-trigger temper, for example—lessened. And, with the fire of gubernatorial longing reduced to embers, he became more reflective, as much about the future of Texas as about his own. If an aide asked him how he should handle a particular situation or problem, instead of blowing up and waving his *A Message to Garcia*, Bullock would sometimes reply, "Do what's good for Texas."

Some old habits died hard, though. The previous year, he had spent 11 days at the Pritikin Institute in Santa Monica, California, trying, without success, to shed his nicotine addiction. At work, too, he remained as driven as a street rod. He arrived at his office earlier than anyone else, but now, at midafternoon most days, he filled a brief case with documents and headed home to read and nap. Most days, he also filled a cardboard box with documents, which he expected a staffer to read and digest by the time he returned from his siesta.

For the most part, his work of transforming the comptroller's office was complete. He had expanded the agency's budget from $15 million to more than $80 million a year, but the prevailing thought in the Legislature was that it had been a good investment. He had a crack revenue-estimating division, an efficient enforcement crew, and a research operation capable of turning out reports on anything political or economic. He was vainglorious enough about the agency he had built that he exchanged friendly jabs with Ann Richards, the state treasurer, belittling the job she held. "I could operate that office with a phone and two clerks," he told her.[7]

Joy Anderson described Bullock's stormy relationship with Richards as "clashes of the Titans, sometimes." He so agitated the treasurer that she adopted one of his own favorite tactics for dealing with adversaries. "Ann bought a voodoo doll and stuck a pin in it to try to get him to change his ways," Anderson said.[8]

A combination of marital contentment and sobriety may have had a personally soothing payoff for the comptroller, but events and the aftermath of the 1985 legislative session also could have given him pause, if not indigestion. Bullock had removed himself from the governor's race nearly a year earlier, when it appeared that White was the man of the hour. Suddenly, the tides turned against the governor, and Bullock was stranded on an island of his own making.

First, Lt. Gov. Hobby, under vehement lobbying by the higher-education community, announced plans to forgo most of the planned cuts in college and, instead, to adopt Gov. White's suggested increases in a variety of state fees. Also, he proposed to double tuition from $4 to $8 a credit hour the next year, and another $4 the year after that—a position that put him at odds with White, who was fighting any measure that smacked of another tax increase. White was virtually alone in opposing the tuition hikes, but he haltingly agreed not to veto them if other provisions were made for loans and scholarships for low-income students.

Then, the cash-strapped Legislature came up with the idea of a cigarette tax to finance indigent health care. It would take effect only if the federal government lowered its cigarette levy. Rather than so blatantly break the promise he had made during the 1984 special session, White offered to surrender a portion of his budget to deter a tax bill. Politically, he might have been better off to allow the taxes, and when the other party made an issue of them, he could stake out the high ground by pointing out that he was willing to pay for education, highways, and indigent care, and that the Republicans were not. But, he was snared in the age-old political trap of making promises he couldn't, or shouldn't, keep.

White's threat to veto the cigarette tax stalled action on a bill to finance indigent health care until the dying hours of the session, and even Democrats turned against him. The House endorsed the tax by a wide margin, and the Senate approved it unanimously. A conference committee report was formally filed at 9:57 p.m., but under House rules, the compromise version could not be debated for two hours after it was submitted. Facing a midnight adjournment deadline, the House had only three minutes to debate and vote on it. Rep. Bill Cerverha, a Dallas Republican, spoke against the bill and easily ran out the clock. A new tax was dead, but so was indigent health care. Supporters of the bill were as angry with the governor as they were with the Republican representative who talked it to death.

White momentarily regained the high ground by huddling with his closest aides and a few legislators before announcing that he was calling a special session to begin immediately. Indigent health care passed, but without the cigarette tax, and it seemed that White had landed on his feet again. As he had promised, 1985 had produced no *tax* increases. What the session did produce was a tripling of college tuition and a painful swelling in a variety of state fees. The line between fees and taxes may be too fine for the average citizen to draw the distinction.

Less than a week after the session ended, it was reported that the latest Texas Poll put White's "excellent" or "good" rating at 46 percent. Twenty-nine percent of those questioned rated his performance "fair," and 15 percent deemed it "poor." Bullock may well have interpreted those numbers as evidence he had acted prematurely in bowing out of the gubernatorial race. The political wisdom held that for an incumbent to be safe, his "excellent" and "good" ratings should be twice that of his "fair" and "poor" ratings. White's were about equal.[9]

The poll, conducted by the Public Policy Resources Laboratory of Texas A&M University, did not reveal the reasons for the governor's mediocre numbers, but as time passed, a few pockets of hostility took shape. There was a backlash from teachers angry over the lack of funding for their incentive pay system and the basic skills test they were required to pass—both the results of the education reform bill of 1984. The 96,000-member Texas State Teachers

Association, which had been instrumental in White's election in 1982, announced that it would withhold its endorsement in the 1986 gubernatorial primary. Another provision of the education reform—no pass, no play—angered many coaches and parents. The prospect of having to bench a star quarterback for low grades would take some getting used to in a state that lived for autumn Friday nights.

Another Texas Poll released late in December 1985 revealed that White's "excellent" or "good" rating had slipped to 36 percent. He was deemed "fair" by 35 percent of respondents and "poor" by 17 percent.[10] At that level he looked vulnerable enough that five Democrats decided to file against him in the primary. Against such unknowns or little-knowns as Sheila Bilyeu, Andrew C. Briscoe III, A. Don Crowder, Bobby Locke, and Ron Slover, White barely avoided a runoff, picking up 589,536 of the 1,096,552 votes cast, or 53.8 percent.

Had Bullock been in the race, he might well have landed in a runoff with the governor. Instead, he coasted through a reelection year in which he would be unopposed in the Democratic primary and unopposed by the Republicans in November. An anonymous "prominent Republican" explained to the *Fort Worth Star-Telegram* why the party had no stomach for taking on an official with a history of turbulence in his personal life and criminal investigations into his official conduct: "There is just no reason to run against him. I think he is pretty much an institution."[11]

By the end of 1985, however, the state comptroller was the one man in government nobody wanted to hear from. He never had anything good to say, and each succeeding utterance was more despairing than the last. At the end of October, he predicted that when the Legislature reconvened in 1987, it would be looking at a biennial budget shortfall of $3 billion—meaning that taxes would have to be increased by that amount to "keep up with our inflation and population trends."

"The easy days are over," he told the Select Committee on Higher Education.[12] Speaking to the Texas Association of Taxpayers, a business organization, he said, "We need new revenue. Yes, I'm talking about an income tax. It is political death to everyone who mentions it, but you have to think about it."[13]

As he spoke, a barrel of Texas oil was selling for about $27. Three months later, a barrel was going for less than $15 and heading for $10, dragging the real estate and financial institutions with it. Texas was facing a harsh reality, and the dwindling price of oil was not the whole of it. Low production also was a factor. Between mid-1985 and mid-1986, the number of active rotary rigs in the state fell 60 percent, and drilling permits dropped by half. Production declined by 51.1 million barrels, costing the state $35.5 million in severance taxes alone. In the West Texas fields, derricks and other equipment were stacked along the highways like so much scrap metal.

Scrap also defined the gubernatorial race. The voters had the choice of Bill Clements, who had promised more than he could deliver in 1978 (trim the state payroll by 25,000 and return $1 billion to taxpayers), and Mark White, who had promised too much in 1982. A Texas Poll in May, shortly after the primaries, made Clements the favorite, 47 percent to 33 percent. White, running for the first time as an incumbent, appeared to suffer from what political consultant Chuck Dean called Reverse Reaganism: the un-Teflon governor. Everything stuck to him. A glaring irony was that he took heat over an issue on which he had shown the strongest leadership: education. Polls showed that a larger majority of Texans favored the reforms, but disliked the man who had brought them about. Teachers disliked some of the reforms, and their opposition to White was so strident that he apologized for the "stress" inflicted on them by the legislation that required them to take a basic skills test in order to keep their jobs.

Clements chose to make White's credibility the focal point of his campaign, but quickly ran into his own credibility trap. As the state's revenues continued to decline, he urged White to call a special session to cut spending to keep the $37.2 biennial budget in balance. He was quoted in newspaper stories saying that he had a *secret plan* to solve the budget crisis and would reveal it if White summoned the Legislature. He may have been gambling that a governor trailing in the polls would not call a special session that was sure to result in another tax increase. White, as well as the legislative leadership, said a special session was not necessary. That changed in June, when Bullock disclosed that the shortfall for the current budget would be $2.3 billion, not the $1.3 billion he had predicted after oil prices collapsed in February.

White had little choice but to call a special session for August. Clements admitted that he had no secret plan.

White got a bounce from the special session—a Gallup poll published in late September had him running even with Clements—and the race turned into the much-anticipated mud-wrestling rematch. Clements staffer Karl Rove called the governor a "jerk," but later another Clements aide, Reggie

Bashur, explained "it's nothing personal." White aide Mark McKinnon called Clements a "cold, heartless son of a bitch," but later explained that "it was a humorous reference, not meant to be pejorative."[14] All of that was expected, but the campaign closed with a dirty trick that came out of nowhere. A month into October, state and federal cops announced that they were investigating an illegal listening device found in the office of Rove, Clements's chief political advisor. Two private detectives with Knight Diversified Services of Fort Worth, the company hired to "sweep" the office, reported that they found the devices, about the size of a matchbook with short antenna wires, behind a framed needlepoint red, white, and blue elephant on the office wall.

Initially, it appeared that someone on White's side had planted the bug, and Rove went to some lengths to make sure the voters drew that inference. "I do know for certain who benefits most from the kind of knowledge that you'd get from listening to my phone conversations, that's our political opposition," Rove said accusingly. "I'm not accusing anybody. I'm simply offering the very strong observation that our political opposition would benefit from hearing phone conversations that they would hear from having that bug four feet from my desk."[15]

Ten days later, however, an unnamed source involved in the investigation told reporters from the *Dallas Morning News* that the probe was focusing on the private detectives, Gary Morphew and Bruce W. Scott. Instead of calling the police to Rove's office, they removed the transmitter and took it to their hotel, possibly spoiling any chance of determining who was on the receiving end, officials said.

It turned out also to be a curious choice for an eavesdropping gadget. A Dallas dealer in electronic surveillance equipment told the *Morning News* that it appeared to be a common, inexpensive model with a short battery life and capable of transmitting only several hundred feet. That meant that the person listening in on Rove's conversations had to be in the building or in the adjacent parking lot.

Was it a hoax perpetrated by a political consultant trying to make his client's opponent appear to be a dirty trickster? Or a fraud conceived by a zealous private detective wanting to please a client and bask in the accompanying publicity? The questions were never answered. Scott, an investigator who worked for Knight Diversified Services, agreed to take an FBI polygraph exam. He told reporters that he "performed satisfactorily." Morphew, the owner of the company, declined to cooperate for "personal reasons."[16]

Federal authorities, aware of the political ramifications of the case, wanted to finish the investigation and take it to a grand jury before the November 4 elections, but were unable to do so. Instead, they tried to dull the political edge by announcing that they had "virtually ruled out" involvement by either campaign. "The bulk of the remaining interviews are outside the political realm," Byron Sage, agent in charge of the Austin FBI office, said. "We've finished with the campaigns, pretty much."[17]

It was an intriguing distraction, but in the end it may have had little impact on a race littered with negative ads and personal attacks.

Clements reclaimed the governor's office, beating White 1,813,779 to 1,585,515. Clements got 52.7 percent. But it was a dubious prize. By then, Bullock was predicting that the budget shortfall could hit $6 billion for the 1988–1989 biennium. Being governor wasn't going to be as much fun as it used to be.

CHAPTER 20

EYES ON THE LIEUTENANT GOVERNOR'S OFFICE

B ill Clements had not even been sworn in when he announced that this was his last hurrah. He would serve one last term and then fade away. The announcement gave some credence to what the White campaign had been saying for months—that Clements was running for governor not because of what he wanted to do for the state, but to exact revenge on White for evicting him from the mansion four years earlier. It also was a statement of the times. Texas was in an economic slump, but it still had a growing population with growing demands. With shrinking revenue, there was little room for bold or creative governance, only immense opportunities to alienate the populace with cuts in services or a more onerous tax burden. The best a governor could do was tinker at the margins, and Clements, who had built a global oil-exploration company, was not a patient tinkerer.

After a decade or more of running a rapidly expanding agency, Bullock, too, had been reduced to tinkering. First the growth stalled, and then it was followed by downsizing to accommodate the new economic realities. Like Clements, he was not one to putter. "I kind of likened it to being a painter painting a picture," one former aide said. "When he's first doing it, he can lay the paint on in broad brushes and accomplish a lot. You get to the point where you're sort of embroidering on the edges. I think that's why he sometimes gets restless being comptroller—because he's a guy who likes to make great changes."[1]

Being of like disposition now brought a calm to what had once been a stormy relationship between two of the most antagonistic political figures of their era. "You and I have something in common," Bullock said when he met with Clements just after the Legislature convened for the 1987 regular session. "You're not running for governor again, and I want you to know I'm not running for governor either. I have no desire to be governor of Texas. It's gone. But I do have a desire, for the next four years, to try to do what I can to get Texas out of some really difficult times. I've got the best research staff in Texas government, and it's at your disposal and the disposal of the Legislature to help you solve these problems. I've got no political ax to grind with you, mister."[2]

It was unlikely that Bullock could provide the help Clements needed. The governor again had been elected on a promise he was unlikely to keep—balancing the budget with no new taxes. He acknowledged as much three weeks into the session, when he told the Legislature he would not close the door on tax reform. But *reform* implied *tinkering* aimed at raising revenues.

The next day, Bullock, who had been putting together his own economic plan—a set of options for expanding the tax base—to offer to the Legislature, issued a press release in praise of the governor. "The longer we put off overhauling our tax base so it reflects the Texas economy, the bigger the fiscal time bomb we're building on a daily basis," he said. "As a matter of fact, we've got a draft bill that's ready and waiting for the governor and the Legislature that will reduce the sales tax rate, expand the base, and spread the burden evenly and fairly."[3]

He also released to lawmakers studies of lotteries and corporate gross receipts, both controversial. Anti-gambling sentiment was strong in the state, and not all of it was found in the pulpits. Some secular social scientists maintained that it was a voluntary tax paid mostly by those of lower income, and some businessmen feared that it would drain money from other segments of the economy. Corporate gross receipts? Another term for income tax, the boardrooms wailed. Then, speaking to the Senate Finance Committee, he once again uttered the words no one wanted to hear.

A headline over an editorial in the *San Antonio Express* read:

BULLOCK BREAKS INCOME-TAX ICE

Texas Comptroller Bob Bullock finally has ended the pussyfooting around and declared that Texas should consider a state income tax.

After Walter Mondale committed a similar faux pas in 1984 (the Democratic presidential nominee vowed to raise taxes), we

didn't expect to hear such loose talk from a politician for at least
a few more years, but here's what Bullock told the Senate Finance
Committee:

"You might as well talk about it; you might as well think
about it." "It" is a Texas state income tax. No one we know *wants*
to increase or create taxes, but now that Bullock has broken the
ice, we can expect to hear more discussion about a state income
tax. Texas is one of only seven states without one. . . . Texans
have had it pretty good, but these are hard times. . . .

Bullock should be praised for having the courage to lay the
cards on the table. While we stop short of calling for a state
income tax, all the options have to be considered.[4]

The editorial spoke volumes about Texas's inability to come to grips with
an issue as important as taxation, to discuss it with anything less than contort-
ed logic and servile denials. Since 1973, Bullock periodically had insisted that
an income tax belonged in the mix of revenue options. No *pussyfooting*, only
deaf audiences. After finally hearing him, the editorial writer condemned his
message as a "*faux pas*" that demonstrated "courage" for which he should be
"praised." Such apoplectic seizures were typical of the discourse that came
with the hard times. No wonder Clements had no interest in another term.

Since his election as lieutenant governor in 1972, Bill Hobby had bided
his time, awaiting the opportunity to follow in his father's footsteps. W. P.
Hobby, Sr., was the lieutenant governor in 1917 but became the state's chief
executive when Gov. J. E. "Pa" Ferguson was impeached and removed from
office. Hobby was elected governor in 1918, served his two-year term, and
then departed from politics. No one with a political nose doubted that the son
wanted the governorship and that if it wasn't his for the asking, it was his for
the taking. He was personable and knowledgeable, presided gently over a
Senate going through the angst of two-party puberty, and allotted power to
the chamber's few Republicans on a proportional basis. What he lacked was a
taste for the brawl.

"Since I've been around, there has not been the opportunity to run
for governor without running against an incumbent—whether Briscoe or
Clements or White—with whom I've worked. And I just couldn't hardly
ever see myself doing that," he said in an interview with the *Austin
American-Statesman* at the beginning of 1987. "To run against an incumbent,

you've got to run around the state saying that so-and-so is sorry and no good—which they're not."[5]

With Clements out of the 1990 picture, that would be his year, the first time since the advent of four-year terms in 1974 that an incumbent governor was not seeking reelection. He declared his intentions less than two months after the 1986 elections, as all statewide officeholders were beginning new terms, setting off an early scramble for the next cycle.

"God forbid, have we already started on another governor's race?" wrote Carolyn Barta, a columnist for the *Dallas Morning News*.[6]

Indeed, we had. Hobby, she noted, "threw down the gauntlet in his inaugural speech by insisting there can be absolutely no cuts in public education and that higher education funding should be increased"—a position that put him squarely at odds with Clements, who preferred "fine-tuning" in an attempt to stretch the budget. She described Hobby "digging in his heels, drawing the line in the dirt" in the path of Clements's ideas about assuming budget execution authority. He also blamed the governor's no-new-tax stand for the state's inability to correct, under threat of federal court penalty, its prison overcrowding problem. "That Hobby has started out [the legislative session] so confrontational comes as a surprise," Barta wrote. "That's not his normal, laid-back statesmanlike, let's-work-it-out style. . . . Perhaps he wants to establish himself the 'main man'—for the benefit of Jim Mattox and Henry Cisneros and Garry Mauro and other potential Democratic candidates, so that they back off a primary fight."[7]

If that was his objective, he misjudged some of the field. Cisneros, the high-profile mayor of San Antonio and rising Democratic star, assured Hobby he would not run against him, but Jim Mattox, a former Dallas attorney, was not so accommodating. He liked nothing better than political fisticuffs, and he savored the underdog role. "Junkyard tactics" was a common description of his style. In 1972, he won a seat in the Legislature by defeating fellow Democrat Sam Coats, a first-term House member who had just been named the outstanding freshman by his colleagues. In 1976, against the advice of friends, Mattox took on Wes Wise, a popular mayor of Dallas, and won a seat in Congress. Six years later, he was the last candidate to enter the 1982 race for attorney general, but, casting himself as the "People's Lawyer," won in a runoff.

So, while Hobby was playing rough with Clements in the Senate, Mattox was raising money and promising that the 1990 primary would be "a classic

race between the country club set vs. the people."[8] He derided the gentleman-
ly, multimillionaire lieutenant governor—Hobby inherited a publishing and
broadcast fortune and then made another fortune of his own—as a prissy,
horsey-set blueblood disconnected from *the people*.

Hobby, not being in campaign mode, largely ignored Mattox's needling.
Besides, he had his hands full with a legislative session that was thundering
like cattle toward a cliff. By the session's midpoint, Bullock was projecting a
$5.8 billion deficit by the summer of 1989, and his own plan to deal with it
was being ignored. Clements was standing firm on his anti-tax pledge, and
Hobby was equally determined not to gut state services.

When Bullock learned that legislators planned to carry a $1 billion debt
into the next biennium, he stunned them with a request for a legal ruling
from the attorney general's office. Would the scheme violate the constitutional ban on deficit spending? "Devastating," said House Speaker Gib
Lewis, adding that an adverse ruling by Mattox "could put government at a
complete standstill."

Once again, Bullock had thrust himself into the legislative process in a
way guaranteed to earn enmity. "I can't help it if they get disturbed," he
shrugged.[9]

In a formal opinion that smacked more of politics than law, Mattox
ruled that the Legislature could carry over the deficit without violating the
constitution, but he warned that their actions would violate the intent of
the state's founders. That momentarily calmed the furor, but did nothing
to resolve the budget impasse. Not surprisingly, the session ended without
passage of a budget bill, and Gov. Clements was forced to call a summer
special session to write a budget before the fiscal year ended on August 31.
The session began on June 22.

Prior to that session, Bullock met with the governor for two hours to
warn him of the increasingly bleak economic forecast, dealing a serious blow
to Clements's resolve to balance the books with belt-tightening. After the
meeting Clements met with reporters.

"The economic health and the budgetary problems that we're confronted with here are far worse than anyone anticipated," he said. "This whole fiscal mess that we have here, which I inherited, is not good."[10] What he did not
say was that the economic predicament would have been far grimmer had
White not already persuaded the Legislature to raise the sales tax twice. The
budget deficit at that time was $1 billion, and Bullock predicted the shortfall

would be close to $6 billion by 1989. Clements was sobered and swayed by the news, but he did not capitulate entirely. He agreed to accept $2.9 billion in new taxes, but pledged to veto any bill that exceeded that.

Whatever the amount, the Legislature returned to one distasteful certainty. It would have to raise taxes again. Addressing a joint session on opening day, Bullock laid out the latest scenario.

"The last time you invited me to speak, you asked me to talk about money," he intoned, glancing around the House chamber where he had sat as a freshman legislator three decades earlier. "I said at the time that I could make the shortest talk in legislative history: You simply didn't have any. Today, I would say you have even less."

Oil prices had climbed back to about $18 a barrel, but Bullock cautioned that there was little salvation in that trend. A few years earlier, each dollar in the per-barrel price had translated to $100 million in tax earnings. By the spring of 1987, he said, declining production had reduced that to $30 million. "You might like to know that oil would have to go to $40 to $50 a barrel immediately, and stay there for a full year, to make up the $1 billion 1987 deficit."[11]

Short of an income tax, the only solution was to broaden the sales tax, which was the cornerstone of the tax plan Bullock offered during the regular session. Legislators balked at a tax bill then because they feared Clements would veto it, leaving them to explain to their constituents why they voted for something the governor deemed unnecessary. Now, they had little choice. Both houses agreed on a package that extended the sales tax to previously exempt goods and services, such as janitorial contracting, garbage collection, and pest control. Higher taxes on tobacco products were added for good measure. The measure would produce $5.7 billion in new revenue, enough to cover Bullock's projected deficit shortfall, but double the amount Clements had said he would tolerate.

Hobby and Lewis went to work on the governor, arguing that his failure to accept the tax bill would be a blow to public education and other state operations. They had an unwitting ally in their drive to get the deal done—the governor himself.

Clements was being hammered by an athletic department scandal at Southern Methodist University, on whose board he had sat during the four years between his gubernatorial terms, part of it as chairman. It was the usual pay-for-play scheme in which football players were lured to the school by cash and other blandishments. This time, however, it wasn't just a rogue coach at the helm, but several members of the board, Clements among them, who insisted that the payments continue even after the National Collegiate Athletic Association placed SMU's football program on probation. The improprieties were conducted on such an expansive scale and with such breathtaking audacity that the NCAA upped the punishment to the *death penalty*—forcing the university to disband its football program for the 1987 season. During the 1986 campaign, Clements denied that he knew about the improper payments. But on March 3, less than two months after his inauguration, he admitted that he had known about the wrongdoing all along. As the scandal unfolded and the governor's role in it was revealed, Atty. Gen. Mattox opened an investigation, and talk of impeachment became more than idle corridor chatter.

Asked about that possibility, Clements shot back, "Do I look worried?"[12]

In fact, he *was* worried and wanted nothing more than to get the ornery legislators out of town as quickly as possible. Lt. Gov. Hobby said he and House Speaker Lewis went over to the mansion to try to convince Clements to sign the tax bill. Also present was George Bayoud, one of the governor's top staffers, who Hobby said was "the voice of reason" with the cranky governor. "When we left the mansion, I don't think we knew the final result," Hobby said.[13] But, over the vehement objections of diehard budget-cutting Republicans in both houses, Clements signed the largest tax bill in Texas history.

The next statewide elections were three-and-a-half years away, but Hobby and Mattox were not the only ones sizing up the quadrennial dance and maneuvering for early position. Ann Richards was ready to move on from the treasurer's office and was ogling the lieutenant governor's job. Land Commissioner Garry Mauro and Agriculture Commissioner Jim Hightower also were angling for higher-profile jobs. Both had run for down-ballot positions with an eye to moving up, and Mauro was considering several offices, including attorney general, while Hightower was eager to keep Republican U.S. Sen. Phil Gramm from winning a second term. And there was Bullock. He had spent most of the regular session and the special session out of sight and out of mind. But those close to him knew, from observing the boredom that had settled over him like a methane cloud, that he had no ambition to be Comptroller-for-Life. Natural selection suggested that lieutenant governor was the only option available to him, except for returning to private life.

In his years in government—as a gubernatorial aide, secretary of state, lobbyist, and comptroller—he spent about as much time in the Capitol as some lawmakers. He observed the gavel-pounders in both houses and had a keen understanding of, and appreciation for, the powers they possessed. In most states, the lieutenant governor is a ceremonial afterthought, mostly there to broaden the appeal of the person seeking the governorship, to cut ribbons at mall openings, to indulge in lightweight oratory, and to stand by in case something happens to the governor. The Texas lieutenant governor is the most powerful in the country, elected independently of the governor, and, by presiding over the Senate and being granted huge powers to control the agenda by the Senate's rules, can be more powerful than the governor in shaping public policy. That singular division of power was a result of the Civil War. Texas and most confederate states abhorred the top-down rule imposed by radical Republicans during Reconstruction. After the Democrats finally threw the Republicans out, they rewrote the Texas constitution in 1876 to disperse government power. Consequently, several *cabinet* officials—attorney general, comptroller, land commissioner, treasurer—that are appointed in many states are elected in Texas.

Besides the constitutional powers given to the lieutenant governor, which aren't many, Senate rules, adopted to keep things running smoothly, enhanced them like steroids. For example, the longstanding tradition of requiring a two-thirds vote to bring most bills to the floor endows the presiding officer with considerable negative power: With just 11 of the 31 senators aligned with him, the lieutenant governor can block just about anything. If the governor is the captain of the ship, the lieutenant governor is the guy who oils the engine.

By giving up the lieutenant governorship, Hobby provided Bullock an opportunity, but all of the newcomers who had swept into office in the unified Democratic effort of 1982 posed problems for him. Bullock was fidgeting for a new challenge, but so were they. Would he take on an old pal, such as Richards, with whom he had bent many an elbow, or Mauro, whom he had befriended, hired, and mentored? For Bullock, that would not have been a trivial consideration. He had shied away from races before, after taking his opponents' measure and that of their war chests. He had the baggage of a 30-year journey through state politics; they had lighter loads.

In a remarkable twist, Hobby would resolve the conflict for him. Throughout the spring, he endured Mattox's "junkyard dog" behavior that included mocking Hobby for his wealth and some of his "country club" diversions.

"Do you know what putting on the pinks is?" Mattox asked in a June 27 speech to the national League of United Latin American Citizens. "It's probably not part of your heritage, nor mine either. Putting on the pinks is when you go out there and put on your little red riding coat, and your little pants, your high-top shoes, and chase the foxes through the woods. Then you go back and eat your wine and cheese. . . . The fact is, we've got too many people that are worried about putting on the pinks, and not worried about . . . whether the average man and woman can feed his or her family and pay his taxes. Some of these people have had the gold spoon in their mouth so long that they forget what it's like for the average person."[14]

He never mentioned Hobby by name, but then, he didn't have to. Everyone got it.

Hobby was tiring of the derision. A week after that attack, he responded, but not in kind. At a Democratic fund-raiser in Houston, Nene Foxhall, a reporter for the *Houston Chronicle*, asked him about potentially facing Mattox in the 1990 primary, and he mustered a response that was tepid, but passed for acrid in Hobby's world: "A weaker candidate than Mattox one could not imagine."[15]

A week later, Hobby made a shocking announcement. He would not run for governor, or anything else, in 1990. By the time his current term ended, he would have held office for 18 years, an eternity in the churning musical chairs of Texas government. "I don't have any more races left in me," he said.[16]

His race against Mattox would have been long and unpleasant, but insiders believed that wasn't the whole story behind his abrupt withdrawal. State Democratic Party Chairman Bob Slagle told reporters that Hobby had been frustrated, worn down, by his contentious dealings with Clements. "Everybody has a fed-up level," Slagle said. "They are only willing to put up with so much garbage."[17]

Sen. Bob McFarland, a Republican from Arlington, may have seen closer to the truth: "I'm not sure Bill Hobby ever wanted to be governor of this state. I think many people assumed that he did and were pushing him toward that, suggesting it was a natural fulfillment of the legacy that should be there because his daddy was governor."[18]

Now the Democratic primary was once again wide open. Mattox was in, Henry Cisneros had an exploratory apparatus in place, and Ann Richards was the subject of considerable speculation. As the gubernatorial field expanded, the crowd around the lieutenant governor's race thinned.

Bullock was hunting doves in South Texas on September 10 when his office issued a two-sentence press release: "State Comptroller Bob Bullock said Thursday that he intends to run for lieutenant governor in 1990. All visitors are welcome."[19]

CHAPTER 21

KING KONG'S ALREADY IN THE RACE

A t the time of Bullock's announcement, several state senators were also coveting the Senate gavel, but potential rivals easily could have been discouraged by the swift editorial response to the man who, with a 22-word press release, was anointed not just as the front-runner, but seemingly as the only runner. No one else had time to crank out a declaration of candidacy before many small newspapers around the state virtually installed Bullock in the higher office he sought. His habit of campaigning at the forks of the creek had paid off yet again.

The *Andrews County News* swooned over the economy of his declaration: "Any politician who can be that brief in announcing for office deserves consideration from every citizen. And we'll vote for the man. Ask any public official, city, county, or state, and they'll tell you that Bullock runs the best agency in Austin. He and his staff put out more real and meaningful information about the Texas economy and Texas taxes than all the other agencies combined. He runs a tight ship with an able, competent, and professional staff."[1]

An editorial page headline in *The Record*, published in Canadian, Texas, was just as blunt: "Bullock for Lt. Governor."[2] Wrote the editor of *The Free Press*, in Diboll: "You have our support, B. B."[3]

Reminding its readers of the "clockwork efficiency" with which Bullock ran the "finely tuned" comptroller's office, the *Victoria Advocate* stopped just short of an outright endorsement: "It is good that a person of his caliber seeks to succeed one of the best lieutenant governors in Texas history. We salute him."[4]

Morris Higley, writing in the *Childress Index*, expressed his belief that Bullock was not aiming high enough. "I'm sorry that he is going to make that race," he wrote. "I'm sorry that he didn't seek the governor's office."[5]

Harry Bradley had worked on several political campaigns, and eventually worked for state Sen. Grant Jones, a conservative Democrat from Abilene, who rose to be chairman of the Senate Finance Committee in the mid-1980s. Bullock didn't have much use for Jones initially, though he later came to respect him. After Jones was upset in the 1988 Democratic primary, Bradley went to work for the Texas Water Development Board. Still, he itched to get into another political campaign.

It was 16 months before the 1990 primary election. He called Gay Erwin, a friend with whom he'd shared an office when he worked for Gov. Mark White. He said Bullock had always interested him, he liked him, and he thought he would probably be the state's next lieutenant governor. Bradley told Erwin he had decided to volunteer in Bullock's campaign, which had opened its office in a two-story house at the corner of 14th and Nueces Streets, three blocks from the Capitol.

"Go today," Erwin advised.

"Why?" Bradley asked.

"You'll be the first volunteer," Erwin answered.

"So what?"

"Bullock remembers things like that," Erwin said.

"She was right," Bradley said later. "Years later, Bullock would say, 'You were the first.' So I worked my way in. I used to get there at 5 a.m. Sometimes I'd get there at 4:30 a.m."

He cleaned the bathrooms and did other odd jobs before heading out to be in his state office by 8 a.m. There was a system for everything at the headquarters, Bradley said. "They had a system for cleaning the bathroom. They had one for taking out the trash, that included policing the area in a 60-foot radius from the dumpster. They picked up the trash every hour. When they hung pictures, they used two nails, not just one, for extra support and security. When you took Bullock a cup of coffee, you had one Styrofoam cup inside another—I guess in case one leaked. Bullock was mostly impressed by whether you worked hard and you did it right."

Once, while he was using the first-floor restroom in the campaign headquarters, "All hell broke loose," Bradley recalled, laughing. "I didn't know that the main-floor bathroom was only for Bullock." He never used it again, instead sharing the second-floor bathroom with 30 other people.

Bradley was the file clerk who ran the copying machine. "I never got any money," Bradley recalled. Sometime after he'd begun his volunteer work, he got a late-night call from Steve Rosales, Bullock's travel aide. "He told me I had to be at headquarters at 4 a.m.," Bradley said.

Boxes of printed materials were stored in an outdoor closet waiting to be mailed that day. They had to be assembled by 6 a.m. in order for the staff to get them done. When Bradley showed up, Rosales was there in a suit, waiting for Bullock to go to a breakfast in San Antonio, 75 miles to the south, that had suddenly been added to the schedule. Bradley was busy hauling the boxes into the headquarters when, suddenly, it started pouring. Bradley kept working.

"I'm wet as hell," Bradley recalled. "Bullock pulls up at 5:15 a.m., and sticks around for about 15 minutes before leaving." Bradley finished his chore, and other workers began showing up. Completely soaked, including his shoes, he headed home to change clothes before going to his office. When he got to the office, there was a message on his desk that Erwin had phoned. He called her.

"Where have you been?" she asked.

Bradley explained what he'd been doing.

"She said, 'Tell the story again. Who was there?'" Bradley did so.

"She said, 'That's the best thing that ever happened to you. Bullock will never, ever forget it, because that's the kind of thing he remembers.'"[6]

Anyone who ran against Bullock would run uphill, and there seemed to be no one with adequate legs lining up at the blocks. With Hobby out of the governor's race, Ann Richards entered it. Garry Mauro turned toward the race for attorney general, and Jim Hightower took aim at Phil Gramm's U.S. Senate seat. Therefore, his most likely primary opponent, if any, would come from the ranks of senators, none of whom had run statewide campaigns or had significant name recognition outside their districts. A statewide poll in October revealed that 88 percent of the respondents recognized Bullock's name, and 65 percent said that "despite past personal problems" he had done a good job. Would the Republicans put up a serious fight? The *Quorum Report*, an Austin political newsletter, thought not. "Bullock's standing among Republicans is so strong that they were not expected to field an opponent against him for comptroller again in 1990. Bullock was the only statewide elected Democrat expected to receive that treatment."[7]

Still, Bullock took no chances. He followed up his announcement with 200 or more phone calls to line up support from lobbyists, politicians, and other political players and set out on a frenzied road trip to visit newspaper editorial boards. "We haven't seen him this excited in years," one of his aides told the *Quorum Report*. The newsletter also suggested that the Old Bullock had been revived—the driven, impatient, intimidating Bullock that predated marital contentment and sobriety. One Houston House member told Bullock he wanted a few weeks to consider his request for support. "Fine," Bullock snapped. "In a few weeks I probably won't need your support."[8]

A few critics—including potential primary opponents—found it absurd that Bullock was running so hard so early. Two of them, Sen. Hugh Parmer of Fort Worth and Sen. Chet Edwards of Duncanville, said they were happy to let Bullock run solo for months, maybe years. "I don't think anybody is going to be able to sew up the nomination this early," Parmer told the Associated Press. "You won't find people making firm commitments three years in advance."

That analysis was not universal. George Christian, LBJ's former press secretary and a leading Democratic activist and strategist, figured that Bullock's early entry might influence others. "King Kong's already in the race," he said.[9]

Bullock was having success in lining up money and political backing, but it didn't scare everyone away. Edwards, a scrappy 36-year-old senator with a record of battling powerful lobbyists, began a low-grade campaign—described by political columnist Ron Calhoun as "guerilla warfare"—to chip away at Bullock's support. Despite his youth and Boy Scout looks, Edwards demonstrated that he could lob hand grenades as proficiently as his battle-scarred adversary.

"I've been told by a lot of Bullock supporters that I shouldn't run against him because he's mean and vindictive," he told Calhoun. "A lot of my supporters have asked me if I'm tough enough to run. I don't wear meanness on my sleeve, but I am very competitive. It will be a very colorful race."[10]

By the end of 1988, however, Bullock had heavy money lined up behind him, thanks to an army of lobbyists who were convinced that he was a shoo-in. On January 16, he reported a war chest of $1.5 million, all but about $300,000 of it raised in the second half of 1988. Edwards raised about $385,000 during the same period, bringing his total to $851,000.

After he formally declared his candidacy in July 1989, Edwards prepared to fight on Bullock's terms. He hired Mark McKinnon, a young strategist and image-maker, who had served with Mark White during his scathing reelection skirmish with Bill Clements. McKinnon urged Edwards to hire as his campaign manager Bob Munson, a veteran of political combat in Louisiana and the strategist behind Buddy Roemer's gubernatorial upset victory over a much better-known and better-financed Gov. Edwin Edwards, the most storied Louisiana pol since Huey Long. "He knows what it takes to unseat an early favorite," advised McKinnon, who also had worked in Roemer's campaign.

What it would take, they estimated, was to go straight for the jugular. Edwards accused Bullock of "putting the thumb" on his contributors by using veiled "intimidation" to shake more money from them. He accentuated Bullock's reputation for erratic, explosive management. "Bill Hobby has spent the last 18 years building up a tradition of fairness and even-handedness," Edwards said. "I think whoever follows in his footsteps should continue that style. There are already jokes going around that Bullock would be changing committee chairmen every week." He characterized Bullock as a practitioner of "the patron [boss] system," out of step with a populace "tired of the old politics of fear and intimidation."[11] He accused Bullock's staff of harassing his supporters with frequent phone calls to let them know "the Bullock camp was watching."[12]

"Chicken Chet Edwards" was one of Bullock's colorfully terse responses to his antagonist. It was a reference to a contribution Edwards received from East Texas chicken mogul Lonnie "Bo" Pilgrim, who walked onto the Senate floor during a 1989 Committee of the Whole meeting on workers' compensation and handed out $10,000 checks to several senators. Edwards later returned the money, but the incident gave Bullock a handy retort whenever Edwards accused him of being "in the back pocket" of utility companies.[13]

For Bullock, everything was on the table. He would be 61 years old by election day, and if he lost this race there would be no comeback. He ran like a man possessed, making over 450 campaign stops during 1989. Edwards had a staff of 12 and about 4,000 volunteers working the state for him, but most of the time they were outflanked and upstaged by Bullock's crew.

A case in point: Sen. Carl Parker's annual Labor Day picnic in Beaumont was a time for Democratic candidates and hordes of their volunteers to strut their wares and enthusiasm in an environment of friendly rivalry, cold beer, and grilled meat. In 1989, Bullock's team showed up a day early and pitched their campaign table in a shady spot near the entrance. They placed campaign posters on chain-link fences and were ready the next day to greet each arriving car with lapel and bumper stickers. At Edwards's table, in a less conspicuous spot a few yards away, volunteers "tried to give away his brochures—to union members already wearing the Bullock logo on their jackets," observed Anne Marie Kilday, of the *Dallas Morning News*.[14]

It was, as Edwards expected, an uphill run, but the grade steadily grew steeper. By the end of November, Bullock had the formal endorsements of 17 of the 23 Democrats in the Texas Senate, and 65 of the 90 Democrats in the Texas House, even though the filing deadline was still a month away. When U.S. Rep. Marvin Leath, a Waco Democrat, announced on December 1 that he would not run for reelection, Edwards saw another career path, one that would be less expensive and less bruising, and would hold a greater probability of success. Three days later he hinted that he would seek Leath's seat; two weeks later, he pulled out of the lieutenant governor's race to run for Congress, and, as is often the way of politics, endorsed Bullock for lieutenant governor.

"Thank God," said McKinnon. "It saved us from having Bullock tear off our heads."[15]

That left Bullock with no opponent in the Democratic primary and a young, relatively unknown Republican Houston oilman to face in November. Rob Mosbacher, Jr., was chairman of the Texas Department of Human Services. His previous run at elective office was for the seat being vacated by U.S. Sen. John Tower, in 1984. But Mosbacher finished in the single digits in the GOP primary, behind U.S. Rep. Ron Paul of Lake Jackson and U.S. Rep. Phil Gramm of College Station, a controversial headline-grabbing former Democrat who won without a runoff.

For Bullock, it looked like another easy stroll for a veteran official who had never lost an election. "He clearly has an enormous advantage," said pollster James Dyer, whose survey showed Bullock with 80-percent name recognition and Mosbacher, whose multimillionaire father was the U.S. Secretary of Commerce, with less than 30 percent. "I don't see he has any problems. In a race like this, that will generate less publicity and interest than the governor's race, it is going to be hard for someone to make up the difference in name recognition."[16]

Bullock apparently agreed. He elected to put his campaign in sleep mode and save his ammunition for the final stretch. It could have been—nearly was—a fatal miscalculation. The campaign of 1990 was extraordinary, with complex variables and calculus. It was a true political fruit-basket turnover: for the first time since four-year terms were adopted in 1974, there was a strong possibility that there would be no incumbent running in any of the major statewide races.

The political shuffle that Gov. Clements precipitated by announcing at the outset of his term that he would be retiring in four years was profound. Since other officeholders below Clements on the political ladder were looking to move up, the notion of several open jobs was the equivalent of wafting juicy steaks by the noses of a pack of hungry dogs.

Vying to replace Clements in the governor's mansion were Atty. Gen. Jim Mattox, Treasurer Ann Richards, and former Gov. Mark White, still itching to get back into the gubernatorial limo.

Since Mattox was running for governor, Land Commissioner Garry Mauro had all but announced he was running for attorney general. He was not alone. Other Democrats who had indicated interest at various points leading up to the January filing deadline included U.S. Rep. John Bryant of Dallas, Harris County Democratic Party Chairman John Odam of Houston, State Rep. Dan Morales of San Antonio, Texas Supreme Court Justice Lloyd Doggett, and Travis County District Attorney Ronnie Earle of Austin, who had gained some notoriety through ethics investigations of several state officials, including Bullock in the 1970s.

Agriculture Commissioner Jim Hightower had indicated that he would take on Republican U.S. Sen. Gramm, whose six-year term was up for renewal in 1990.

By the time the filing deadline passed, Mauro and Hightower had shelved their ambitions to move to other jobs, and sought reelection to their current posts. Most of the other potential candidates for attorney general had followed Mauro's lead, leaving only Morales and Odam to duke it out in the primary. The only Democrat brave or stupid enough to try to capture Gramm's U.S. Senate seat was Hugh Parmer, a state senator and former mayor of Fort Worth. Railroad Commissioner John Sharp, a popular former legislator, was the odds-on favorite to take over Bullock's job as comptroller.

But most eyes were focused on the governor's race. While Bullock was on autopilot in his Democratic primary race for lieutenant governor, the battle for governor turned out to be one of the bloodiest, most brutal ever—in a state in which, as Lloyd Bentsen, Texas's Democratic senior senator, used to only half-joke, "we consider politics a contact sport." The combative Mattox had had the gloves off for years, if indeed he had ever had them on. He seemed to be gaining traction by promoting a state lottery in television ads, at the suggestion of consultant James Carville, who had successfully used that tactic in governor's races in Georgia and Kentucky. Meanwhile, White's grisly television ads, produced by consultant Ray Strother, featured him walking past huge mug shots of convicts who had been executed during his days as governor.

But then Mattox took the brutal tactic of accusing Richards in television ads of a history of drug use. Richards's response to reporters was that as a recovering alcoholic, she and others active in Alcoholics Anonymous did not discuss publicly what type of substance they had abused. It was a relatively lame statement—but her problem was well in the past.

In the first primary, Richards outpolled Mattox by just over 34,000 votes—39 percent to Mattox's 36.7 percent. But since White and three minor candidates got enough votes to deny a majority, Richards had to face Mattox in an April 10 runoff.

Meanwhile, in the Republican primary, self-financed Midland oilman Clayton Williams, Jr., had deluged the state with TV ads claiming that as governor, he would have prisoners "bustin' rocks" instead of watching television. Despite the fact that his six opponents included three fairly well-known names—Railroad Commissioner and former Lubbock Congressman Kent Hance; Dallas attorney Tom Luce, who had been executive director of Ross Perot's school-reform study program in 1984; and Jack Rains of Houston, a former secretary of state—the folksy Williams stunned them all, getting almost 61 percent, thus avoiding a runoff.

Mattox's consultant Carville recommended that in the runoff, Mattox go back to plugging the lottery, which had improved his numbers in the first primary. But Mattox ignored him; he preferred to keep on hammering Richards with the drug ad. But it had the impact of creating sympathy for Richards, who had kicked whiskey almost a decade before.

The question repeatedly put to Richards by reporters was whether Mattox's charge that she had used drugs was correct. But as Texas political columnist Dave McNeely wrote in the *Austin American-Statesman* on April 10, the day of the runoff, "Yes, she should've answered the question, and if the answer was 'no' we'd probably have heard it by now. But it's been ten years."[17]

Apparently, the Democratic voters agreed. Turnout dropped by almost 365,000 voters in the runoff, yet Richards increased her vote from the first primary by more than 60,000 votes. Mattox's total, however, dropped by more than 64,000 votes. Richards got 57.1 percent, and began to plan for what was expected to be an uphill general election. It was a volatile year for politics, and Republican strength was steadily growing.

George Christian, the former LBJ press secretary who did political public relations and lobbying, had helped Ben Barnes when he and Preston Smith squared off in the 1972 governor's race. But when Bullock decided to run for lieutenant governor, "I started helping him," Christian said. "And he really appreciated it."

But Christian thought Bullock was making a mistake in thinking he had a cakewalk. Mosbacher, his Republican opponent, came from a rich family. He'd run statewide before. Republicans were gaining. Lots of political leaves were in the air. "I just insisted that he hire Jack Martin to run his campaign," said Christian, who'd worked with Lloyd Bentsen in his campaigns that had been run by Martin. "He didn't know Jack Martin. He was going to let Otice Green, the same old bunch of Preston Smith's guys, he was going to bring them back in to run his campaign. They knew how to do it. I asked him to meet with Jack Martin."

"Why do I need to do something like that, when I don't even know this guy?" Bullock said.

"Because it sends a signal, Bob, to the Democrats and potential opponents that you've got a credible campaign. And you've got to do that," Christian said. "Jack had run Bentsen's stuff, and some other things, and was big with the Democratic party in the state. And you've just got to show that kind of flag."

Bullock consented to a meeting, but it did not go well. Bullock behaved as Bullock, Christian said, and "chewed Martin out worse than I ever heard a man chew out another man. I was astounded and, of course, it really hurt Jack's feelings."

Tony Proffitt tried to smooth things over. "Don't worry about that. It was just your turn," he told Martin. *Nothing personal. Just your turn. Everybody gets a turn.* Martin agreed to run the campaign.[18]

Greg Hartman, who had managed John Sharp's campaigns for the Railroad Commission in 1986 and his campaign for comptroller in 1990, had also been drafted by Martin to oversee Unity '90, the Democrats' more recent stab at a coordinated campaign.

Hartman's phone rang, he answered it, and without so much as an answering hello, a torrent of abuse came out of the earpiece. It took Hartman a little while to recognize the voice as Bullock's, but the string of obscenities, accompanied by accusations that he was wasting and misspending Bullock's campaign dollars, made it quickly clear who was on the other end of the line. It was, Hartman said, the most vicious ass-chewing he'd ever experienced— before or since.

"I was almost crying," Hartman said. When he got off the phone, he called Martin. "I guess I ain't doing this anymore," Hartman said, presuming that the tirade meant he was fired.

"No, that's a good sign," Martin said. "That means he recognizes that you're doing this. If he'd never called you, then I'd be worried."[19]

Bullock's duel with Mosbacher was not unlike what it would have been with Edwards: age verses youth; the past versus the future; the old guard versus a changing of the guard. Mosbacher was no pushover, and he matched Bullock negative ad for negative ad. One particularly harsh television spot opened with a photo of Bullock, who was 61 and wore a hearing aid, cupping his hand around his ear, as if to hear better, while a voiceover described him as "old Bob Bullock."[20]

Bullock didn't dodge the age issue. One of his spots opened with a Little Lord Fauntleroy look-alike (unmistakably representing Mosbacher) playing in a sandbox and threatening to demolish a sand-castle replica of the state Capitol while an announcer's voice suggested, falsely, that Mosbacher was responsible for the $340 million shortfall in the Department of Human Services' budget. The ad was misleading because the welfare department's shortfall was caused by rising numbers of welfare recipients and changes in federal requirements for some programs.

Words and phrases such as "mudslinging," "morally bankrupt," and "outrageous lie" flew between the two camps like mortar rounds. They fought over experience and management skills, over tax policy, abortion, school funding, environmental issues, and personal lifestyles. "Junior Mosbacher" traded blows with "old Bob Bullock" with enough efficiency that a month before the election, three Democratic state senators joined the fray on Bullock's behalf. At an Austin news conference, Senators Gonzalo Barrientos of Austin, Eddie Bernice Johnson of Dallas, and John Montford of Lubbock—all members of the Finance Committee—criticized Mosbacher for asking for a $2.5 billion budget increase for the DHS without suggesting a way to pay for it. But the surprise element of the attack had nothing to do with budgets.

"Who knows, but you know that we can take the gavel away," Barrientos said. Since almost all of the lieutenant governor's powers are conferred in the rules by the Senate over which he presides, they could be revoked and given to a senator, who would run the chamber as president pro tempore. Since Democrats held a majority of seats, Mosbacher could have been forced to sit on the sidelines and watch the show being run by a party whose candidate he had defeated. "Regardless of who is elected, if that person is unreasonable, illogical, and does not deserve to be president of the Senate, we the senators will take his little gavel away. Or big gavel," Barrientos said.

Johnson and Montford said the possibility of taking away the lieutenant governor's powers had been discussed over the years, but more as an academic debate. It had never achieved enough critical mass to bring it about—partly because many of the senators realized they needed a referee, and partly because many feared the consequences if they planned a coup and it failed. The last time it had been proposed was in 1972, by Sen. Oscar Mauzy of Dallas, when Ben Barnes was a lame-duck lieutenant governor. It was "probably not" a likelihood if Bullock were elected, Montford said, adding, "I think in all candor, if Mr. Mosbacher were to be elected, it would stir up a partisan fight."[21]

They were sending a message not to their Democratic constituents, but to Republicans, who, despite their admiration for Bullock's performance as comptroller, might allow partisanship to trump esteem: reject Bullock, and you may end up dealing with another Democrat, one about whom you know far less, and who may be more partisan than Bullock would be.

Mosbacher attacked Bullock for failing to rule out an income tax. "Bob wants to leave the door open to a state income tax," Mosbacher said in a statement. "If that is what he wants, he needs to explain just how much of our income he wants to take away. Not only will I close the door on an income tax, I'll nail it shut."

Bullock's spokesman, Rafe Greenlee, said Bullock was opposed to a state income tax. "He's not afraid to talk about it," Greenlee said. "He wants to have an open debate about Texas's tax structure. He wants to have an open debate on tax cuts."[22]

Bullock's ads blamed Mosbacher, whose family owned a barge company, for oil spills in the Gulf, and continued to blame the shortfall at the welfare department on him. "He makes a mess, and you pay to clean it up."[23] Inaccurate, maybe, but Bullock's ads served the purpose of keeping Mosbacher on the defensive.

In the governor's race, Claytie Williams couldn't keep his boot out of his mouth. His offhand comment to reporters at his ranch in the spring during drizzly weather, comparing rain to rape—"If it's inevitable, you might as well relax and enjoy it"—had continued to reverberate. He managed to survive the summer, but committed, on purpose, what turned out to be a huge gaffe before a rare joint appearance with Richards before the Dallas Crime Commission. That it was premeditated was made clear by sensitive television cameras that recorded him quietly telling a friend, "Watch this, we're going to have a little confrontation."

Williams was irked because Richards had questioned whether his ClayDesta bank in Midland was involved in laundering drug money.

Williams walked over to Richards at the Dallas event, with cameras grinding.

"Ann, I'm here to call you a liar today. That's what you are. You lied about me. You lied about Mark White. You lied about Jim Mattox. I'm going to finish this deal, and you can count on it."

"I'm sorry, Clayton," said Richards, obviously surprised by his speech. She put out her hand to shake. He turned away and said, "I don't want to shake your hand."[24]

Williams, perhaps, was trying to copy the example U.S. Sen. John Tower had set in 1978, when he refused to shake Democratic challenger Bob Krueger's hand at a joint appearance at a luncheon in Houston. But that was a man refusing to shake a man's hand. For a man who prided himself on his cowboy ways, the idea of refusing to shake hands with a woman, deserved or not, turned out to be a huge blunder. The pendulum of sympathy swung back toward Richards. Then Williams delivered the final self-inflicted wound on an East Texas steam-train ride, designed as a photo opportunity. Williams told reporters that the economy after the oil bust of the 1980s was so bad that he paid no income taxes in 1986.

The Democrats had the statement on radio ads all over the state within hours. Voters obviously paid attention. The election results had Richards outpolling Williams by almost 100,000 votes, winning with 49.5 percent of the vote.

Bullock, who got 75,000 more votes than Richards, and 260,000 more than Mosbacher, won with 51.7 percent. It was closer than he had anticipated, but his victory string nonetheless remained unbroken. All the other Democrats were elected, with two exceptions: Agriculture Commissioner Jim Hightower was upset by Rep. Rick Perry, a former Democratic state representative from Haskell who'd switched parties to make the race, and former state Rep. Kay Bailey Hutchison was elected state treasurer to replace Richards.

With Bullock's victory came one problem: while the comptroller's salary was $74,698 a year, the lieutenant governor's was less than a tenth that much. He would get the same salary as legislators, $7,200 a year. He said he was considering joining the law firm of his father-in-law, Dan Felts, of the firm of Robinson, Felts, Starnes, Angenend & Mashburn. By mid-December, he chose instead to draw his state retirement pay and work with a private alcohol- and drug-abuse program, ViewPoint Recovery Centers, which had treatment programs in seven Texas cities. "I feel I have something to contribute by helping people who are trying to turn their lives around, and this is the kind of work that can be done as time permits," said the recovering alcoholic in a news release.[25] The firm, based in Beaumont, was owned by multimillionaire plaintiff's attorney Walter Umphrey.

Meanwhile, the folks in the Texas Capitol held on to their hats; with Bullock about to be back in the building, anything could happen, and probably would.

CHAPTER 22

I'M IN CHARGE HERE

P aul Hobby, the 30-year-old son of the outgoing lieutenant governor, got a phone call at his home in Houston, where he was an assistant U.S. Attorney. The caller introduced himself and said, "Do you know who I am?"

"Yes," said Hobby, who had been forewarned by his dad that the call probably would come. He definitely knew who Bob Bullock was. They had met in passing during his father's 18-year tenure, but mostly he knew him by reputation—the good and the bad.

"I'd like you to come up here to Austin and talk to me about being my chief of staff."

"Yes, sir," Hobby said. "What time would be good for you?"

"Oh, I think there's a six a.m. flight, so seven tomorrow's good with me."

That night, and for most of the short flight to Austin, Hobby formulated questions in his head and wrote down the five most important he wanted to ask Bullock, questions about the scope of his authority as chief of staff and other mechanics of the job. But he also anticipated something of a psychological reading of his prospective boss. He admired Bullock's energy, dedication, and dynamic genius, but he also was aware that while his wild days seemed to be behind him, there were still two Bob Bullocks: the reasonable and gracious political virtuoso, and the explosive and vengeful despot. On a given day, no one knew which one would show up at the office. If the wrong Bullock showed up too often, he could cause intolerable working conditions and staff disruptions—possibly even a revolt among senators. As comptroller, Bullock commanded a staff of more than 3,000; as lieutenant governor, he would have a staff of 25. "Bullock fires that many in a day," went a popular Capitol wisecrack.

Unlike the comptroller's office, the Senate was not a body that could be ruled by autocracy. From observing his father, Hobby knew that tact and diplomacy were vital. Did he, or anyone else, for that matter, have enough of those qualities to offset Bullock's deficiencies in them? If it worked out, the job could be invaluable schooling for Hobby's own political future—if he chose to have one. But first, he was committed to due diligence. *Did he really want to—could he—work for this guy?*

Bullock was waiting when Hobby arrived at his transition office, a small limestone house with peeling green walls several blocks west of the Capitol. Hobby had his written questions in his pocket and several others queued up in his mind, but didn't get a chance to ask even one of them. Bullock held the floor for most of the meeting.

"He literally answered the questions in order before I could ask them," Hobby said. "He had forethought the meeting. He knew what someone like me would ask someone like him, and he literally answered them before I could ask them."

It went further than that. Bullock spoke of his past with a disarming candor that shocked the younger man. "He confessed to me the most heinous personal and professional sins that you can imagine," Hobby said. "I was agog. I had just met this guy, and he is telling me the worst things he had done."

Bullock owned up to behavior and decisions that were compromised by drink or libido, by anger or greed or revenge—the same catalogue of iniquities he had once shared with reporters on the patio at Scholz's. Hobby listened uncomfortably until, at length, Bullock concluded his confession, leaned back in his chair, and said, "Paul, there is nothing left for me to do but what's good for Texas."[1]

Was this the Bob Bullock who was about to take over the most powerful position in state government, a man who asked that his sins be washed in redemption, whose crimes were forgiven by the statute of limitations and who, from now on, would *do what's good for Texas*? Or would the other Bullock appear? During the campaign, the kinder, gentler Bullock—the one often observed in his last years as comptroller—gave way to the reemergence of the sleepless, frenetic, demanding, and restless persona of old. Hours that had once been spent in saloons were available for serious work, and Bullock drove his staff like a charioteer and went at his adversaries like a chainsaw. During one confrontation, campaign aide Steve Bresnen stood up to him and

declared, "I'm not going to take an ass-chewing for something I didn't do."
Bullock, Bresnen later told *Texas Monthly*, got "right up in my face" and said,
"Damn you. Get the fuck out of here." Three days later, Bullock called and,
with no apology, ordered him back to work.[2]

There was no reliable way for Hobby to know which lieutenant governor
was trying to hire him, but as Bullock talked about the issues facing Texas, it
was apparent that there was much he wanted to do. Reassured, Hobby accepted the job and arranged a one-year leave from the U.S. Attorney's office.

His inaugural address was part populist manifesto, part libertarian longing, and part lofty idealism, a statement of humility *and* a call to arms:

> When I think about the honors and opportunities that have
> come to me—a person born and raised in the small town of
> Hillsboro, a person rich in human frailties but poor in worldly
> goods, who just assumed the second highest honor in Texas—
> I think about the kinds of opportunities and dreams that I
> want to see become reality for every man, woman, and child in
> Texas. Today, that reality does not exist for thousands—if not
> millions—of our fellow Texans; not for the baby born with
> birth defects which might have been prevented with adequate
> prenatal care, not for the working Texan who is unemployed,
> not for the small business owner smothered by over-regulation
> and over-taxation, and not for Texans with disabilities whose
> state offers few services and even less compassion. But that reali-
> ty can become a dream for all Texans if we, who are entrusted
> with high office, conduct our duties with no agenda save the
> agenda of a better Texas.

He spoke of the need for a new financial course, strong ethics legislation,
excellence and equality in public education—"not to satisfy some court mandate, but to honestly, effectively, and efficiently educate every child in
Texas"—as well as the urgency to safeguard the environment and reform
criminal justice. He quoted John F. Kennedy ("It may not be finished in the
first hundred days nor in the first thousand days, but let us begin") and the
Apostle Paul ("Run the race before us with courage looking always to the
author of our faith").[3]

Hope. Determination. Faith. Compassion. Justice. The good Bob Bullock was onstage, but the evil twin was lurking in the wings and about to introduce himself to the Senate.

> Capitol denizens are eyeing Bob Bullock these days as though he is the other shoe. Indeed, few around here claim to think Texas's new lieutenant governor is going to go much longer without stomping some political toes, and most think the falling shoe is more likely to resemble a bomb than footgear when it hits. About the only questions, besides when, are: On which political toes is the veteran politician's first shoe-bomb going to fall and what will be the long-term impact of its detonation?

—Jane Ely, in the *Houston Chronicle*, January 27, 1991 [4]

Indeed, one of Bullock's first acts was to stomp on some toes by discarding the bipartisan accommodation Hobby had made with Republicans as their numbers increased in the Senate. Unlike most state legislatures and the U.S. Congress, where the majority party holds all committee chairmanships, Hobby made proportional assignments. With nine members (nearly one third of the Senate), Republicans were given about 30 percent of the chairs. It served two purposes: It helped the lieutenant governor, by currying favor with the senators, to hold on to the powers they granted him in their rules, and it discouraged partisanship from trumping principle.

Bullock not only removed the Republican chairs and replaced them with Democrats, he was openly disdainful of the opposition party. Sen. Cyndi Krier, a moderate Republican from San Antonio, had—not unreasonably—supported Bullock's Republican opponent for lieutenant governor. Bullock instructed his staff not to address her as "Senator." He so disliked Republican Sen. Jane Nelson that for the entire session he refused to recognize her to speak on the Senate floor.

After Chet Edwards's election to Congress, a special election was held to fill his Senate seat. The Texas Medical Association backed Republican David Sibley, a dental surgeon turned lawyer who also had been mayor of Waco. Bullock supported Democratic State Rep. Betty Denton, and he frequently called Kim Ross, lobbyist for the TMA, urging the organization to switch its endorsement.

"Sibley is a good guy," Ross insisted. "You'll like him."

"I can't stand another Republican in the Senate," Bullock said.[5]

Sibley won.

Although he was never cozy with the party hierarchy and never held much enthusiasm for linking his campaigns to those of other Democrats, Bullock was ardently partisan, as illustrated by an Andrew Jackson Day speech he delivered in Dallas. "I do not believe that Old Hickory would be one bit surprised 160 years later that the national Republican Party still cares more about big banks than about little people . . . that the Republican Party is still opposed to helping working people who have been victimized by Republican economic policies and victimized by Republican insensitivity to the damage those policies have done to working people, small businesses, poor people, retired people, disabled people, students, minorities, and sick people." He rapped Texas Republicans' record on workers compensation, welfare, and school funding. "Republicans in the Legislature have taken the luxury of opposing taxes because they have always known that a responsible majority of Democratic legislators would bear the burden of doing what had to be done," he said.[6]

More Republicans in the Senate, he believed, would only obstruct his legislative program. It was an ambitious agenda, and Bullock was in a hurry. Besides the fundamental challenges of reversing the declining quality of public education, fixing an overcrowded prison system, reforming an antiquated and inequitable tax system, and redrawing congressional and legislative districts, Bullock was prepared to compound the workload. He wanted to create a new department of environmental quality, a performance-review process for assessing and reforming state agencies, and pass strong ethics legislation.

Though angered at being marginalized by Bullock's partisanship, the Republicans did not have the numbers for a counterattack. There was little they could do except sit on the sidelines and leave Bullock to his own devices. It wasn't much, but it would turn out to be enough to teach the new lieutenant governor the downside of despotism.

No toes of either party were immune to his boot heels. He was an active volcano, and the eruptions were always intense, usually brief, and wholly unpredictable. They could occur anywhere—in his office, on the Senate floor, in a corridor—and senators began to refer to his tirades as "drive-by ass-chewings." Many senators and Senate staffers became convinced that they were calculated, almost scripted. Rationalizing his conduct as cunning was more palatable than the alternative explanation of borderline lunacy.

This is how a few senators, as well as other state officials, received their indoctrination into the style of leadership Bullock was bringing to the chamber.

Sen. David Sibley, the freshman:

> Bullock is at the podium, machine-gun gaveling one bill after another to passage. Sibley tries to be recognized to protest that bills are coming up before senators have a chance to study or debate them. Bullock ignores him, but Sibley persists. At length, Bullock resentfully relents. "The chair recognizes the crybaby from Waco," he says.
>
> In Bob Johnson's office adjacent to Bullock's, Sibley, anxious to learn the ropes, chats with Johnson, Bullock's friend since their House days of the late 1950s and now Senate parliamentarian. While they talk, Bullock bursts into the room, rants at Johnson for a few minutes, and then fires him. After Bullock leaves, Johnson returns to his work.
>
> "Wait a minute," Sibley says. "What just happened here?"
>
> Johnson shrugs and says, "Hell, I get fired probably twice a day."[7]

Sen. Bill Haley, a Democrat from Center, whom Bullock appointed chairman of the Senate Administration Committee:

> Bullock's punctuality is legendary, and he expects no less from those around him, regardless of extenuating circumstances. He sends out the word that he expects members to be at their desks when he gavels the session to order, usually at 11 a.m. There are no excuses—not constituents who show up unexpectedly, not ill-timed phone calls, not committee meetings delayed by witnesses. There is no great consequence to being a little tardy, since the Senate's first order of business is the morning call, which is primarily housekeeping matters.
>
> A few days after receiving Bullock's on-time edict, Haley arrives in the Senate chamber at six minutes past eleven, just in

time to observe Sen. Carl Parker rising from his chair and declaring, "Due to lack of interest on the part of my colleagues in today's session, I move we stand adjourned until eleven o'clock tomorrow morning."

Bullock glares at Haley, slams down the gavel, and apologizes to the Rev. Paul Thompson, the Hope Presbyterian Church minister who was there to offer the morning prayer.

"I'm ashamed that there are not enough here to conduct the business of the State of Texas," Bullock says.

He disappears into his office and, a few minutes later, his secretary, Rhetta Butler, steps into the chamber and motions to Haley. "The lieutenant governor wants you to come to his office," she says.

Like a wayward student summoned to the principal's office, Haley follows her to his fate. Once there, Bullock stands, walks to the outer door and closes it, then goes to the door leading into the Ramsey Conference Room and closes it. He turns and approaches Haley until their faces are inches apart. He yells at the top of his voice. He curses and scolds, a feral blaze in his eyes.

Stunned, Haley is frozen for a few seconds and then begins to yell back, louder than Bullock—loud enough to be heard in the outer office. "You can't insult the members of this Senate!" Haley shouts. "They are not your employees! They have busy schedules that they can't always control!"

Now it is Bullock who is stunned. He listens to Haley's rant and then walks behind his desk and stares out the window. "It's over," he says quietly, and slumps into his chair. "You can leave."

"No, it's not over," Haley says. "You can't treat senators like that, and I won't stand for it."

"You don't care about the State of Texas, only yourself," Bullock says.

"Well," Haley says, "I'm not the one who has a personal valet on the state payroll."

Again, Bullock is momentarily speechless. "It's over," he repeats.

Haley walks around the desk, extends his hand, and says, "Okay, it's over."

Bullock stares at the hand for a long beat before reaching out to shake it.

The next morning, all but one of the 31 senators are at their desks. As the roll is called, several answer with a rousing "HERE!" Bullock smiles. "Wonderful attendance this morning," he says.

He never raises his voice at Haley again.[8]

Rep. Bruce Gibson, a moderate Democrat from Godley, southeast of Fort Worth, a legislator for more than a decade:

> The House of Representatives is far more likely than the Senate to be charged with disorderly conduct, but, as a rule, its brawling is internal. Its members are not accustomed to being bullied by their own Speaker, much less an outsider, such as the lieutenant governor. But now, a school finance bill is stumbling and Bullock is testy. He wants, as much as anything, to resolve an issue that has vexed the Legislature for a quarter of a century. He wants a permanent fix and publicly belittles the efforts and motives of the House in opposing a Senate remedy. In a room full of legislators and lobbyists, Bullock dresses down Gibson, a member of the conference committee, in terms that some witnesses describe as "verbal abuse." A fistfight nearly erupts. When the House convenes later, Gibson goes to the podium and invites Speaker Gib Lewis aside for a private talk.
>
> "I'm taking this personal," he says. "I've had it. You just don't treat people that way. I'm going to bust him."[9]

Newly elected Atty. Gen. Dan Morales, a Democrat and former member of the House:

> Redistricting has been described as the DNA of politics, and it never goes down easy. There are always issues of favoritism, parochialism, race, constitutionality, and political punishment, and 1991 is no different. It is serious enough that the senators hire an outside redistricting legal expert, Dave Richards (ex-husband of the governor), to look after their interests. Morales is offended. "Paul," he says to Hobby, "how do you think it feels? I'm supposed

to be the lawyer for the state. These guys don't have the authority
to hire separate counsel. We've got lawyers to do that. How do you
think it feels to be the first statewide elected Mexican American
and have this sort of slap in the face?" He asks for and gets a meeting with Bullock and Gib Lewis, in Lewis's office, to discuss it.
Bullock becomes irritated by Morales's incessant complaints and
physically challenges him by bumping against him with his chest
and lightly backhanding him. "You skinny-assed son of a bitch,
you're squealing like a pig stuck under a gate," he tells the attorney general. Fully believing that blows will be exchanged, Hobby
steps between them.[10]

Andy Sansom, director of the Texas Parks and Wildlife Department:

Relatively new in his job, Sansom is to meet the newly elected
lieutenant governor, with whom he will have to work closely on
policy and budget matters. Sansom is escorted by board member
Bob Armstrong, who was Texas's land commissioner for 12 years,
and who knew Bullock well. Bullock had a special interest in
Sansom's agency, both because he was an avid hunter and because
he had a paternal affection for the old forts and other historic sites
that the agency managed. Sansom, young but serious, is on record
about his intentions to strictly enforce field and stream laws.
Bullock is ready to test him.

"You're going to enforce these laws . . . the fish and game
laws? You're serious about that?"

"Yes, sir," Sansom nods.

"Tell me about your plans for enforcement," Bullock says.

Sansom gives him a brief rundown.

"Game wardens," Bullock says. "You going to need more of
them?"

It goes on. Like a courtroom lawyer setting up a witness for
the gotcha moment, Bullock draws out Sansom's unequivocal
commitment to cracking down on poachers or sportsmen who take
more than the legal limits.

"Now that you've told me all that," Bullock says, "let me tell
you about the time I killed 325 quail in one day." This was more

than 20 times the bag limit of 15. "What are you going to do about it?"

Sansom is incredulous. It is a true confession, but Sansom suspects Bullock is making it up to test his reaction.

Armstrong bails him out. "At least you are not trying to get on the Parks and Wildlife Commission," he tells Bullock.[11]

Bullock may have been making harmless sport of Sansom, or disingenuously testing his commitment to game-law enforcement. More likely, he was letting the new, young agency head know who carried the big stick in state government.

"Most people used MBO—management by objective," said Ralph Wayne, who had been his chief of staff in the comptroller's office. "He used MBF—management by fear."[12]

Paul Hobby, with his front-row seat and close encounters with Bullock, developed his own theory about the boss's behavior, one that dismissed the notion that Bullock's routine was an act. It may have been MBF, but it was involuntary. *The truth is, you don't hold those things against Bullock any more than you hold the fact that a child wets the bed against the child,* he believed. *It was like a stiff summer storm. It would blow by, and it would be over. Don't hold it against him, because it is a physical handicap; it is outside his control.*[13]

CHAPTER 23

ANN RICHARDS
Friend or Enemy?

"Hairy-legged lesbians" is how Bullock came to refer to Gov. Richards and her female staff.

Certainly, the inauguration was a Bullock-Richards love-fest, but it wilted quicker than a rose in the desert. Bullock sized up the governor's staff as incompetent, indecisive, too cautious and, in one respect, too fiscally conservative. One thing that didn't help was that the new lieutenant governor had offered a job to Susan Rieff as an environmental advisor. Rieff had accepted, but then was asked to go to work for the new governor. She chose to work for Richards, and Bullock, to say the least, didn't forget.

Richards instituted the ritual of having the lieutenant governor and the House speaker to the governor's mansion each Monday morning for breakfast and policy discussions. Bullock found the menu decidedly petit. After one breakfast, according to Speaker Gib Lewis, Bullock had about $100 worth of groceries delivered to the governor's mansion, along with a note: "Next time, I'd like to be fed."[1]

Some of those close to Bullock felt that his resentment of Richards involved more than her breakfast menu or the performance of her staff. He had held some of the most important positions in state government for three decades but couldn't seize the gold ring. She had risen quickly from a lowly county commissioner to the insignificant position of state treasurer to governor, and was a rising star in the national Democratic Party to boot. *It should have been him.* With an eye on the political future, Richards tried to avoid controversy; with no political future, Bullock was as brash and impatient as ever. The clash of styles was inevitable.

Early in the session, Bullock attended a gathering at the governor's mansion, where Richards was entertaining newspaper editors and editorial writers from around the state. On the turf of a governor dancing in glass shoes, he sported steel-toed boots.

"Texas needs an income tax," he declared from the grand staircase in the governor's mansion, responding to the editors' questions about the unhappy budget prognosis.[2] He had said it before, had he not? Not exactly. Not so emphatically. For a quarter of a century, Bullock had been warning the Legislature that an income tax "should be looked at" or that it was "inevitable" as Texas ran out of revenue options. Bullock's predecessor, Bill Hobby, had called for an income tax in late 1989, but as he was on his way out of office and not facing another election. Now, Bullock was saying the time had come, saying it in the governor's new house in the presence of influential opinion-makers. He was the polecat at the prom, and the odor of an outcast topic was as welcome as fire ants.

The reaction was swift, clamorous, and negative. "We literally had two fax machines melt into the corner over the weekend," said Paul Hobby, Bullock's chief of staff.[3]

Rumors started to circulate that Bullock was terminally ill. Why else would he so forcefully attempt political suicide? So convincing were the rumors that friends called his office to inquire about him. Word of his imminent passing reached his old friend Clinton Manges, the South Texas rancher whose on-the-edge financial dealings had landed him in bankruptcy court. "Hey, Bullock," he said, "I got two hundred grand stashed away that nobody knows about. Let's go around the world. One last good go."

Hobby was impressed by the devotion of Bullock's pals. "Here was Clinton Manges, admitting to fraud on a federal court to take his friend Bob Bullock around the world and blow his last two hundred grand," Hobby said. "That tells you about . . . the way people felt about him."[4]

Some of the storm also blew against Richards's door. Bullock's dropping of the income tax bomb in the governor's mansion was greeted with about as much enthusiasm as if he had fouled himself. Richards hadn't campaigned against an income tax, and hadn't ruled it out. But her stock response when asked about it while campaigning was that she didn't think one was necessary. For Bullock to have outed the idea in that gathering of newspaper folk, where it was sure to zoom around the state like a ricocheting laser beam, not only upstaged the governor, but was going to make an issue-packed legislative session even more difficult. A number of people thought it was a good idea, and agreed with Bullock and Bill Hobby that it was long overdue. But if there's a right time for the right idea, this wasn't it. Richards was still testing her wings as governor, and now Bullock had provided a large and turbulent headwind. *How dare he!*

For weeks, Bullock tried to peddle the idea in speeches and interviews and by writing guest columns for newspaper op-ed pages, arguing that the Texas Supreme Court had ruled "not once, but twice, that . . . relying on *local* school property taxes to support the state school system is unconstitutional, [and] the bottom line is that the state must *replace and/or redistribute* local school property taxes on a statewide basis."[5]

It was a reasonable argument with legal intricacies that probably went over the heads of most taxpayers. The state constitution prohibited a statewide property tax, raising questions about the Legislature's ability to redistribute *local* property taxes. Therefore, as long as property taxes were the major source of school funding, unconstitutional district-to-district revenue inequities would continue. It was no small quandary, but one the Legislature spent decades avoiding.

"Full implementation of a state income tax would let us completely eliminate the school property tax on all residential property," Bullock wrote. "A Texas income tax would apply to people and corporations from out of state who do business and make profits in Texas. For the first time, out-of-staters would be paying a Texas tax on the money they make here."[6]

Gov. Richards said an income tax's chances were "slim to none." House Speaker Lewis said that fewer than 40 of the 150 House members would vote for it.[7] House Ways and Means Committee Chairman James Hury, a Democrat from Galveston, predicted that it would be "political death" for a legislator to vote for one. "You have to recognize that it's an unpopular vote now," Hury said.[8]

They were right. Despite its logic, Bullock's crusade was futile. Even as his aides were putting together the details of an income tax bill—a five-percent rate to head off an oppressive increase in property taxes—the notion was sliding toward oblivion. Gov. Richards didn't want to talk about it, and House Speaker Lewis said that "politics and reality" would not allow it to happen. Texas, for a while, would continue to fund schools with a regressive sales tax, some of the gasoline tax, and some of the highest property taxes in the nation.

Much of Austin was wary of Bullock, and not just for his verbal outbursts. He came to the job with more knowledge of state government than perhaps any of his predecessors, but he also brought along a keener understanding of power and its applications than anyone before him. In his world, knowledge and power fattened off each other, and Bullock seemed unable to get enough of either.

Frivolous knowledge was no exception. In a town where gossip is the underground language, Bullock insisted on holding the biggest dictionary. He was convinced that all of his employees were sleeping around, and that those who occupied cubicles below ground level were singularly lascivious. He insisted that Hobby give him a daily "fornication report"—his words—and accused his young aide of participating in the basement debauchery.

"Governor," Hobby told him, "I'm at a loss for when you think I might do these things, since you and I are up there on the second floor together, total sixteen hours a day. Who's got time for fornication?"[9]

It was the serious knowledge, however, that gave Bullock his force. His box of nightly reading included every report issued by every government agency, federal reports, newspaper and magazine articles, and books on Texas history. He continued to badger aides at impossible hours, and it was rare that anyone beat him to the office.

Bullock and his lieutenants, usually in strained tandem with Gov. Richards, pursued an ambitious agenda that most legislators—Democrats, at least—felt was worthwhile. Republicans resented their loss of power under Bullock and the dismissive treatment they received from him, but they lacked the votes to do much about it. Even among his allies there was an uneasy sense that he was reaching for imprudent omnipotence.

Bullock proposed a performance review process in which the comptroller's office would assess the efficiency and effectiveness of each state agency, but then went a step further by proposing to create a state budget policy committee consisting of himself, Gov. Richards, and Speaker Lewis—a "troika," as it quickly was dubbed—that would decide which state agencies and services were vital and which were not, which should be reorganized, consolidated, or abolished. The committee would get staff assistance from the Legislative Budget Board, the state auditor, the Sunset Advisory Commission, the governor's planning and budget office, and the comptroller's office. The legislation creating the committee would freeze state salaries, the hiring of outside contractors, equipment purchases, and the leasing of office space unless approved by the troika. When the Legislature was in session, the committee would make funding and reorganization recommendations. When the lawmakers were not in town, which was most of the time, the committee would have the authority to make whatever decisions it liked.

It would have been an unprecedented concentration of power, and nobody doubted which member would have dominated the troika's actions. Bullock would eat Ann Richards's taco and have Lewis's enchilada for dessert. He had, House members agreed, the effrontery, farsightedness, and sheer determination to shake up the state bureaucracy, to wire around the logrolling and pork-barreling that slowed, if not derailed, the legislative process. But even those who agreed with his ideas balked at installing him as Emperor of Texas.

The troika proposal went quietly and mercifully to its tomb. Bullock would have to wield his power the old-fashioned way.

During the financial crisis of the 1980s, Bullock studied ways to stream-line and increase the efficiency of various agencies. During the 1989 session, while still comptroller, he urged the Legislature to create a new department to oversee environmental matters. It went nowhere then, but things were differ-ent now: he held the gavel. With Senate and House sponsors, he revived the proposal into a 300-page bill creating a state Department of the Environment, a super-agency that would take over all functions of the Texas Water Commission, Air Control Board, Texas Water Development Board, and Water Well Drillers Board, as well as pluck environmental management, reg-ulation, and research functions from other agencies, such as the General Land Office, the Agriculture Commission, the Railroad Commission, and the State Health Department.

It met the predictable opposition of officeholders and bureaucrats reluc-tant to have their authority eroded. Agriculture Commissioner Rick Perry, for instance, objected to relinquishing control over pesticide regulation. Utility companies lashed out at the proposed five-percent tax on their gross receipts to pay for low-level nuclear waste disposal. With opposition coming mostly from the House, the bill sputtered and died during the regular legislative ses-sion, but was revived in a special session a few weeks later.

Again, Sen. Carl Parker, a Democrat from Port Arthur, was the Senate sponsor, and the bill cleared that chamber by a unanimous vote. In the House, however, another Democrat, Rep. Robert Saunders, of La Grange, was draft-ing a different version, one that would exempt environmental-protection functions of the Land Office, the Railroad Commission, and the Department of Agriculture from being folded into the new agency, and it was considerably less muscular than the Senate bill. For instance, the House repeatedly reject- ed provisions requiring landfills to be located at least 500 feet from homes and 1,500 feet from schools. Tom "Smitty" Smith, Texas director of Public Citizen, a government watchdog group, declared: "It's a very weak bill that protects the polluters and not the people."[10]

When the two bills landed in conference committee, Bullock again found himself butting heads with Bruce Gibson, who told him the votes were not in the House to pass the bill.

"Just send me something," Bullock told him.[11]

What came back to the Senate was heavily revised and far weaker than Bullock wanted. And, thinking the package would be rejected anyway, Gibson whimsically gave the new agency a tongue-twister name—the Texas Natural Resource Conservation Commission, thereafter known as *ten-rack* by most people, or *train wreck* by the lobbyists opposed to it—to enter into the bureaucratic lexicon.

"Passage of the . . . bill is bittersweet progress," Bullock said. "The short- comings mean we still have a long way to go in effectively implementing good environmental action."[12]

Bittersweet success was better than no success, and this was a session in near collapse.

Lt. Gov. Hobby, said Sen. Ken Armbrister, was a "controller," inclined to kill bills of which he disapproved by declining to recognize the Senate spon- sor, thereby keeping the bill from reaching the floor. Bullock, Armbrister observed, was an "expediter." If a senator wanted a vote on his bill, Bullock would make it happen.[13] His own agenda dealt with the sweeping measures of governmental reform. The routine business bills that most senators brought forth interested him little, and he was happy to hasten them through the process. In his first session as presiding officer, the Senate became known as "The Bullock Train" for the rocket speed at which he gaveled bills through the chamber.[14] More than one senator privately complained about Bullock's habit of interrupting the vote-count roll call after a few names had been called, and declaring, "There being 31 ayes and no nays, the bill passes to engrossment."

He also was impatient with the haggling, dickering, lobbying, and counter- lobbying that usually accompanied routine legislation. If a dispute arose, his

standard procedure was to usher representatives from both sides into a conference room. *Write a bill you can agree on, or I'll write it—and you may not like the
one that I write.* He would leave the room, leave the door ajar, and allow no
one else to depart until a deal was cut.

But in his first session, MBF largely failed him. The deals that were cut
were not the ones that were most important to him. He was not able to gavel
through much of significance. His first effort at being lieutenant governor, at
trying to broadly reform state government, was disappointing. Wrote *Texas
Monthly*:

> The best that can be said about the long struggle of the Seventy-
> second Legislature is that it is over. That was a year when
> the Legislature was as bad as the public has always suspected.
> Eight months of work produced only patches on leaky tires:
> a school finance law that hurts as many schoolchildren as it
> helps; new prisons but no change in the practice of crowding
> them with nonviolent felons; and new taxes on the same old
> taxpayers. The Legislature . . . must be judged on the gut-check
> issues—and on these, it failed. The main reason is that none
> of the legislative leaders was willing to demand that it succeed—
> not Gov. Ann Richards, not Lt. Gov. Bob Bullock, not Speaker
> Gib Lewis.[15]

It is likely that the critique had a profound effect on a politician unaccus-
tomed to failure, one accustomed to giving orders and seeing immediate
results. Possibly, Bullock may have concluded, he had been too nice in that
first session. If so, it was an error he would not repeat.

Unfinished work from that session, planned in advance by the governor
and legislative leaders, required the governor to call a special session—primarily to pass a biennial budget. Before that called session, a leadership summit—the governor, lieutenant governor, House speaker, Legislative Budget
Board, and a few support staff—convened at the Wynne Lodge on Matagorda
Island on the Gulf Coast to write a budget away from the public and press.
Reporters, who assembled on the mainland, howled about violations of the
state open-meetings law. Some rented boats and tried to crash the summit, but
had to settle for photo ops and clipped interviews.

In privacy, the state's leaders gathered on a screened-in porch and wrote a budget bill that included—among some tax adjustments—the controversial state lottery. Richards was on record for a lottery. Bullock said that it was a sleazy way to raise revenue but, since his income tax had fizzled, he went along with it.

When they returned to Austin, Bullock summoned a large contingent of lobbyists, who had worked to kill a tax bill during the regular session, to a meeting at the Capitol. "The state of Texas has gone as far as it can go without additional revenue, and I am going to take a little chunk out of each of your asses and put a tax bill together," he said. "If you whine, I'm going to take a big chunk out of your asses. So you just decide what you want."[16]

It was an easy decision. The tax bill passed during the special session with little interference from the lobbyists.

Bullock had dealt with redistricting before, as a member of the Legislative Redistricting Board that got the chore in 1981. But as lieutenant governor in 1991, the task took on different overtones. As a Democrat in charge of a Senate dominated by Democrats, he wanted to make things as comfortable for his party as possible. At the same time, the federal Voting Rights Act, and particularly its affirmative action clause that sought to maximize minority representation, limited the running room. Any map had to be pre-cleared by the U.S. Department of Justice or by a federal court.

Bullock put his old friend from the Preston Smith days, Sen. Bob Glasgow of Stephenville, in charge of redistricting the Senate. Bullock was in a hurry to get redistricting behind him, because he considered it a time-consuming distraction when there were plenty of other issues—the budgets, prison expansion, and school finance among them—that he thought were higher priorities. At the same time, he also realized that for the individual senators, a considerable amount of their time in Austin was spent trying to make it as certain as possible that they'd be able to return. Bullock saw it as his job to protect as many of the Democratic incumbents as possible. They, after all, were the ones who granted his large powers through passage of the Senate rules.

Glasgow said, even before redistricting passed the Senate and then the House, that he expected it would wind up in court, and he was right. In a challenge to the map brought by lawyers for the Mexican American Legal Defense and Educational Fund, state District Judge Mario Ramirez of Edinburg agreed that it had undercounted minorities. That led to negotiations between the attorney general's office and the plaintiffs, which produced a settlement agreed to by 19 of the Democrats in the Senate. The judge decreed that the settlement was acceptable.

That sent the Republicans into a howling rage. How could 19 senators assume a job that supposedly required the assent of a majority of not just the Senate, but also the House? They appealed the judge's ruling to the Texas Supreme Court. Meanwhile, on a parallel track, a three-judge federal court was also reviewing the Senate map.

Sure enough, in December 1991, the Texas Supreme Court agreed with Republicans that the settlement did not pass muster. That opened a window for the federal court, which quickly imposed its own Senate map—even though Gov. Richards called a special legislative session to begin the second day of 1992. Too late, the federal court ruled—in a decision and manner that later would cause Judge Jim Nowlin to recuse himself after being admonished for getting help drawing the map from Republican state Rep. George Pierce of San Antonio, with whom Nowlin had served in the Texas House before his appointment to the federal bench.

The court-imposed districts were used in the 1992 elections, but by 1994, the Senate had returned to its earlier map. The result was that all 31 Senate districts, instead of just half of them, were on the ballot in 1992 *and* 1994. In some ways, the redistricting fiasco may have been an inadvertent windfall for Bullock, because it kept the senators off balance and left him with some leverage into the middle of the decade over Senate districts, while his own district was all of Texas. It was not until the 1996 elections that the dust settled on Senate redistricting.

Hobby's one-year leave of absence from the U.S. Attorney's office was nearing an end and, frayed by a tense year with Bullock, he was anxious to get back to Houston. He still had respect and admiration for his boss, but his mental and emotional endurance had been sorely tested.

Bullock would scold him one day for assuming too much responsibility ("Hey, Buster, you weren't elected to anything; I'm the lieutenant governor") and scold him the next for assuming too little ("Why are you bothering me with this? You don't deserve responsibility if you don't claim it").

Mental warfare, calming Bullock's tantrums, enduring his mood swings, and mediating his blowups with senators and other state officials exhausted him and tested his tolerance. When the regular session ended, Hobby got home about one o'clock in the morning and told his wife, "I might kill him. I literally might use my bare hands and kill him."[17]

After several months, after first offering the job to former state Sen. Kent Caperton of Bryan, Bullock picked as Hobby's replacement Bruce Gibson— the former state representative whom he had chewed out mercilessly just the year before. Gibson needed a press secretary and hired Reggie Bashur, the former press secretary to Gov. Clements, to deal with the media. It was just a few days before a special legislative session in December.

Within three days, Bashur realized he'd made a mistake. He told Gibson he had changed his mind.

"I was mad," Gibson said. "The way you resigned in those days with Bullock was to turn in your pager. I told Bashur he was going to have to turn it in to Bullock himself, and marched him into Bullock's office. Bullock proceeded to give him the worst ass-chewing I've ever seen. It was brutal.

"'Reggie,' Bullock said at one point, 'You're not from around here, are you?' Reggie, who grew up in New York, said, 'No, sir.' Bullock said, 'I can tell the blood of William Barrett Travis doesn't flow in your veins. If you were at the Alamo, you'd have gone over the back wall.' Bullock then proceeded to chew on Reggie for ten minutes. When he finally finished and we walked out of his office, I told Reggie, 'Man, I'm sorry. I was mad at you. But not now. We're even.'"[18]

CHAPTER 24

SECOND SESSION IS A CHARM

Seldom if ever has one person so dominated a legislative session as Lieutenant Governor Bob Bullock, who ran the Texas Senate like an evangelist on speed. His agenda for the session amounted to addressing every problem facing Texas that he could think of. When the session was over, he had cleaned his plate. A budget that increased spending without raising taxes. A school finance plan that staved off a court order to close the schools, and tough new penal laws were just the beginning; turf wars that had paralyzed the Legislature for years, from trucking deregulation to the Edwards Aquifer, had been resolved.

Topic A was how Bullock had done it. The Capitol was full of street-corner psychologists analyzing his obsession with detail. His compulsion for work, his drive to seal a deal, his impulse to chastise, his need for vote margins that reflected near-unanimity. People queued up outside Bullock's office, grumbling that he was a control freak who dictated when the Senate inhaled and exhaled; then they went behind closed doors and asked him to dictate a solution to their battles. Bullock was desperate to lead and everybody else, the Senate included, was desperate to be led.

How did he get his way so often? Through incessant use of facts, flattery, rewards, old-fashioned threats. He trusted underused senators with major assignments, and they were afraid not to succeed. He communicated with unmistakable intensity, boring his unblinking eyes in uncomfortably close to a senator's face in a

manner reminiscent of Lyndon Johnson. He always knew the substance of an issue better than anyone else, and he had, as always,
an unsurpassed feel for politics. Far from being weakened by a large
Republican minority, he was strengthened by it; coalition building
was essential, and no one can assemble coalitions like Bullock.
Underlying everything else, he had a public spiritedness that was
genuine; when he demanded that senators do what was best for
Texas, they knew he meant it. He dominated the Senate because
the Senate knew it could not have done what it did without him.[1]

—*Texas Monthly*, July 1993

R endered by the same magazine that had pronounced Bullock's maid-
en session a dismal performance, that assessment was a definitive
summation of what the Capitol—the entire state—could now expect
from the lieutenant governor for as long as he held office.

It wasn't a particularly pretty session. As *Texas Monthly* noted,
there were "raucous debates over sodomy and handguns, attacks on
sex education, and a rodeo war between Mesquite (honored as the Rodeo
Capital of Texas) and Pecos (honored for its Oldest Rodeo in the World)."
Bullock himself added a touch or two to the whimsy.

Less than two weeks into the session, he attended a breakfast meeting
of the Texas Chamber of Commerce to speak on a serious subject: Human
services programs for needy children and women were being threatened
by the state's budget crunch. He arranged for Sen. Judith Zaffirini, a Democrat from Laredo, whom he had appointed to chair the Senate Health and
Human Services Committee, to be present. His message was lost to the noise.
Acknowledging Zaffirini's presence, Bullock tossed out an aside meant, no
doubt, as humor and as a compliment.

"She could get any legislation passed if she cut her skirt off about six
inches and put on high heels," he said.

Bullock had lived his life well behind the political correctness curve and
rarely suffered a scratch for it, but this time Republicans thought they smelled
blood. Karen Hughes, the executive director of the state GOP, called the
remarks "blatantly sexist."[2] Beverly Kaufman, president of the Texas
Federation of Republican Women, said, "Women, whether conservatives or
liberals, don't like to be offended or demeaned."[3]

Zaffirini told reporters she was not offended. "I guess I'm getting used
to his sense of humor," she said.[4] Even Gov. Richards defended him. "Quite

frankly," she said, "he is one of the most ardent defenders of equal opportunities for women."[5] The incident quickly vanished, and for the rest of the session, Bullock stood mostly above, or outside of, whatever silliness beset the Legislature. It was, as the *Texas Monthly* tribute suggested, the defining session of his tenure. Richards was deferential on legislative matters, and the House had a new speaker, Pete Laney, who was still learning the ropes. That left Bullock to set the legislative agenda and make things happen.

He succeeded under what should have been circumstances more trying than his first session, when he and his party had nearly full rein over the Senate. In the 1992 elections, the Republicans picked up four seats, bringing their total to 13—enough, under the Senate's two-thirds rule, to block legislation and gubernatorial appointments, break quorums, and otherwise frustrate the process. Stripping Republicans of their committee chairmanships in 1991 had backfired, possibly contributing to the general failure of the session. This time around, he moved some of them back into leadership positions and made good use of their talents.

Among other things, they taught him the arts of accommodation and conciliation. Sen. David Sibley, who became what *Texas Monthly* termed the "unofficial minority leader," led a Republican boycott of a judicial redistricting bill, which he considered too partisan. With no quorum, the Senate brakes were on. After Bullock's assurances that the Republicans' concerns would be addressed, Sibley ended the walkout. The ramifications of this new paradigm were large—for Bullock more than anyone. He ruled the Senate by consent, which could no longer be taken for granted. That was not enough to blunt his spikes, but it forced him to rethink his tactics. Sibley would become one of Bullock's go-to guys and a member of his inner circle.

In dealing with the bureaucracy, Bullock also became craftier and strategically less officious. Part of it was that more and more former Bullock staffers from his comptroller days were showing up in key positions in state government and the lobby. Equally important, if not more so, was the sheer force of Bullock's management style.

Andy Sansom, the Parks and Wildlife Department executive director, concluded from their first encounter that Bullock was now the power in state government, meaning that he would have to deal with him on his terms. Sansom's plan for increasing his budget was to persuade the Legislature to double the two cents of the cigarette tax that was earmarked for Parks and Wildlife. To his dismay, the Senate included in its budget a provision to cut his share of the cigarette tax to zero. He went to John Montford, chairman of the Senate Finance Committee, and asked what he could do to avoid losing that revenue.

Montford shrugged. "The guy in control of that is Bullock," he said. "He's the man you need to talk to."

Bullock was chain-smoking as Sansom sat in his office and tried to make his case for a larger share of the cigarette tax.

"The cigarette tax should be earmarked for cancer research and treatment," Bullock said.

"What are my options?" Sansom asked.

Bullock leaned toward him and replied almost in a whisper, "Suicide."

When Finance Committee hearings were held, Sansom arranged for nearly 200 witnesses to speak on the need to *maintain* the two-cent earmark. In the committee's deliberations at the end of the hearing, Montford, as the first order of business, gaveled through the restoration of the two-cent allotment.

"I later figured out that what he had done was keep me off balance," Sansom said. "I was trying to double the earmarked cigarette tax, and Bullock's move to reduce it to zero had the effect of causing me to spend all of my effort not on *increasing* the tax take, but avoiding having it cut."[6]

Facts, flattery, rewards, and old-fashioned threats remained the most visible components of Bullock's arsenal, and as *Texas Monthly* stated, fear of failure drove senators to succeed at the tasks he assigned them. He dispatched Sen. Armbrister to resolve the thorniest and testiest issue of the session: creation of a water district to regulate apportioning of the Edwards Aquifer waters. It pitted farmers against urbanites, and the battle was as emotional and unyielding as a jihad. With an eleventh-hour, marathon negotiating session, Armbrister kept both sides up all night, working without a break, and by sunrise had forged a deal he could fearlessly take to Bullock.

The model for Bullock's willpower and determination, however, was the adoption of a school finance bill capable, at long last, of surviving court scrutiny.

A series of Texas Supreme Court decisions had held that the system was unconstitutional because of the disparity in the resources of rich and poor districts. Despite the judicial mandate, the Legislature repeatedly refused to enact a fix—a statewide tax that could equalize school district spending. In 1984, the high court toughened its order and threatened to close the state's schools if the funding disparities were not corrected. Various schemes were put forth, and each was found wanting. After the Legislature's failure to act in the 1991 session, the court set a deadline—June 1, 1993. No bill, no schools.

During the second half of 1991 and most of 1992, Bullock worked with Gov. Richards and House Speaker Lewis on a plan that contained the only option available to them, a proposal Bullock referred to as "recapture." Later it was declared the "Fair Share Plan." That sounded better than "Robin Hood." But Robin Hood it was. The state would take money from wealthy school districts and distribute it to poorer ones.

State leaders campaigned hard for the proposal, explaining to voters that its failure could result in the courts shutting down or taking over public schools. "The Fair Share Plan guarantees every school district in Texas a better than average return on its tax rate," Bullock, Richards, and retiring House Speaker Lewis wrote in a joint plea offered for publication in newspapers late in 1992. "To ensure that kind of equality, the plan asks a little over 11 percent of the state's wealthiest districts, containing only six-and-a-half percent of Texas schoolchildren, to share some of their good fortune with the state."[7]

But, doing that would require an amendment to the state constitution, which since 1982 had prohibited a statewide property tax. An amendment was drafted and scheduled for a statewide referendum on May 1, 1993, near the end of the legislative session. A separate bill to implement the redistribution had been ready since before the session opened.

It was a hard sell. Wealthy districts fought against being forced to send their tax dollars out of town. Some teacher groups opposed it because neither the amendment nor the accompanying distribution bill contained a specific appropriation. The amendment was defeated 1,293,224 to 755,417, or almost two to one. The Legislature, scheduled to adjourn in 30 days, was under the gun, if not the howitzer.

Scrambling for a fix, Bullock summoned Sen. Bill Ratliff, one of the previously *underused* members he now relied on. Ratliff was a Republican, but one had to scratch deep to expose his partisan bones. Bullock made him chairman of the Senate Education Committee. A soft-spoken engineer from Mount Pleasant, Ratliff was contemplative, intelligent, unflappable, and gracious, the quintessential citizen legislator given to respectful discourse rather than persuasion by decibel. He had observed Bullock in nose-to-nose shouting matches and found it discomfiting.

He was spared that experience in 1991, probably because he had not been one of Bullock's appointed team members. But his time, inevitably, would come. Arriving at Bullock's office to discuss a fix to the school problem, he anticipated brainstorming the Legislature's options. Instead, only a few minutes into the conversation, Bullock inexplicably detonated. "He jumped on me horribly, with really vicious profanity," Ratliff said.

Rather than respond, Ratliff stood up and said, "I'm ending this conversation."

He walked out of the office and found Senate parliamentarian Bob Johnson. "I want you to tell your boss something," Ratliff said. "I'm 57 years old, and I don't take well to having my ass chewed. I will bust my butt to try to help him solve these problems, but if he ever raises his voice at me again, I'm out of here."

Johnson confronted Bullock and told him if he didn't ease up, "you're about to lose a good one." Ratliff, he said, would quit the Senate rather than be treated that way.

Three hours later, Bullock called Ratliff and apologized.[8]

Buck Wood also got a phone call. It had been years since he had worked for Bullock, and months since he had seen him. But, he knew well that no one ever really stopped working for Bullock, who was quick to call on friends, ex-employees, casual acquaintances, and anyone else whose help he needed. Usually, he didn't ask for a favor; he issued an order.

"I need for you to get with Jim Shear and come up with a constitutional school finance plan," he told Wood. Shear was the employee that Comptroller Bullock, as a member of the Perot Commission, had assigned to become an authority on public education. He, too, no longer worked for Bullock, but he still knew public schools better than anyone in Austin.

"Well . . ." Wood hesitated, pondering the magnitude of the chore.

"I want to pass it before the session is over."

"Bullock, we've got less than a month," Wood said.

"I want it in three days," Bullock said.

Wood was incredulous. In the three previous legislative sessions, three different school finance bills had been passed—all deficient in the view of the Supreme Court—and it appeared there was no option left, not one the Legislature would swallow.

"Three days?" he said. "Bullock, people have been trying to do that for thirty years."

"You call Shear and get over to his house. Y'all stay there and you get anybody else you need and you spend any amount of money you need until you come up with something."

After six hours of scratching their heads, Wood and Shear thought they had considered every possibility and still had not come up with a way to shuffle money from rich to poor districts.

Suddenly, Shear said, "Okay, take Eanes. They're a rich district. If we just took Barton Creek Mall out of Eanes's school district and put it into Hays Consolidated, we could bring their wealth level down to an acceptable level and increase the wealth of Hays Consolidated by the same amount."

Wood snapped to the potential. "Well, school districts don't have to be contiguous. We can take property in downtown Austin and give it to San Marcos."

It would be purely a paper transaction, having no impact on students or teachers in any affected district. There were noncontiguous districts in the state, and they were legal. Why couldn't San Marcos tax Congress Avenue?

They briefed Ratliff, whose bemused response was, "I don't know why we didn't think of it before." They invited Mark Yudof, dean of the UT law school, to a Tuesday meeting at the Capitol, and he, too, was taken by the simplicity of the idea. "I'm going to run it by some of my people [at the law school], and I'll have a memo for you on Wednesday."

"It'll work," Yudof informed them the next day.

Ratliff secluded himself in his office and typed up the legislation on his personal computer. Two days later it went to the Senate floor. At Bullock's invitation, Wood and Shear were present for the vote. After quick passage, he invited them to the podium. "These are the people that did it," he told the senators. "It's amazing what you can do if you really put your mind to it and you don't care who gets the credit."[9]

Of course, not everyone in Texas liked the "Robin Hood" plan, but for the first time in decades, the state had a school finance system that would pass the test of constitutionality.

It was commonly seen as a political ruse to calm jittery constituents, but it just as easily might have been called Bullock's Revenge. After the beating he took over advocating an income tax in 1991, Bullock waded back into the issue two years later—on the other side. Texas would get an income tax when one of two things happened, he said. One, a Russian submarine sailed into the Houston Ship Channel; two, the business community demanded one. He began gathering support in the Senate for a constitutional amendment that would bar the Legislature from passing an income tax unless voters concurred

in a statewide referendum and dedicated the money to education and property tax reduction.

One interpretation was that Bullock had taken that issue away from the
Republicans and rehabilitated himself in the process. That may have been an
accurate reading, but there was more to it. Bullock had been preaching for
years that the state was running out of tax options, and was rebuked each
time. He still believed that an income tax was inevitable, that property and
business taxes would become so oppressive that businessmen would be for one.
Other taxes also would max out, and to keep the government running, politicians would beg for an income tax. In effect, he created a scenario under
which he might one day have the pleasure of watching his critics beg.

At a casual glance, it appeared that Bullock's plan would forever close the
door to an income tax, and there were those in the Capitol who argued just
that. In reality, his amendment left the door to future action open wider than
it might have been. An amendment providing an absolute prohibition of an
income tax could be reversed only if two-thirds of the House and Senate
agreed to put the matter before voters.

Bullock's amendment did not constitutionally ban an income tax; it merely required that the Legislature get voter approval before enacting one. A simple majority—not two thirds—of both houses could submit that referendum to
the people. He did not want to make an income tax impossible, but he may
have wanted to make it difficult enough that when it became unavoidable, it
would require the broad and deep support of businessmen, Republicans, and
conservative Democrats—his perennial antagonists on that issue. Most, if not
all, would have to get on board. Few, if any, would have a place to hide.

Almost 70 percent of Texans who voted in the November election
approved Bullock's amendment—a vote of 775,822 to 343,638.

Republicans had been sharpening their sabers on the income tax issue in
preparation for the 1994 elections. Now they had to sheathe them and scout
for other lanes of attack. As the session closed, there were few to be found.
Bullock had been uncommonly efficient in getting the Senate to perform difficult tasks. Equally as important, House Speaker Laney rewrote House rules
to move the deadlines for the legislative process earlier in the session. That
avoided the last-minute crush of legislation that customarily contained nearly as many errors and oversights as it did laws.

For the first time since 1979, the governor had no need to call the
Legislature back into special session.

Even with the Republican drums beating louder across the state, Bullock's power, stature, and command of the times was complete. Still, he was gnawed at by the fiends of manic depression, the mood swings that hurled him back and forth between the raw and lucid application of his might and the abject abuse of it.

A sign of the former:

In November 1993, Andy Sansom, having failed to increase his share of the cigarette tax, again made an appointment to meet with Bullock to talk about the budget for the Parks and Wildlife Department. He spent two months preparing his presentation. He might as well have gone fishing. Bullock seemed relaxed and jovial at first, talking at length about two of his favorite pastimes—hunting and fishing. Sansom listened deferentially and occasionally glanced at his watch. He was afraid that his time would expire before he had made his pitch. Finally, when Bullock paused, Sansom gently interjected, "Well . . . governor . . . I wanted to talk about my budget . . ."

Bullock abruptly stood and said, "You're the most disloyal sonofabitch I've ever known. Get out of my office, and don't ever come back to this side of the Capitol again."

Shocked, Sansom left the office, but was not sure precisely what had happened. That evening, he talked to Bullock's close friend and confidant Jack Martin and described the incident. What should he make of it?

"If it's any consolation," Martin said, "Jan called me this evening. Bullock was putting on a tuxedo [to attend the Senate Wives dinner] and was having trouble with the studs on his shirt. She said he was out of control and asked me to come over and calm him down."

Martin, who lived two blocks away, was accustomed to this drill. He talked Bullock down, installed the shirt studs, and saw him off to a formal evening. It may not have been much consolation for Sansom, but it was all he would get.[10]

A sign of the latter:

Sometime in the 1990s, a transformation was taking place in the way college athletic programs were financed. Conferences, rather than central organizations (the NCAA, the College Football Association), began negotiating their own television contracts, leading the more powerful schools into a superconference mentality. The stronger the conference, the more lucrative the contract. After Arkansas bolted from the Southwest Conference for the Southeast, athletic directors from the Southwest Conference and the Big 8 began discussions about their own superconference. The talks centered on

Texas and Texas A&M joining the Big 8, leaving TCU, Houston, Rice, Baylor, Texas Tech, and SMU to fend for themselves in a much weakened Southwest Conference.

The athletic directors overlooked a few critical factors. Bob Bullock and Gov. Richards were Baylor grads. Bullock was also a Texas Tech grad, as were House Speaker Laney and House Appropriations Committee Chairman Rob Junell. Sen. John Montford, chairman of the Senate Finance Committee, represented the school. Stiff-arming them would not be easy.

Bullock, invigorated by the triumph and praise of the previous legislative session, summoned Bill Cunningham of UT and Herb Richardson of A&M to his office early in 1994, when the conference shuffle—converting the Big 8 to the Big 10—was on the verge of being a done deal. Glaring at the two men, he said, "You're taking Tech and Baylor, or you're not taking anything. I'll cut your money off, and you can join privately if you want, but you won't get another nickel of state money."

The university representatives apparently believed the subject was open for discussion, that they had a negotiating position. When they expressed hesitation, Bullock cut them off. "If you want to try me, go ahead," he said.

"Governor, we understand," Cunningham said.[11]

At that moment, for all practical purposes, the Big 8 became the Big 12.

CHAPTER 25

HERE WILL LIE BOB BULLOCK

Death was never far from him. He saw to that. Bullock was fascinated with cemeteries, so much so that when he was courting his fifth and final wife, burial grounds were common dating destinations.

"He'd pull off the road and go into the cemetery and look at all the markers," Jan Bullock was quoted in the *San Antonio Express-News* in 2001. "At first I thought it was morbid. What a depressing thing to do. But he completely changed my way of looking at things. I became so enthralled with history because of him."[1]

Love of history undoubtedly accounted for a share of his urge to walk among the dead, but morbidity was just as likely a contributor. From midlife on, thoughts of his own mortality were his perpetual and dispassionate companion. He didn't mourn his anticipated destiny, just acknowledged it.

"Bullock always thought he was going to die young, and he talked about it," said Buck Wood. "If you'd asked him when he was 50 if he'd make it to 60 or 70, he'd have said, 'No chance.' He really believed that."[2]

He was wrong. By May 1994, when he joined the funeral procession of former legislator and chemical industry lobbyist Harry Whitworth to the Texas State Cemetery, Bullock was approaching his 65th birthday. The clock still ticked, but here it ticked louder. All around him were the monuments and tombstones of friends and enemies past, of a few of Texas history's giants and a slew of its forgotten. Hallowed but unkempt ground. Besides inattention to landscape and road maintenance, rusting monuments and a broken ornamental fountain, the gravesites of some individuals could not be determined, and some headstones were wrongly positioned.

Back at his office, Bullock summoned the heads of several state agencies—Department of Transportation, Department of Criminal Justice, Parks and Wildlife, General Services Commission, Capitol Preservation Board, and others—for a meeting, which had overtones of an emergency. Soon, workers from each agency and state prisoners were trimming and touching up the cemetery. Bullock wanted more than grooming and cosmetics.

Writing in the *Dallas Morning News* in the summer of 1994, Christy Hoppe described a stroll through the aging burial ground with him, where he demonstrated a sense of Texas history and of sensing his own mortality:

> The 143-year-old cemetery is not neglected, but neither is it pristine. The drainage is bad, headstones have shifted, a fence has buckled, and the magnolia, maple, and cedar trees are overgrown, infected by mold, and generally in need of care. . . .
>
> "This was supposed to be the Arlington [National Cemetery] of Texas," Bullock says. "But it's just been forgotten."

They passed the highest hill, where lay the remains of Stephen F. Austin, the Father of Texas, and walked beside the tombs of Confederate generals and the cross-marked graves of 1,500 Confederate soldiers. Eleven governors are buried here, as are long-forgotten officeholders and a few famous Texas authors. It isn't an exclusive roll call, but membership isn't cheap. Only elected officials, confirmed appointees to state boards, and individuals approved by gubernatorial proclamation or by a majority of both houses of the Legislature are eligible.

> "Everyone in here contributed something to this state," Bullock says. "I'd like it fixed up so people can be as proud of where we've been as where we're going."[3]

When the epic 1993 legislative session ended, the major issues that had preoccupied him were off his plate and in the archives. Like a fireman who couldn't spend downtime waxing the engine, he needed projects, challenges, and problems to solve. He found his fire among the deceased icons of Texas legend.

The agency heads Bullock had drafted to spruce up the cemetery sat in uncomfortable silence as he railed against the lack of progress. Things had gotten worse, not better, he complained. Clipping shrubbery and moving dirt around did little to elevate the nobility of the place Bullock planned for his earthly self to spend eternity. His impatience was approaching ire when Sansom, considering himself already in the doghouse after being booted out of Bullock's office earlier, figured he had nothing to lose by speaking up. "We need a plan," he said.

"What?" Bullock snapped, piercing him with an icy gaze.

"We need to hire someone who has done historical preservations of cemeteries and get them to draw up a plan," he said. "We can all chip in and work on it."

Bullock softened. "Okay, who will head this up?" he asked.

There was another long silence. Sansom figured Parks and Wildlife was as good as any. "We can do it," he said, placing himself under one colossal Sword of Damocles. *Blow this one, and you might as well blow town.*[4]

Lake/Flato Architects, Inc., which had a consultant who had refurbished historical sites in Boston and elsewhere, was hired, and elaborate plans were drawn up, including 31 pillars to be inscribed with the names of famous Texans who, though deserving, were not buried in the state cemetery. The House eventually killed that idea, but other work proceeded apace. Harry Bradley, who had a long history of working in political campaigns—including Bullock's—as well as holding state and municipal government positions, was pulled from his recent job at the General Services Commission and installed as director of the cemetery.

Throughout the rehabilitation, Bullock showed up at Bradley's office daily, usually during the lunch hour, offering criticisms and suggestions. Sometimes they purred across the grounds in Bullock's car, while he ranted at Bradley for one shortcoming or another. Bullock, on one of his lunchtime visits with his former aide turned beer lobbyist Mike McKinney at the wheel, got Bradley inside his car, and they drove around the cemetery for 28 minutes. McKinney spent the whole time laughing while Bullock mercilessly scolded Bradley for cemetery deficiencies. "He got mad at me one day and took my cemetery plot away," Bradley said of the parcel bestowed upon him by gubernatorial decree. "Three weeks later, he called and gave it back."

On another visit, Bullock grumbled about the condition of the roads and placed a call to the Texas Department of Transportation. At 6:30 a.m. the following Monday, Bradley arrived at work to find several yellow TxDOT trucks lined up outside the gate, waiting for someone to let them in. The District 14 engineer personally accompanied the crew to oversee their work. One road was quickly repaved, but it got another upgrade a year later, after it was declared State Highway 165 to qualify for federal funds. "The shortest state highway in Texas," Bradley said.

As the work progressed, Bullock took a personal pride in the refurbished acres. He brought other state officials around—some of them future occupants—to show off his handiwork. He called Bradley one sweltering afternoon and announced that he would be at the cemetery in 15 minutes with Joe Kilgore, a former U.S. congressman and a close friend of the late Gov. Connally. "You get Joe a [burial] spot by Connally," Bullock said.

"But Governor," Bradley sighed, "there aren't any spots near Connally."

"Find one," Bullock snapped.

Bradley paced the area around the former governor's tombstone and confirmed what he had told Bullock. No vacant plots. There was, however, space between some of the graves—the right-of-way of a four-inch water line.

When Bullock and Kilgore arrived, Bradley escorted them to the site of Kilgore's future place of eternal repose. "Great," Bullock said.

"I didn't tell him about the water line," Bradley said. "It was going to be a lot easier to move the water line than to deal with Bullock."

Later, Bullock again upbraided him because no flagpole had been installed. "I didn't send you out there to mow grass and trim hedges," he said. "All I ever sent you out there to do was put up one goddamn flagpole."[5]

It was becoming apparent that the flagpole was a nonnegotiable imperative. He turned to Paul Hobby, his first chief of staff and a recent Ann Richards appointee to chair the General Services Commission, and Andy Sansom. "I want the tallest flagpole in the state," he said.

They met the landscape architects and relayed the demand.

"We can't do that. It's not in the plan. It'll look out of context," one of the contractors said.

"We don't give a damn," Hobby said.

"It does not meet our aesthetic design," said the contractor, who had never had the experience of telling Bullock he could not have what he wanted.

"How many times do I have to tell you? Do what you have to do," Hobby insisted.[6]

Still, the contractors balked. Wind loading would make it a hazard, they said. Federal Aviation Administration rules would prohibit it, they said.

"Look, guys," Sansom said firmly, "just help us here. Find a flagpole!"[7]

Bullock, the assumption was, wanted the flag to be visible from the Capitol, preferably visible from his second-floor office in the East Wing. That, it turned out, was an impossibility because the Zavala State Archives Building blocked the view. However, a flagpole was found in San Antonio that was tall enough that it could be seen from a Senate office on the *third* floor, directly above Bullock's office. That would have to do.

It was a massive structure—165 feet tall and the diameter of a car tire at its base—that had to be planted 15 feet into the earth and erected in sections. Three men were required to attach the 40-by-26-foot flag to its lines.

On the day it was being installed, a light mist fell on Austin, making the pole slippery and the work dangerous. At 6 p.m., Rocky White, the San Antonio contractor, told Bradley it was time for his crew to quit for the day.

"No, you can't do that," Bradley said. "You've got to get it done tonight."

"I'll have to pay my men quadruple time," White said.

"No problem," said Bradley, who then left to buy lunchmeat, bread, and soft drinks for an impromptu dinner for the workers. Bradley stayed until the work was completed, about 11 p.m. He returned to the office the next morning at 4:30 to put the flag aloft before sunrise and Bullock's arrival at the Capitol.[8]

Unlike most Bullock ventures, the cemetery caused little public controversy, except to reopen the question: Is Bullock dying? Now and then, a reporter would call Hobby and ask, "Isn't Bullock just sprucing up his own final resting place?"

Hobby's standard answer was "So what if he is?" *Whether there's a personal benefit to Bullock after death is less important than whether there's an immediate benefit to all the people of Texas,* he thought.[9]

In time, the lieutenant governor was satisfied with the restoration. One afternoon, he leisurely toured the immaculate grounds with Dan Van Cleve, a go-between for Parks and Wildlife on the cemetery and other matters with Bullock. The crusty leader seemed almost eager to take his place among the Lone Star patriots. "It's a shame you can only be buried here with one wife," he said.[10]

If his preoccupation with the cemetery fueled speculation about his health, which had been ongoing since his lung removal two decades earlier, through his hemorrhoidectomy, heart attack, aneurysm, and the more recent back and shoulder surgery, events in the late summer of 1994 heightened it.

With the general election less than two months away, on September 16 Bullock checked into Seton Hospital for single-bypass heart surgery, performed by Dr. Emery Dilling. His staff was taciturn, as was his physician,

Dr. Kent Beasley, who said only that it was not the result of a heart attack or any other medical emergency. It was "recommended" because of test results from a routine examination, he said. The reticence of Bullock's staff was mostly a political calculation. He had a weak, under-funded Republican opponent, but there were no guarantees, as Mary Lenz noted in the *Houston Post*:

"In the world of Texas politics, Lt. Gov. Bob Bullock is the proverbial 10,000-pound gorilla. He's been in public office for 27 years. He sits at the helm of the Texas Senate. And, he's got almost as much name recognition as the Alamo. . . . But, in Texas politics, anything can happen. Bullock, 65 and a heavy smoker, underwent heart bypass surgery Friday. . . . Although doctors say Bullock came out of the heart surgery just fine, uncertainty over his health raises a question mark over the race most observers expect Bullock to win."[11]

Dave McNeely, the *Austin American-Statesman* state political columnist, took a more detached look at the surgical event, exploring not how it affected the lieutenant governor and his reelection prospects, but how it potentially affected state government. Given the power of the office, succession was a complex and important, but rarely discussed, subject.

"He is expected to recover fully," McNeely wrote. "That said, some in political circles wondered what would happen if Bullock . . . were to die in office. Here are the answers: Because the ballot was certified on Sept. 14, 55 days before the election, Bullock's name will be on the ballot even if he dies before election day. If he had died before Sept. 14, the State Democratic Executive Committee could have replaced him on the ballot. . . . If Bullock were to die before the election and still get a majority of the votes, then the office of lieutenant governor would become vacant."

He cited the constitutional provision for dealing with a vacancy: "The president pro tempore of the Senate shall convene the Committee of the Whole Senate within 30 days after the vacancy occurs. The Committee of the Whole shall elect one of its members to perform the duties of the Lieutenant Governor in addition to his duties as a Senator until the next general election."[12]

The column went on to explain that if the governor should die in office, the senator who had taken over the lieutenant governor role would then become governor, and the Senate would pick another of its members to replace him as its presiding officer.

As clinical as it was, the column, to Bullock, contained inflammatory words or phrasing. *Die. Die in office. Die before election day.* A full year would

pass before McNeely would grasp the depths of Bullock's umbrage at the public allusion to his death.

Bullock agreed to the interview to discuss his role and influence in state
government and the forces that had impelled him and shaped his sensibilities.
He walked into the conference room adjacent to his office, and sat down across
the table from McNeely. Bullock's press secretary Cindy Rugeley, a former
Houston Chronicle reporter who had been a press assistant to Gov. Richards, sat
there too. McNeely took out his notebook and turned on his tape recorder. He
had been reporting on Bullock's activities for more than 20 years and, knowing his sensitivity to the press, took no chances with inaccuracy.

Bullock was cordial but cautious—almost reserved—and at first the
interview progressed routinely. Why shouldn't it? In the intervening year,
McNeely had written other columns about Bullock, had received the perfunctory biting responses. Everything, in other words, was normal. Suddenly,
something long pent-up burst out of Bullock.

"I don't know why you want to write this story in light of what you've
written all these years. I think you've got something up your sleeve. My relationship with you ain't been too good. I thought that story—when I told my
wife I was going to have an interview with you, she ate my ass out. She had
real hard feelings towards you, and my family does, for that article you wrote
when I had that heart attack. And so do I."

The color drained from Rugeley's face.

He ranted about "callous disregard," "irresponsible act," and added, "I'm
being as nice to you as I can, 'cause this is a public building."

"Well, I'd just as soon you go on and continue being nice, Governor,"
McNeely responded evenly.

"I'll be nice to you in a public building, but the less I have to do with you,
the better off I am. I won't kiss your ass like a lot of politicians do. I think you
are so full of—egotist, the biggest egotist. I think you're slanted in your writing. You let your personal feelings enter your writings. You know, I don't have
no use for you."

I'm finally witnessing a Bullock meltdown, McNeely thought.

"I'm sorry to hear that, Governor."

"I'm just giving it to you straight. That's the way it's always been with
you. Nothing in the law and nothing religiously says I have to like you, and
nothing says you do me. There are some people that come along, and they've

got a little personal deal and they've got a little pen that they can write with. And you use it to hurt people. And I think that's wrong."

"I'm sorry you feel that way, Governor."

"That's the way I feel. That was an awful article. A man in the hospital, with a heart operation, open-heart, and you write that kind of article, that was terrible. Absolutely awful. And my dislike for you ain't nothing compared to my wife. And I love her very much."

"Sorry to hear that, Governor."

"I'll bet you're just sorry to hear that I love her very much. . . . Because you've let your emotions control that pen you've got. What you've talked to me about today has been in the press 30 times—30 times. If you had wanted to do your homework, you could have gone back and looked at the former employees that formed an association when I ran for lieutenant governor to help me. You could've got all the information you wanted. There's some other reason you're here. I don't know what it is. I don't really care."

"Well, Governor . . ."

"I will not, I will not waste my time on somebody like you. And you don't have to waste your time with me."

"Would you like for me to ask you some of the other questions I had?"

"You can ask me anything you want to. I can't do anything more about that than the way you write it. But I tell you one thing: If I ever meet with you again—and I'm not looking forward to it, but you write for a newspaper that's important to Texas—I'll have me a tape recorder there."

"I'd be happy for that to occur."

"Happy or not, I'll have one. Now, what's your questions?"

McNeely returned to the interview. But before long, Bullock returned to what was on his mind.

"I don't think you ought to write about me, David. I don't think you're objective anymore."

"I'm sorry you feel that way, Governor."

"When you get down on your hands and knees tonight, you pray to God for him to give you a little objectivity because you ain't exhibited it. You see, I think a reporter—when two people don't care for one another, and you don't me and I don't you—I don't think it's fair for you to write about me."

"Duly noted."

"You're not supposed to. I think that's the ethics of the newspaper business, if I'm not mistaken. If there is any, anymore."

"Let me ask you one more question, Governor."

"In light of what I just said?"

"Sir?"

"In light of what I just said, you want to still ask me a question?"

"Yes, sir, but you don't have to answer it."

"You don't have to *yes, sir* me."

"I was going to ask you if there were any . . ."

"Although I am a little older than you and probably have a little bit more wisdom."

"The question I was going to ask was whether there are any particular axioms or rules or sayings by which you live your life and do your business, things that sum up your approach to how . . ."

"Well, you've summed that up through the years. Read your own column."

"Well, Governor . . ."

"You can have all the say you want to. I'm sitting here. In fact, if you wish to say anything, you go right ahead. But that article you wrote when I was in the hospital, shame on you, David. Shame on you. You've had no idea how you can hurt people, or another reporter can hurt people. And you know, God didn't give you any gift, or judgment, any more than anybody else. Didn't give you any more objectivity than those of us in public office. He hasn't touched you divinely to be objective. You're a human being and I'm a human being. And if I didn't like, for example, a member of the Senate, I'd have no business going out here and writing about that senator. You have no idea the hurt you can do to people, and you have done to people. And that might make you feel good, but it doesn't make me feel good. I don't want to be hurt by it. I want to do a job. And I can do it without the likes of you."

"Well, thank you, Governor, for that vote of confidence."

"You're welcome. I ain't giving you anything, David. I don't think you should be writing a column. I think you're prejudiced, man. I don't know how I can make it any plainer. You've got favorites you write about—that phone you and visit with you and that you're buddies with. And it shows in your writing. And that's the reason that nowadays people have such low esteem of reporters. . . . They don't believe you anymore."

McNeely steered Bullock back to talking about Preston Smith, easier times—there was no tax bill from 1973 to 1984—school problems, bird hunting.

"Well, Governor, I appreciate your time. Most of it."

"David, I just told you how I feel . . ."

"That's fine."

". . . and how I see it. I don't think you've got any business writing about me . . ."

"Well, I appreciate what you say."

". . . and I'll feel that for a long time."[13]

Bullock could readily discuss his own mortality. But when others did so, his skin was very, very thin.

CHAPTER 26

GEORGE W. ARRIVES ON THE SCENE

A t every level, 1994 was shaping up to be an unkind year for Democrats. Nationally, President Bill Clinton was facing his first midterm congressional elections, and it was not pretty. Tagged with some unpopular issues like gays in the military, federal gun-control efforts, and a health care plan developed in secret by his wife, Hillary, he was like a scampering mule deer in a canned hunt. Virtually every Republican running for Congress, and some for state and local office, was running against him, and deep-pocketed lobbyists were gunning for him. The National Rifle Association targeted not just Clinton but state and congressional Democrats with harsh advertisements in rural areas. Republican Congressman Newt Gingrich of Georgia and Texas Congressman Dick Armey were developing a revolution guided by a "Contract with America."

Gov. Ann Richards faced a significant challenge from presidential son George W. Bush—masterminded by Republican wunderkind Karl Rove. Richards had a record of accomplishments to run on: a difficult school finance bill, a prison-building spree that reduced crowding, a state lottery, and a tax increase that helped the state stay in the black. The problem was, most of those issues cut both ways. The school fights had generated controversy. The prisons cost money to run. The lottery, though popular in some circles, was strongly opposed by many in the religious community, and Richards had backed it only after being goaded into it in the 1990 Democratic gubernatorial primary. Any tax increase, even though it kept the state's systems running, was fraught with peril—particularly in increasingly conservative Texas.

Republicans, fattening on the rapidly growing suburbs of the state's major cities, were lining up candidates and shelling out money to increase their numbers in the Legislature and throughout government. No Democrat, it seemed, was invulnerable. Except Bullock.

Two relatively unknown Republicans, Louis Podesta of San Antonio and Randy Staudt of Leander, declared intentions to run against him, but pulled out early in January when a higher-profile candidate, Harold J. (Tex) Lezar, jumped in on the final filing day. Lezar had been an aide to President Richard Nixon from 1971 to 1974. He had served in the U.S. Attorney's office under President Ronald Reagan from 1981 to 1985 and claimed responsibility for the federal prison-sentencing guidelines that required judges to hand down sentences that inmates had to serve in their entirety, effectively ending parole for federal crimes. He tried for the Republican nomination for attorney general in 1990, but finished a distant third, with just 15.2 percent. Lezar also had been a founder and president of the Texas Public Policy Foundation, a fledgling ultraconservative think tank. He resigned that job to run against Bullock.

Despite his resume of public service and political aspiration, Lezar seemed to pose no great threat to Bullock, then at the height of his power. Nonetheless, given the atmosphere of the season, Bullock took nothing for granted.

Jack Martin, the head of Public Strategies, Inc., and manager of Bullock's 1990 campaign, saw to it that one of his employees, the young image-maker Mark McKinnon, who had worked in Chet Edwards's campaign against Bullock in 1990, was on board.

"It was sort of ordained that I was going to work for him," McKinnon recalled.

A get-acquainted luncheon was arranged, and McKinnon picked Bullock up at the Capitol. Wearing sunglasses and a dour expression, Bullock got into the car and, without shaking hands, slumped against the passenger-side door. *Weird*, McKinnon thought.

They drove in silence for a couple of miles. Suddenly, Bullock seemed to uncoil like a snake, grabbed McKinnon's arm, leaned close to him, and shouted, "You remember all those goddamn lies you told about me?"

McKinnon, unsure if he should bail out of the moving car or check the glove box for a weapon, said nothing. Bullock stared at him in silence for what seemed an eternity before leaning back against the door. "Well, I hope you haven't forgot how to do that," he said.[1]

Bullock also brought his considerable fund-raising prowess to the party. Like those of no one else in Texas politics, his fund-raisers drew a broad and diverse crowd from across the state, from all interest groups and parties. Many were longtime friends and supporters, and some were there to be seen, to show that they were players in the legislative power game. Many were there out of fear.

"I want to get up there and shake his hand and get out of here," one legislator-turned-lobbyist confided at a Bullock shindig.

At such gatherings, his staff arrived as much as six hours early. Contributors and well-wishers sometimes arrived early and lined up for a two-hour wait to greet the candidate. "Mob scenes" was the way Ralph Wayne described the fund-raisers to *Texas Monthly*. "If you didn't go, you got somebody to pick up your name tag, because he would have an aide pick up the unused name tags so he could see who didn't come, and he would call you the next day."

One on one, he was just as effective and intimidating, as evidenced by a pair of items in *Texas Monthly*:

When a trade association sent him $1,000, he returned it with a note: "Here's your check back, and I'm sending you a $500 check from myself. I didn't know your association was in such bad shape. I hope this $500 will help you." The association upped its ante.

Two plaintiffs' lawyers sent him letters complaining about the campaign support he had given to Republican Sen. Ratliff.

"I'm sorry you were disappointed in me," he responded in writing. "I supported Bill Ratliff because I thought he was good for Texas, but I would never allow you to believe that I'd misled you." He said he'd checked his records, and found that one had given him $10,000 over the years, and the other $3,000. He enclosed refund checks to both.

A few days later, Bullock received a reply from one of them—his check marked "void" and an additional contribution enclosed. "Bullock showed it to me," Ratliff recalled, "and said, 'You think I don't know how to raise money?'"[2]

Lezar couldn't find much traction on state issues and, more importantly, he didn't have much campaign money, by Texas standards, for a statewide race. With the lieutenant governor's huge ability to affect state laws and state spending, contributors preferred to back the guy who was already in the chair and likely to stay there rather than the ideologue trying to kick him out. So, he copied the national theme of the Republicans. In a campaign of memorable ineptitude, he ran more against Clinton than Bullock. It was a distant echo of Republican Bill Clements's race for governor in 1978, when he pledged to hang then-President Jimmy Carter around Democratic candidate John Hill's neck like "a rubber chicken." A major difference was that Clements had great personal wealth, and was willing to spend it. Lezar didn't, and couldn't.

As the battle moved into the fall, Lezar had about half a million dollars. Bullock had raised ten times as much. Lezar could afford only a limited radio-advertisement buy, primarily on conservative talk shows, where the hatred of Clinton approached irrationality.

"Bill Clinton is wrong for America," Lezar's 60-second ad proclaimed. "He's unethical, he's liberal, and he's two-timing us all with sound bites. . . . This November, let's vote Bill Clinton's liberal friends in Austin out of office."[3]

Bullock, who had made rapid response a trademark, shot back through aide Tony Proffitt, the former newspaper reporter who was Bullock's longtime chief political aide.

"Sometimes we call him Tex, and sometimes we call him Harold," Proffitt told *Dallas Morning News* columnist Carolyn Barta, who wrote that Lezar had been called "Tex" since he was two days old. "Harold wants to run against Bill Clinton because he's not popular in Texas. . . . Whatever Harold wants to do is fine, but he ought to just save his money and run against Clinton for president in two years."[4]

One Dallas news station thought Lezar ads that said "This is the Whitewater news update with Tex Lezar" could mislead listeners into thinking it actually was a news broadcast. Lezar's handlers called the Federal Communications Commission, which informed the station that the communications acts say a broadcaster "shall have no power of censorship over the material broadcast" in candidate ads.[5]

Lezar's bigger problem was that he couldn't get his message out much anyway. He could afford only a tiny amount of television time—barely enough to say that he had some. Bullock, on the other hand, was on radio and television for weeks leading up to the election.

There's an old saying in Texas politics: If someone does you wrong, just tape your deer rifle to a tree, and eventually they'll wander back into your gun sight.

That was the situation that Max Sherman, the former senator who had become dean of the Lyndon B. Johnson School of Public Affairs, found himself in after Gov. Richards asked him to chair the board of the Department of Health and Human Services.

"I told her I was willing but that I was not sure the lieutenant governor would approve," Sherman said. He was one of the 11 senators who had voted to bust Bullock for the State Board of Insurance more than two decades earlier. He was certain that Bullock's deer rifle was loaded and that Bullock, an apparent shoo-in for reelection, would not hesitate to pull the trigger. "She said she was aware of that concern, but was convinced it would not be a problem."

Richards notified Chuck Bailey, Bullock's chief of staff, of the appointment, and Sherman assured her that he also would place a call to Bullock.

"Up to that time I had never approached him for anything and had never been in his office," Sherman said. "But for the governor of the State of Texas, I would not have on this occasion. I called Rhetta, Bullock's assistant, and told her I needed to talk with the lieutenant governor."

Before long, the call came from Bullock.

"I picked up the phone, and here are the first words from Bullock: 'Senator, the worst thing that can happen to a man is not to be confirmed by the Texas Senate.' I then held the phone a couple of inches from my ear for several minutes as he leaned in on me. He said, 'I want you to know that I remember that you were one of the senators who voted to bust my appointment to the insurance board back in '72, and I want you to know that that was one of the worst things that ever happened to me in my life—to be busted by the Senate of Texas. I went home and cried like a baby. No man should have to go through what I went through. And because of that, I will support your nomination. You will be confirmed by the Texas Senate, but you'll need to clear it with Senator Barrientos [in whose district Sherman resided].'"

Sherman knew what Bullock meant: By letting him know that he could have busted him, but graciously wouldn't, Bullock was telling Sherman "You owe me."

Trying to help his friend the governor during a tough reelection battle, Sherman took the job anyway and served for several months, until after the November elections. A recurrence of prostate cancer led him to resign before the Senate could consider his nomination.[6]

Bullock was also tightening his hold on the machinery of state government. In the spring of 1994, John Hall, chairman of the TNRCC, was summoned to the lieutenant governor's office. Senators were getting too many complaints from business owners, farmers, and others that the environmental agency's permitting process was slow and unfair. Not acceptable, Bullock said.

Hall limped out and called his former boss, Land Commissioner Garry Mauro, a former Bullock aide and deputy comptroller, for advice.

Hire a Bullockian, Mauro said.

Before long, Dan Pearson was hired. For the previous five years, he'd been vice president and chief operating officer of the Texas Guaranteed Student Loan program. More importantly, for the 13 years before that, he'd worked for Bullock in various capacities in the comptroller's office. Pearson got the environmental trains running on time, and the agency's image improved—at least with the Senate's presiding officer.[7]

After Chuck Bailey had moved up from general counsel to succeed Gibson as Bullock's chief of staff, he called Andy Sansom, the executive director of Texas Parks and Wildlife. Bullock's aide Joey Parks had done various chores for Bullock for perhaps a decade. But Parks had gotten married and had two small children, Bailey explained, and Bullock concluded that it was time for him to get a real career.

Sansom agreed to interview him. Parks showed up without even a resume, or any idea what he could do for Parks and Wildlife. Sansom told him to go back and get someone to help him with the resume, and to think about what he could do for the agency.

Parks came back with the resume, was dutifully interviewed, and Sansom concluded that there wasn't really a place for him. But he had fulfilled Bailey's request of him to interview Parks.

Three days later, Bailey called. "Mr. Bullock wants to know when Joey's going to start." So Parks went to work for Parks and Wildlife.

As it turned out, it was wonderful, Sansom said. They had hired someone who had walk-in privileges at Bullock's office. There were five major things that Sansom hoped to accomplish that legislative session. He asked Joey to see what he could do. Bullock set them all for action as soon as Parks asked him to, Sansom said.

"Our folks wondered," Sansom said, "how did we get so brilliant to hire this kid?"[8]

Bullock was also conciliatory toward his former antagonist Ronnie Earle, the DA who nearly indicted him. Earle's Public Integrity Unit was bound to alienate politicians and, therefore, keeping it intact was an ongoing struggle. After that unit focused on House Speaker Gib Lewis in the late 1980s, there was a move to either strip it of state funding or move it elsewhere, away from Earle's control. That effort continued well into the 1990s.

To fend off the latest assault, Earle took one of his assistants, Rosemary Lehmburg, and went to see Bullock at his home. They sat at the kitchen table while Earle pleaded his case and, with no resistance, Bullock assured him he would not lose the PIU.

"You remember when you were investigating me years ago?" Bullock asked.

"Yes," Earle said, not sure what was coming next.

Bullock puffed on his cigarette. "I was guilty as hell," he said. The statute of limitations had long since expired.[9]

Bullock's move away from the strong Democratic partisanship he had demonstrated during his first year in office paid dividends. He invited the 13 Republican senators to his mid-September fund-raiser at the Four Seasons Hotel in Austin. Conservative Christian groups backing Lezar warned of retaliation against the GOP senators if they went. Lezar demanded that the senators skip the event.

"Sadly, there are a handful of Republican state senators who think going along to get along will keep them in power and in a position of privilege in the state Legislature," Lezar told *Houston Chronicle* reporter R. G. Ratcliffe. "The liberal Bob Bullock must be defeated, not catered to."[10] Those warnings had about as much effect as Lezar's attempts to attach Bullock to Clinton.

"I plan to go," said Sen. Bill Ratliff. "I answer to the 550,000 people in Senate District 1, and I am not accountable to anyone else. The people in my district support those who are trying to avoid partisan gridlock in our state government."[11]

Sen. Jerry Patterson of Houston said he was going, even though he planned to vote a straight Republican ticket. He even predicted, without quite saying so, that Lezar would lose anyway.

"The likelihood of me being reelected and Bob Bullock being reelected is good," Patterson told Ratcliffe. "I need to be in a position to work with Bob Bullock for all of my constituents, not just the Republican ones."[12]

Bullock castigated those who were protesting the senators' attendance. "The threats and intimidation are coming from a small group of party hacks, political has-beens, and advocates of gridlock," Bullock said. "These hacks have shown that they care more about their party than their state."

He also sent letters to the GOP senators saying they did not have to attend if it might harm their reelection chances. "My respect for you won't be diminished one bit if your political safety prevents you from attending this event," Bullock's letter said. "If your political well-being is threatened, you would be well-advised not to attend."[13]

Most of the senators ignored Lezar's line in the sand; 10 of the 13 indeed showed up. Two others said they had long-scheduled events in their districts. Several days later, when the State Republican Executive Committee was meeting, and some of its members felt they had no choice but to censure the treasonous senators, Lezar had cooled his jets. Saying he "wasn't too happy" about the senators ignoring his demand, he nonetheless asked that no "formal action" be taken. Despite the fervor among some of the committee members to retaliate, others said it could be like assembling a firing squad in a circle.

"Let's don't make idiots of ourselves," cautioned member Bonnie Maynard of Amarillo. "After all, 10 of our 13 [Republicans in the Senate] attended the event."[14]

With some grumbles, the committee finally settled for a measure saying it was "disturbed and upset" at the senators' behavior, but stopped short of censure.[15]

Bullock followed up his Tuesday evening fund-raiser by having the recommended heart bypass operation on Friday. Lezar took the day off from his own campaign events and sent prayers from him and his wife to Bullock and his family. By early October, however, Lezar was charging that Bullock was ducking events because of his health. Lezar and Bullock had been scheduled to debate in Dallas on October 17, but Bullock, citing doctors' orders, canceled the appearance.

After Lezar charged that Bullock "has been seriously incapacitated," Bullock put out an angry news release. "Besides being a total lie, his comments were terribly irresponsible. I am hereby ignoring my opponent for the rest of the campaign. I am also canceling all campaign events between now and November."

Bullock's doctor, Kent Beasley, predicted "a full and complete recovery [but] he must rest a reasonable period of time before resuming a normal schedule." Despite his absence from the campaign trail, Bullock's television and radio ads continued.

Bryan Eppstein, a Republican political consultant, while complimenting Lezar's intelligence, questioned his campaign tactics. "He is a very sharp, sharp guy," Eppstein told Mary Lenz of the *Houston Post*. "But his campaign is being run in a juvenile, sophomoric fashion. It's a cheap PR ploy, and it's inappropriate and insensitive."

Lezar had plenty of other issues on which he could run—the "Robin Hood" school finance system, Bullock's previous support of a state income tax, the fact that taxes had gone up. "The issue is Bob Bullock's record, and if Lezar can't run against that record, he has no business running for that office," Eppstein told Lenz. "Bob Bullock does not have to appear at a debate."[16]

Of course, had Lezar been elected, the senators almost certainly would have stripped him of much of the power afforded the lieutenant governor. But no danger there. A Texas Poll conducted the second week of October, about a month before the election, showed Bullock with 54 percent and Lezar with 23 percent.[17]

Bush's polls were showing the likelihood that he was going to beat Richards, and he privately expressed nervousness about dealing with the volatile lieutenant governor. Three weeks before the election, Bush requested a meeting, for reasons that he explained in his memoir, *A Charge to Keep*, published during his campaign for president. Of "Bully," the nickname he bestowed upon the lieutenant governor, Bush said:

> Bullock was the last remaining giant of a past era, when Texas politicians and their personalities seemed larger than life. Adjectives cannot describe him. He was a man of outsized passions and famous faults. He was frequently outrageous, sometimes crass, often funny, always cunning. He was unpredictable in his language, rough-hewn, yet surprisingly tender-hearted. . . . Bullock was not of my party or my generation; he was a crafty master of the political process, not inclined to think much of a rookie like me. Yet I knew that if I became the Governor of Texas, somehow, I would have to get along with him. Visiting his home the final weeks of the 1994 campaign was the first step. I thought I was going to win, and I hoped Bullock would be impressed by my overture. We spent a couple of hours talking about our mutual

> love for Texas; we talked about policy, not politics. Mostly, I lis-
> tened and he talked. Conversations with Bullock were often a
> monologue.[18]

As Bush had hoped, Bullock was impressed with the overture and
how Bush handled himself. He told Chuck Bailey, "I think we can work
with that boy."[19]

They got their chance to find out. Bush retired Richards from public life
by getting 53.5 percent of the vote. Bullock, with 61.5 percent, easily crushed
Lezar. Bullock ran 614,915 votes ahead of Richards.

Bullock was credited with being the "stopper" for the Democrats—the
point on the ballot where a considerable number of people who had voted for
Sen. Kay Bailey Hutchison and Bush crossed back over to the Democratic column. They reelected not just Bullock, but the four Democratic incumbents
immediately below him on the ballot—Attorney General Dan Morales,
Comptroller John Sharp, Treasurer Martha Whitehead, and Land
Commissioner Garry Mauro. But when voters got to the next race, where
Republican Agriculture Commissioner Rick Perry was the incumbent, they
crossed back—and stayed there. Republicans won every race below that in
which they had a candidate—including defeating two incumbent Texas
Railroad Commission members, Jim Nugent and Mary Scott Nabers, and
Court of Criminal Appeals Justice Charles F. Campbell.

After Bush was elected, there was definitely some nervousness about getting along with the lieutenant governor. The pre-election visit had been a
courtesy call, but a long-term strategy was necessary.

Bush had the good judgment to hire as part of his legislative liaison effort
Cliff Johnson, the conservative Democratic House member from Palestine
who had served under Gov. Clements and had then been appointed by him
to the Texas Water Commission. Johnson, with the personality of a 220-
pound Labrador retriever puppy, had a sixth sense about how the Legislature
and the Capitol worked.

When virtually anything came up early in Bush's administration, including what the weather would portend, Johnson would counsel, "Call Mister
Johnson." That was Bob Johnson, Bullock's longtime friend from their House
days and now his parliamentarian in the Senate, affectionately known as
"Big Daddy."

"Why?" Bush asked, puzzled.

"Governor," he told Bush, "in this place, relationships are everything. Trust me, call Mister Johnson."[20]

For Bush, whose one-on-one ability was good, that was a good thing. He took the advice.

The cigar-chewing Big Daddy always answered the phone with a gruff "Johnson." Soon, Bush was responding with an almost equally gruff "Bush." They became good friends. Johnson was the counselor to literally dozens, if not hundreds, of legislators over the years, and most knew that he was one of the few keys to Bullock.

Some senators described him as Bullock's one-man bomb squad, to protect bystanders when the Bullock Bomb was about to go off. Johnson would pull Bullock off to the side, put the black lead cape over him, and Bullock would detonate with a minimum of harm to nearby innocents.

Bush also sought the counsel of Paul Hobby. Invited to the governor's office, Hobby thought the purpose was to talk about his agency, the General Services Commission. It quickly became evident that Bush had something else on his mind.

"People tell me you're the guy who can tell me how to get along with Bullock," Bush said.

"Governor," Hobby sighed, "when it happens, if it doesn't happen in public such that you don't have to defend your office, let it go. Turn the other cheek, nothing to it. It's just a temporary eruption. It's a sugar imbalance. It's whatever you want it to be. But don't take it personally. Don't take it seriously. It's just going to happen."

Bush listened patiently, possibly incredulously. *Was it in his job description to be dressed down and chewed up by the lieutenant governor?*

Hobby continued: "I don't know how, when, or where, but it's going to happen. He's going to lay into you, and it won't be pretty and it won't be fun. But you know what? It's not a big deal. And if you take it and come back the other side of it still smiling at him, he'll admire that."[21]

CHAPTER 27

YOU'VE GOT TO KISS ME FIRST

The new year brought with it a new world.

Bill Clements had been the only Republican governor since Reconstruction, but now there was another, and the promise of others to come. Republicans had picked up two more Senate seats and enough House seats to signal the impending end of Democratic dominance there. Bipartisanship was no longer a rhetorical abstraction and noble goal; it was increasingly a necessity, the stuff of a new life form if anything was to be accomplished. Republicans had the votes to shut down the Senate and hamstring the House, and Bush could veto anything that slipped through.

Obstructionism serves its purpose, but it doesn't make for legislative success. Bush and the Republican legislators needed the collaboration of the Democratic leaders and the majorities they held to avoid the appearance of bungling incompetents—and for Bush to allay a common suspicion that he was a lightweight with a heavyweight name. It was a year when the trains weren't going to move until all the principals were on board.

After the election, Bush called Bullock and House Speaker Laney to reiterate his willingness to "work with them for the good of Texas." Two days later, he met with Laney at the Four Seasons Hotel and received a reciprocal avowal. "Governor," Laney said, "we're not going to let you fail."[1]

It was not a decree of capitulation. The Democratic legislators had no reason to want this Republican governor to flounder. He had picked up their ball and already was running with it. Bush's campaign platform had four essential planks, all poll-tested: strengthening the juvenile justice code to abate the soaring youth crime rate; reforming tort laws to cap personal-injury lawsuit judgments; overhauling welfare; and reforming education. It was the agenda the Legislature, still meagerly held by Democrats, had already set for itself. Interim studies had been conducted on three of those issues, and bills were being prepared to implement them. Everyone might not get all they wanted, but it would be no trick for everyone to at least look like a winner.

"Bullock and Bush needed each other," said Mark McKinnon, the political ad man who had worked for Richards, Bullock, and later Bush. "Bullock was the aging veteran who provided the institutional knowledge and history of Texas government. Bush was the eager rookie full of charm, energy, and vitality."[2] For Bush to appear successful, he needed cooperation from Bullock and Laney. For Bullock and Laney to hold on to their leadership jobs in the face of Republican growth, having a friendly relationship with the GOP's leader helped them keep the partisan political dogs at bay.

Gathering in Bush's transition office, the three leaders agreed to hold weekly breakfast meetings during the session to help keep everything on track. In his memoir, Bush recalled that the first was held at the governor's mansion, but that Bullock "complained that the food was too healthy, not greasy enough." Subsequently, the sessions alternated between Bullock's and Laney's kitchens on opposite sides of the Capitol. Eggs, sausages, biscuits, gravy, and pancakes became the standard fare. The pancakes were for Bush.[3]

In a session that would test bipartisan sincerity, compromise was on everyone's lips, if not in their hearts. Bullock demanded flexibility of others but, in his own passions, could be as unbending as a cinder block.

Sen. Rodney Ellis, an African American from Houston, had introduced a bill in the 1993 session that would have resulted in more black judges getting onto the bench. It failed, and he came back in 1995 with another, this one to appoint some judges in larger counties. Bullock knew the bill would be difficult and controversial, so he sent Sibley, Armbrister, and Montford to meet with Ellis and work out a compromise. Ellis considered their proposal but decided to stand firm.

He got a call from Bullock.

"They tell me you didn't want to compromise," Bullock snapped.

"No, I didn't," Ellis said.

"Well, fuck you, you black motherfucker," Bullock shouted. "You've got to show some leadership. You can't have everything you want."

Startled, Ellis tried to calm him. "Governor, I've always supported you," Ellis said.

"Fuck you," Bullock said.

Ellis invoked the name of Mickey Leland, a popular African American former legislator and congressman on whose congressional staff Ellis had once worked. Leland, one of the black legislators who had forgiven Bullock for his segregationist votes when he was a House member, was killed in a plane crash in Africa in 1989.

"Fuck Mickey Leland, too," Bullock said.

Ellis was so distraught that he left his office and walked around the Capitol grounds for a long time, trying to figure out what to do—about Bullock and his judicial-appointment bill. He talked to Sen. Eddie Bernice Johnson, another African American, who told him, "Do what you've got to do." He decided he would not compromise just to get along with Bullock. But how would he get along with him? He called Jack Roberts for advice.

"Ellis, if he cusses you out, that means he likes you," Roberts assured him.

Rather than keep Ellis's bill from advancing to a vote, Bullock presided over its passage in the Senate but, to no great surprise, it died in the House. Bullock later called and told Ellis, "You're a great Texan." He confided that he had stood with Ellis on that bill "to make up for voting for that poll tax" in the late 1950s. He invited Ellis and his wife to join him and Jan on a trip to South Africa after the session closed.[4]

Gov. Bush also received the *it* Paul Hobby had foretold. *It* was precipitated by Bush's appointment of Catherine Mosbacher, the wife of Bullock's 1990 Republican opponent, to the Department of Human Services board. He had no legal obligation to consult with Bullock, but giving him a heads-up courtesy might have avoided *it*. While Bullock was still smoldering over the Mosbacher affair, Bush showed up in the Senate uninvited. Governors don't have Senate floor privileges, though that prohibition is generally ignored.

Bullock, watching Bush meander from desk to desk during a floor debate, laid down his gavel, stepped down from the podium, and walked over to the governor, got close to Bush, and said, "You're a cocky little motherfucker, aren't you?"[5]

Bush, taking Hobby's advice, smiled and moved on.

Bullock went to Waco to speak to employees at the regional Texas Department of Transportation office. Cost-cutting was a high priority, and there were rumors of downsizing, but Bullock told the audience, "As long as I'm lieutenant governor, this office will never be closed."

When he returned to Austin, he learned that Waco was at the top of the list of TxDOT regional offices scheduled for extinction. As it happened, he had a fortuitous visitor at an opportune time.

TxDOT chairman Ray Stoker walked into Bullock's outer office, where Sen. Armbrister happened to be hanging out.

"I've got to see Bullock," he said.

"Ray," Armbrister said, "you don't want to go in there today."

"I've got to see him now," Stoker insisted.

"Trust me, this is not a good day for you to see Bullock," Armbrister repeated.

Stoker persisted until Armbrister relented and said, "Just remember, I told you not to."

Armbrister stepped into Bullock's office and said, "Ray Stoker is here to see you."

Stoker heard the reply: "Tell that sonofabitch to get in here."

Armbrister gestured for Stoker to enter.

Several minutes passed, and Stoker emerged, shaking.

"I've never had anyone in my life talk to me like that," he said. No TxDot regional offices were closed.[6]

That year the Legislature was considering telephone deregulation, and Bullock told Laney that "we ought to make these companies do something for Texas" in exchange for being liberated from government control.

"How about wiring up rural Texas?" Laney asked. Bullock agreed. Also, the telephone companies should pay $1.1 billion for fiber-optic cable to aid schools and libraries. Moreover, they agreed to establish a Telecommunications Infrastructure Fund to pay for additional computer and Internet resources at public institutions. A House bill was prepared that called for the industry to pay $75 million into the fund over a six-year period, and the industry was prepared to accept that.

The head of AT&T met with Bullock and Laney, believing they would seal the deal.

"How much do you think the industry should pay?" Bullock asked.

"Oh, how about $75 million a year for six years?" the executive said.

"One hundred and fifty million," Bullock shot back without hesitation. "For 10 years."

Laney watched as the executive swallowed hard and, also without hesitation, said, "Okay."[7]

Six weeks after Bush was inaugurated, nine well-dressed men and women were spotted shuffling down a sidewalk beside the Capitol. Behind them, a block away, was the governor's mansion. They were members of the Texas Supreme Court, returning from lunch with the governor and a few of his key staff members.

"I tried to get Ann to do this for four years," Democratic Justice Bob Gammage confided.

A Hispanic Democratic state senator was seen emerging from the back door to the governor's office on the second floor of the Capitol, a short walk from the front door of the Senate chamber. Where had he been? "The governor called me over to talk about one of my bills," the senator said. He lowered his voice. "That's the fourth time I've been in there since he became governor. That's more times than in four years under Richards."[8]

Initially, Bush may have been dismissed as an interloper, governor not because he should be but because he could be—thanks to his daddy's name and Rolodex. But he proved to be an inquisitive student of state government and the legislative process. He was already a household name across the state, so he concentrated on building relationships inside the Capitol. He used his celebrity—as a former First Son, president of the Texas Rangers baseball team, governor of Texas, and potential candidate for president—to good avail. In the afternoons during that first legislative session, Bush, accompanied by Dan Shelley, a former House and Senate member who served on his legislative liaison staff, would wander among the underground legislative offices, popping in unannounced and introducing himself to legislators and their often-awed staff members. He posed for pictures with anyone who wanted one—knowing full well that the photographs had a good likelihood of winding up on their home or office walls.

He was far more accessible to individual legislators than Richards had been. By two months into his tenure, he had met one-on-one or in small groups with all but six of the 181 legislators—and the six he'd missed were due to their scheduling conflicts, not his.

With the help of state Rep. Ric Williamson of Weatherford, who switched from Democrat to Republican to seek reelection the same year Bush ran for governor, he cultivated a close working relationship with Rep. Paul

Sadler of Henderson, the Democrat who chaired the House Committee on Public Education. But the two people he courted most were the ones most important to Bush's success: the lieutenant governor and the House speaker.

Bush's weekly breakfasts with Bullock and Laney turned into seminars, with Bullock doing most of the talking and Bush much of the listening. Sometimes they sparred and agreed to disagree. Always the talk was about policy. "Gradually, we built trust and friendship," Bush wrote in his memoir.[9]

Perhaps more importantly, in contrast to Richards, who was put off by Bullock's temper and disdain for her staff, Bush did everything he could to feed Bullock's voracious hunger for information. The fact that Bush, unlike Richards, had not been steeped in state government issues for years may have helped keep him focused on big-picture items, leaving the details for Bullock and Laney to work out.

"One of Bullock's and Ann Richards's downfalls was that he wanted to know every piece of gossip," said Carlton Carl, a friend of both. "And even though he and Ann used to be drinking buddies, she didn't pay him that kind of attention, didn't feed him that information."[10]

But the friendship between the new governor and the grizzled, combative lieutenant governor developed into a warm one. "I think that Bullock initially had a very good political relationship with Governor Bush, beginning with the governor's election," said Jack Martin, Bullock's close confidant who managed the lieutenant governor's part of their joint inauguration. "But as time passed Bob developed a true and deep personal affection for the governor. What I saw between those two men was as deep a friendship as I have seen."

"Their friendship was based on straight talk, constant communication, and sharing a public-policy agenda that always placed the people of Texas first and foremost," said Reggie Bashur, a top aide on Bush's gubernatorial staff. "They agreed on many issues, but when they had a difference of opinion on an issue there was an abiding respect and unwavering spirit of cooperation."[11]

One episode early in their joint tenure showed that their friendship could defuse a potentially serious conflict. During one of their weekly meetings, Bush and Bullock were at an impasse over a detail in one of Bush's cornerstone issues. Bullock was unwilling to compromise.

"Governor, on this I'm going to have to fuck you," Bullock told Bush, according to the story told at the time.

Bush stood, walked over to Bullock, and kissed him.

Spluttering and wiping his mouth, Bullock said, "What the hell was that all about?"

Bush smiled.

"If you're gonna fuck me, you've at least gotta kiss me first," Bush said.[12]

The work of the Legislature was progressing with conspicuous alacrity, and Bullock was lauded in the press as a "Texas powerhouse" as he and Laney were credited with orchestrating a session that held partisanship to a minimum.

Bullock was still volcanic, but there were other instances when he got his way without raising his voice, or even saying a word, as when Houston business and civic leaders needed enabling legislation to build a downtown baseball stadium, partly with public funds. Bullock initially was tepid toward the measure, believing that team owners, not taxpayers, should fund professional athletic facilities. After a visit from a Houston delegation that included his old Hillsboro chum Jack Loftis, by then editor of the *Houston Chronicle*, Bullock reversed fields. In his interview for the Baylor University oral history project, Loftis described how the Houstonians prevailed over a recalcitrant Senate.

"Do you have the votes?" Bullock asked Houston Sen. John Whitmire, who chaired the committee considering the bill.

"No, I don't," Whitmire said. "There are two against me, and I . . ."

"Well, I think we can find a way to help you out a little bit," Bullock said.

What he did next was not recorded, but Bullock must have let the opposing senators know he was paying attention. When Whitmire's committee met, one of the opponents failed to show. Bullock walked into the room, folded his arms, scanned the faces of those present, and returned to his office. Just before the vote was taken, the other senator who opposed the bill said, "Senator Whitmire, excuse me. I've got to go to another committee meeting right now."

Houston got its stadium legislation.[13]

Midway through the session, Bullock had to deal with another tragedy, this one deeply and disturbingly personal. On March 30, Parliamentarian Bob Johnson died at the age of 66 during a night of popping nitroglycerin for his heart. He had spent a stressful week after a gambling lobbyist accused him of being crooked, alleging that he had helped his sons lobby on behalf of horseracing interests against casinos.

Fifteen senators took the floor to condemn the lobbyist, former State Rep. Lloyd Criss, of the Texas Association for Casino Entertainment, and Bullock not only pronounced casino gambling dead for that session, but doubtful for the next. "They [casino interests] can take their 20 pieces of gold and go home," he told reporters.[14] "I have a long-term memory."[15]

Johnson's death a week later was more than just the loss of a friend. Arguably, he was the most important gear in Bullock's political mechanism. They had been friends since they arrived in the Legislature in 1957. As with most of Bullock's friendships, it was bonded by contention and edgy practical jokes. As young, hard-drinking House members, they got into fistfights.

In the mid-1970s, as Johnson was moving into his second decade as House parliamentarian and director of the Texas Legislative Council, Bullock found in his files one of his friend's old segregationist campaign newspaper ads, circa 1956, had it enlarged to poster size, and sent copies to each African American member of the House.

For a while, Bullock kept several goats on his spread near Llano, in an attempt to trim the abundant cactus growth. But as Johnson had warned him, they would, among other things, foul his porch. They did. Their destructive appetites compelled Bullock to get rid of them—by shooting them. He reported to Johnson that he'd killed all the goats. When next Johnson went to Llano, he stopped and bought more goats and, while Bullock was away, turned them loose on the property.

Back in Austin, he told Bullock, "I thought you got rid of those goats."

"I did."

"Well, when I was out there last weekend, there had to be a half dozen still there," Johnson said.

Bullock went back to Llano and carried out another extermination. That went on for several weekends, with the same goat assassination result. It's not certain whether Johnson ever told Bullock what he'd done.

Johnson's sons often heard him say of Bullock, "I love him to death, but goddamn he's crazy."

Once, son Rob replied, "Aw, Dad, you know he does a bunch of crazy things."

"No, son," Johnson said. "I'm talking certifiable."[16]

When his son Gordon suggested that he stop being Bullock's parliamentarian, Johnson replied, "I love what I'm doing, and I love doing it with him."[17]

As parliamentarian, Johnson was Bullock's gatekeeper, and it was serious business . . . usually. Lobbyists on the outs with Bullock would slip their bills to Johnson, and he would arrange for them to be introduced without Bullock knowing the source. House members also would come to him if they thought one of their bills would be in trouble when it reached the Senate. "Don't worry, son," Johnson would tell them. "We'll pass your bill." He was a grandfather and godfather to senators of both parties. When Bullock's temper exploded, he tried to absorb the shock wave—or prevent it from ever occurring.

Former Sen. Kent Caperton, a Bryan Democrat, said that after he became a lobbyist in 1991, he'd always check with Johnson before going in to see Bullock. "We had code words," Caperton said. "He'd say, 'The weather's pretty stormy in there.' Or 'It's a clear day.' And he was always right."[18]

Gordon Johnson said his father kept a plastic parrot in his office; you could say something, and the parrot would record it and repeat it. "When people came in to complain about Bullock's behavior, Dad would say, 'Here's how I deal with it.' He'd punch that button, and the parrot would say, 'Fuck Bullock. Fuck Bullock.' When Dad died, they boxed up all his stuff and sent it over—except the parrot. Bullock kept the parrot."

Gordon talked with his father for a couple of hours the night before he died and encouraged him to see a doctor. "Son," Johnson replied, "there's nothing the doctor can do for me. They want me to stop playing golf, quit politics, stop driving my bulldozer, and quit smoking my cigars. That's no way to live."[19]

His passing left a void in the Senate and, more profoundly, in Bullock.

"He was Bob Bullock's best friend," Sen. Mike Moncrief said at the time. "It's going to have an effect on him—there's no doubt in my mind. I think it's going to hurt him deeply."[20]

It was one of the gathering omens that Bullock, better than most politicians, was capable of interpreting. Things were never going to be the same.

In the politically saturated environs of Austin, the most awaited issue of *Texas Monthly* arrived on newsstands and in mailboxes a month after the close of the regular legislative session. It contained the magazine's selection of "the Best and the Worst Legislators." The choices are a difficult smorgasbord: the table of *worst* possibilities is a cornucopia; the buffet of *best* selections, in some years, is close to a famine. Compiled by Paul Burka and Patricia Kilday Hart, both discerning students and scholars of Texas politics, it can be scalding in its censure and fortifying in its acclamation.

Consider this *worst* winner from the 1995 roster: "Frank Corte, Republican, San Antonio, 35. Mercenary. Mendacious. Malicious. Petty. One of the more dismal products of democracy to reach the Legislature in many a year." That summation was backed up with wilting anecdotes.

That same year, the writers seemed almost exuberant to be able to anoint an "All-Star Team," not from the rank and file, but from the bipartisan helm: George Bush, Bob Bullock, and Pete Laney. Bush, it was noted, "passed his entire legislative program without a hitch." Bullock's "single-mindedness guaranteed that the state's business got done." Laney, the populist West Texan, was the "strikeout" ace who sent bankers, insurance companies, and utilities back to the dugout with their heads down.[21]

Undoubtedly, all luxuriated in the warm fuzziness of the moment. Bush had established himself as a governor who could; Laney came into his own as a serene commandant who could take a punch as well as throw one. For Bullock, the glory was tainted by a whiff of the endgame. The loss of Bob Johnson, his own failing health, and the inevitable arrival of a Senate Republican majority weighed on him. A new world had formed around him, and it may have been hard for him to see his place in it. It was a great year, but he couldn't ignore the voice in his head that whispered that this was his last hurrah.

CHAPTER 28

THE LONG DRUM ROLL

Bullock was still basking in the illustriousness of that 1995 session when calamity again came calling. Fifteen days into 1996, Bullock, along with Senators John Montford and J. E. "Buster" Brown and longtime friend and lobbyist Jack Roberts, went deer hunting on Roberts's lease near Uvalde, southwest of San Antonio. After scaling a 20-foot deer blind, a piece of the frame tore and Bullock plunged backward, flailing his arms to break the fall, the weight of heavy rifles pressing against his chest. He lay still for a while, thinking he would have to wait for his friends to find him and help him up. He later jokingly told Paul Hobby that he worried that Montford, who had aspirations of running for lieutenant governor, would find him first and kill him.

When his friends arrived, though, he was leaning against a tree, aching and barely able to use his hands. They took him back to the camp where pain in his wrists, which he attributed to sprains, did not lessen. That same day, he flew to Austin and doctors told him the wrists were broken and that he also had a fractured shoulder.

His office downplayed the seriousness of the accident. Press secretary Cindy Rugeley told reporters, "He has a cast on his right arm and a soft Ace bandage on the other. He has some mobility, and he isn't incapacitated at all. He's running the office. He can still dial the phone. He's doing well." His primary complaint, she said, was that "he can't eat chili dogs right now."[1]

A week later he was hospitalized with pneumonia.

Paul Hobby visited him and told his wife, Janet, that he was concerned. Bullock had been sick before. He had been pessimistic about his prognoses before. *This is different,* Hobby thought. "He was very morose," he told his wife. "This seemed more legitimate than some of the other spells he went through with his health."[2]

Typically, Bullock did not let his condition distract him from business. Immobilized, he had time to think, and what he thought about was an ambition he had harbored for most of his public life: Build a state history museum worthy of Texas. To get things moving, he summoned Gov. Bush and Speaker Laney to his bedside and told them of his plans. He called on his trusted confidant and fellow history buff George Christian, and Dealey Decherd Herndon, executive director of the State Preservation Board, which had overseen restoring the Capitol.

When word of the plan went public, it was not met with universal applause. Museum directors across the state feared that it would suck state money from their budgets and focus attention away from their collections. The *San Antonio Express-News* joined with them, editorializing that "if Texas needs another museum, let private enterprise build it."[3] Little did they realize that only one thing could stop the museum: a dead Bob Bullock. Despite his sagging health, he would live to see the groundbreaking for the museum, soon to be a grand and imposing pink granite edifice holding down a prominent corner across from the University of Texas campus, named for him.

Recovered from the pneumonia, Bullock returned to the Capitol and continued to run things in the manner in which his staff was accustomed— with sound and fury.

If Bullock was looking for the exit, he didn't let on to many people. While he had dangled the idea of succeeding him as lieutenant governor before several people, and indicated to some that he planned to serve only two four-year terms, as he got into the second one, he indicated that he might be running for reelection to a third term. Part of that may have been to keep senators and others off balance, part of it was to put off as long as possible the idea that he was a lame duck on the way out, and part of it may have been a genuine notion that he might indeed run again.

Whatever combination it was, Bullock's behavior robbed at least one senator who was waiting for a chance to succeed him an opportunity to try to. Among the senators closest to him was John Montford of Lubbock, a moderate-conservative Democrat who had done much of the heavy lifting for Bullock as chairman of the Senate Finance Committee. They clashed only once, over a judicial bill that was strongly opposed by judges.

"We had an enormous blowup, and I met him head-on," said Montford, a quiet-talking former Marine and Lubbock County district attorney. "He started working on me in front of [Senators] Sibley and Bivins, who ran out of the room, we were hollering so bad. Bullock staggered out of the room and told Rhetta [his assistant], 'I don't think Montford supports that bill.' We never had another run-in. We had disagreements, but he never jumped me again."[4]

Montford had a desire to be governor or lieutenant governor, and he had stuck around in the Senate for years, waiting for his chance. Bullock had led him to believe that after two terms at the Senate's helm, he would step aside. That would create Montford's opportunity. But later, despite his health problems, Bullock indicated that he planned to seek reelection again in 1998. That was enough for Montford, who decided to leave public office.

When he learned that he might be named chancellor of Texas Tech University in his hometown—certainly a noble enough career shift and one that recognized his fund-raising ability—Montford called Kent Caperton, a fellow lawyer who had served a decade in the Senate and preceded Montford as Finance chairman. Montford had voted to raise the chancellor's salary, and he wanted Caperton's opinion on whether it would be legal for him to accept the job.

"It's legal," Caperton said, "but you should stay put because it is very unlikely that Bullock is going to seek another term."

"No, he's told me he's running," Montford said.[5]

For nearly a year, the corridor buzz was that Bullock was in his last term, that, despite his denials, he had lost the will and the physical vigor to go further. Montford ignored the smart money and took Bullock at his word. He took the job as chancellor and left the Senate in August 1996. Bullock seemed miffed that his Finance chairman, one of his most adept legislative horses, had bailed out before the 1997 legislative session. At the same time, he may have helped arrange for Montford to get the job at Texas Tech. Montford said he still isn't sure which is correct, though given Bullock's mercurial nature, it could have been both. Montford could well have been both victim and beneficiary of Bullock's inner turmoil—the weary recognition that his time had passed, and a primal scream against the dying of the light.

The handwriting was no longer on the wall. It was on the tally sheets that poured into the Secretary of State's office that Tuesday night in November 1996. Republicans had picked up one Senate seat, giving them a 16–15 majority, and were presumed quite likely to add another in a January special election to replace Democrat Jim Turner of Crockett, who won an East Texas congressional seat in the middle of his four-year Senate term. The district had turned conservative enough that his replacement was expected to be Republican Steve Ogden, a wealthy House member from Bryan, whose district occupied the middle of the Senate district.

The Republicans were in position to do more than just obstruct via the two-thirds rule. With a majority, they could rule the chamber by stripping the lieutenant governor of all his powers, except those specified in the state constitution, and install a president pro tempore of their own party. That they would do that, or even attempt it, or even discuss it above a whisper, was unlikely. The faintest stirrings of a coup could leave the east side of the Capitol strewn with the wounded and the heartbroken. Bullock might be outvoted, but it had been rare in his career that he was out muscled or outmaneuvered. Ask the all-powerful lobby.

In 1993, learning that business lobbyists opposed his school finance bill and had testified against it in committee hearings, he instructed Bruce Gibson, his chief of staff, to herd them into his office. When several were arrayed before him, Bullock began with the weakest. "Are you for me or against me?" he asked. His flinty eyes were hard to look into in those circumstances. "Uh, I'm with you, Governor," the first lobbyist crumbled. One by one he stared them down and posed the same question, and one by one they caved. "We passed that bill 29–2 in about three days," said Gibson.[6]

"Bullock wasn't the kind of guy that you wanted to wound and then track him into the brush," said Cliff Johnson, a former Democratic House member from Palestine, who had dealt with Bullock for years as legislative liaison for Governors Clements and Bush. "It had better be a head shot, or you might come out dismembered. Anybody plotting against Bullock, that was dealing with death."[7]

With the new election results in hand, the Republican leadership felt it finally had the heft to petition for a larger portion of the political spoils. Bullock would have suspected as much. He might have suspected worse. The day after the election, he met with four senior GOP senators—Bill Ratliff, David Sibley, Buster Brown, and Teel Bivins—ostensibly to talk about a property tax plan he was developing. He was more interested in how they intended to exercise their newfound majority.

"What do you want?" he asked them. None wanted a partisan meltdown.

"It began very amiably," Ratliff recalled. They explained that they were not going to try to change the rules and remove him from power as the President of the Senate, but they felt "there should be more inclusion," particularly in the number and selection of committee chairmanships. Democrats held eight of the 13 chairs in 1995, but now greater parity seemed in order. Bullock started out calm, but as the discussions progressed he became more and more agitated, darkening like a tropical storm over warm gulf water. Finally, he ordered the senators out of his office, telling them, "Y'all can kiss my ass."[8]

Pragmatically, he was vulnerable. Ratliff theorized that his aggression was premised on the old sports truism that the best defense is a good offense. They moved the ball against him, but not by much. Nonetheless, he named those four senators to chair four of the most powerful committees in the ensuing session. But, Ratliff said, he could not bring himself to acknowledge that they shared in the decision-making.

Was Bush intoxicated by the GOP showing in the November elections, or was he soberly calculating the 2000 presidential possibilities? Whatever his mindset, it was expressed in the oddest political stunt since Clayton Williams and a mounted posse galloped their horses across the Capitol grounds in pursuit of the governor's office.

Eight days after the 1996 presidential election, without consulting the lieutenant governor, the House speaker, or the chairmen of the spending committees in either chamber, Bush declared that an iffy $1 billion in revenue—based on *preliminary* figures from the comptroller—would be used to pay for a cut in school property taxes. The first word legislative leaders received of the plan was in a press release Bush sent to their offices just moments before his press conference.

From a political standpoint, it may have been shrewd. First, it would appeal to voters unfamiliar with the way state budgeting works, which probably was in the range of 99.5 percent of them. Second, it could serve as a long-range missile aimed at the 2000 New Hampshire presidential primary, where tax reform was likely to be a principal issue (Steve Forbes built his 1996 GOP presidential primary candidacy around a flat tax to replace the existing progressive income tax).

From a practical standpoint in Texas, it had the markings of a colossal blunder. Bush had no power to order property tax relief—that is a function of the Legislature—and by making a unilateral declaration, he risked alienating the lawmakers who would have to write and approve any tax bill. He also risked reopening the contentious school finance issue, which was resolved in 1993 and, at long last, upheld by the Texas Supreme Court. If a property tax relief debate became a school funding debate, and Republicans were successful in undoing Robin Hood, the state could end up back in court—an untimely embarrassment for a governor with presidential yearnings.

With Bush driving the issue, tax reform became the dominant issue of the session. For Bush, it might simply have been politics—to say he'd at least called for giving some money back to taxpayers. But Speaker Laney called his bet, and raised it.

Laney decided to piggyback on Bush's tax-cut idea and give teachers a pay raise in the bargain. Laney appointed a select committee on taxes and education—chaired not by his Ways and Means chairman, tax-hating Republican Tom Craddick of Midland, but by Paul Sadler, the steely plaintiff's attorney and moderate Democrat from Henderson, who chaired the House Committee on Public Education. Laney named ten others to the committee, which in addition to Craddick and Sadler, included five other committee chairs.

Although miffed by Bush's audacity in not seeking legislative counsel beforehand, Bullock was still fond of the governor and still convinced of his potential in national politics. But he seemed weary of fighting the tax battle, of trying to make the Legislature face up to fiscal realities. He tried to craft a compromise tax reform bill that would give Bush a face-saving exit from the session, but that effort failed—in the Senate.

Bullock's apathy extended to governing in general. He persuaded the Legislature to enact a water plan to address the state's interminable drought, but otherwise he was often a no-show. In its biennial critique, *Texas Monthly* characterized the session as "A do-little orgy of partisan indulgence. The will to legislate wasn't there. Caught between a Democratic past and a Republican future, the members just wanted to get out of town without casting a vote that could defeat them."[9] Bullock, the magazine noted, "seldom presided over the Senate, he shied away from the property tax fight, and he threw his weight behind only one issue, water, which ended up being much ado about nothing."[10]

His detachment portended the denouement of an epic time in Texas politics.

In the final days of the session, he called Paul Hobby.

"I'm not going to do this again," he said. "You'd better get ready."

He had been talking up Hobby's candidacy for lieutenant governor since 1994, as though he believed it was the young man's destiny to walk in the footsteps of his father and grandfather.

"Governor, don't try to make that decision right now," Hobby said. "You're at the end of a legislative session. You're tired. You've got a lot left to give. Let's finish this session, and then you go to Santa Fe for a few weeks. In July or August, we'll talk about it."

Bullock's decision was made, and he wanted to announce it early. He told Hobby to fly to Austin and prepare to claim the office. It was all set up, Bullock told him. He had someone lined up to do Hobby's media work and other campaign duties. He was not going to actively participate, because he didn't want to politicize his office, but he would contribute money and his database—the highly prized card file that was now digitized.

The 1997 regular session ended on Monday, June 2. Bullock called a press conference on Thursday. Hobby had arranged to be in Austin on the appointed day, but for reasons he never understood, Bullock's announcement came earlier than Hobby had been told. Hobby arrived barely in time to join the crowd of reporters, staff members, legislators, lobbyists, and other state-house denizens—including Gov. Bush—who packed into the large Lieutenant Governor's Reception Room in the East Wing of the Capitol behind the Senate chamber.

It was there that Hobby learned that he was not going to be Bullock's anointed successor after all. Comptroller John Sharp, who had planned to run for governor, veered instead toward lieutenant governor and told Hobby he had lined up the support of all but one of the Democratic senators. Bullock, too, no longer encouraged Hobby to run, and other influential players, such as organized labor, did likewise. *Don't create an intra-party fight,* they counseled. *Wait your turn.* Bullock was out, and it seemed he no longer had the power or the will to control the actions of others.[11]

"I will leave this office with no ill will to anyone, none, but only admiration and respect and love for the people of Texas who made this all possible for me," Bullock said to the crowd gathered for his announcement. "Only death will end my love affair with Texas."

The reaction was a mixture of funereal eulogy, hyperbolic tribute, and heartfelt appraisal of a remarkable political life.

"This is an earthquake across the political landscape of Texas," said lobbyist Reggie Bashur, whose own tenure as Bullock's press secretary had lasted three days.

"The contributions he has made to our state will affect the lives of all Texans forever," said Atty. Gen. Dan Morales, who still remembered getting slapped by Bullock.

"It's an end of an era. There are not many giants, true giants, in Texas history. He's got to be among a handful," said Sen. Ratliff, who, to the benefit of their relationship, suffered only one of Bullock's tirades.[12]

"I couldn't help realize that I was standing behind and listening to a legend," said Gov. Bush, who had capitalized on his relationship with the Democratic lieutenant governor to underline the idea that he could bring a bipartisan spirit to the presidency.[13]

Bullock would serve another year and a half—until January 1999—and in that time, he would continue to nourish George Bush's political ambitions, so much so that old cohorts complained that they rarely saw him because "he was always surrounded by Republicans." In 1998, Bush was challenged by Garry Mauro, the former land commissioner who had been one of Bullock's closest friends and allies. Bullock was the godfather to two of Mauro's children. Running uphill against a popular Republican governor in an increasingly Republican state, Mauro needed all the help he could get, and a Bullock endorsement still had tonnage.

Bullock endorsed Bush.

Paul Hobby, waved off the lieutenant governor's race, ran for comptroller that year. Bullock, who had vowed not to politicize his office by campaigning for Hobby, became chairman of Sharp's campaign for lieutenant governor. Both were defeated in a display of the power of Republican Gov. Bush's coattails.

In retirement, declining health and premonitions of death drained Bullock's time and energy for political activities. He was being treated again for cancer and a failing heart, and he visited the state cemetery often, fretting over the proper burial plots for himself and Jan. He considered four sites before settling on one on the highest knoll, the most historic section of the cemetery. "I'll be right beside that old carpetbaggin' Republican governor E. J. Davis," he said in a December 1998 interview with *American-Statesman* reporter Patrick Beach.[14] Not right beside, but close. Bullock's chosen spot was 16 paces behind the towering statue of Stephen F. Austin, the Father of Texas, and 12 paces from the cemetery's tallest monument, that marking the resting place of *that old carpetbaggin'* Davis. Immediately next to him would be Gen. Edward Burleson, a vice president of the Republic of Texas, founder of the town that later became Austin and the first occupant of the state cemetery, in 1851.

Bullock also spent much of his time trying to repair fractured relationships from the past. He occasionally had lunch with Sam Kinch, one of his old press demons, and sometimes called him to ask about the whereabouts of one person or another—people he wanted to contact and atone for past wrongs or offenses. When Kinch entered treatment for alcoholism in late 1997, Bullock called him repeatedly to check on his progress and give encouragement.

Dave McNeely was the journalist whose 1994 column about what would happen if Bullock died had precipitated a Bullock ass-chewing a year later. But when the breast cancer afflicting McNeely's wife, Carole Kneeland, showed up in her bones, Bullock pulled McNeely aside in the Capitol to offer his plane to fly her to Houston for further tests and treatment.

George Kuempel, who had returned to news reporting in 1978 after walking out of Bullock's comptroller office that year because of nefarious activities, said Bullock never mentioned it when Kuempel dealt with him later. "Bob and I never talked about what happened, and we became friends again even while he was still comptroller," Kuempel said. "He was one of my best sources up to his death."[15]

In mid-May 1999, Bullock went to see Ben Barnes at his downtown office. They talked for "two hours about life, death, grudges," Barnes said.

"Ben, you should have been governor," Bullock told him. "I'm sorry you weren't."

After they were talked out, Bullock stood to leave and said wistfully, "I'll only be here a few more days. I want to get a beer."[16]

Early in June, he walked around the cemetery for the last time. "I'll see you in a little while," he told Harry Bradley, the overseer he had installed during the refurbishing of the grounds.[17]

Paul Hobby got a call from a Bullock aide about a week later. Bullock had been hospitalized for a few days before his doctors concluded that they could do nothing more for him. He went home to die.

"This one is pretty serious," Hobby was told. He also was told that Bullock was not receiving visitors.

"If I had called and said I wanted to come from Houston, they would have said, 'Don't come,'" Hobby said. He went to Bullock's house unannounced and was welcomed and escorted to a bedroom, where he found Bullock looking miserable, physically and spiritually emaciated.

"Paul, the doctors say that I've got a couple of more days to go," he said.

"Yes, sir," Hobby said. "I understand."

"I'm not sure I want a couple more days of this."

Hobby knelt by the bed, and they talked for ten minutes. Hobby tried to assure him of his "legacy and his place on earth and what he had meant to me," but Bullock still had politics on his mind. George Bush would become president, he predicted, and the House would keep going to the Republicans and there "wasn't any saving it."[18]

He breathed through an oxygen nose tube, but his mind was sound and his spirit good as time ran out. He summoned Tony Proffitt to write his obituary and vigorously edited it on his deathbed. In the last 36 hours, though, the world became fuzzier to him, his musings on politics and Texas less coherent.

Sometime after midnight on his last day, his breathing grew labored, and Jan called for a hospice worker from Robinson Creek Home Care and Hospice, which had been assisting them. A nurse was sent to the house, but there was little to do but wait. Bullock died before sunrise.

It was a sendoff that Bullock would have appreciated. A procession of luminaries eulogized him with the loftiest oratory they could marshal. The governor and every living former governor—most of whom Bullock had savaged at one time or another—were there. He might well have wondered if they came to confirm that he was, in fact, dead. Best of all, outside was a gaggle of reporters who had tormented him. While he reposed on a grand, floral altar, they huddled in a strong summer rain.

Bullock stories wafted around the edges of the funeral and burial like smoke from a campfire and continued later at a gathering of battle-scarred Bullockians at Scholz Garten. Anyone who had ever crossed Bullock's path had at least one story. They told them with pride and respect and, now and then, apprehension. Most, if not all, of them had been required by Bullock to carry pagers, and even now some still jumped when they went off, as though zapped with an electric cattle prod from the beyond. *Relax, he's gone. It's safe to talk about him now. Isn't it?*

Later, at the official dedication of the Bob Bullock State History Museum, some old Bullock hands talked with reporters on the condition of anonymity. *He might be listening.*

Months after he was buried, an indigenous granite headstone was set in place. On the front it said "Bob Bullock" and "God Bless Texas." On the back were words taken from his farewell to public life: "Only death will end my love affair with Texas."

Harry Bradley, the first volunteer in Bullock's first campaign for lieutenant governor, who became overseer of the refurbished Texas State Cemetery that became Bullock's pet project, was interviewed several years after Bullock's death by a reporter for a story on the state cemetery and the design eccentricities.

Why, the reporter wanted to know, was Bullock's influence still felt so much?

"That's the way Mr. Bullock wanted it," Bradley said.

"But Bullock's dead," the reporter said.

Bradley smiled, arched an eyebrow, and inquired, "You sure?"[19]

EPILOGUE

Bob Bullock got his deathbed wish. George W. Bush indeed won the Republican nomination for president. Through campaign manager Joe Allbaugh, Bush asked Bullock's widow, Jan, to introduce him at the Republican National Convention in Philadelphia. She was happy to do so.

"It's quite an honor," she said. "My husband would be thrilled to death." She acknowledged that some Democrats would be less thrilled but, she said, "I think all Texans are very, very proud that they're going to have a president from Texas."

Jan Bullock told the convention of her husband's initial wariness of Bush, which quickly melted. In their weekly breakfasts, "Bob saw that George was sincere in his efforts to do the right things for Texas. He also recognized exceptional ability and great leadership potential. Their friendship evolved from mentor and student to friend and friend. . . ."

The Bullocks, she said, "have seen firsthand what kind of genuine people George and Laura are. We have seen his intelligence, his integrity, his sense of humor, his bipartisan spirit, and his dedication to public service. Texans of all political stripes are proud of Gov. Bush and Laura Bush. And Americans will be proud of President George W. Bush and Laura Bush, who, by the way, will make a grand first lady in the tradition of Barbara Bush.

"My husband predicted that George would become president and encouraged him. Tonight, I am honored to join in his nomination. I consider it to be part of Bob Bullock's unfinished business."[1]

Bush went on to win an electoral vote majority over Democrat Al Gore, although not the popular vote, in one of the tightest and most disputed elections in American history, one that finally had to be settled by the United States Supreme Court. After it was finally determined that Bush would be president, in mid-December—more than a month after the November 7 election day—Bush asked Speaker Laney to introduce him in the House chamber to a national television audience. Laney did so.

Three months after Bush's inauguration, he again was called on to remember Bullock, at the April 27 dedication of the Texas State History Museum that had been named for him.

Bush said that in shifting from being a governor dealing with the Texas Legislature to a president dealing with Congress, he had tried to transport some of the spirit of bipartisanship that he and Bullock and Laney had enjoyed.

"There is a way yet to go, but I think we're making some progress," Bush said. "The tone is more civil, the respect is more widespread. I think Bob Bullock would be pleased."[2]

If that was happening, it wasn't that obvious in Washington. The situation Bush faced there was much more contentious and complex. In Texas, he was a president's son who inspired chauvinism even among Democrats, who figured that if a Republican was going to be elected president, he might as well be from Texas. Bush's cultivation of relationships with legislators of both parties produced some genuine affection. His agenda was small, and it was an open secret that parts of it were driven as much by presidential politics as state policy needs. And bipartisanship was a vital ingredient.

In Washington, by contrast, there were 535 legislators, not 181. Despite his professed bipartisan intentions, hardball partisanship had so permeated Congress that Bush was forced to play. With Republicans narrowly in control of the U.S. House, Bush needed their help, rather than the Democrats', to get anything done. Besides that, the chauvinism of Texans proud to have a Texas president was missing; a considerable number of the 535 people on the Hill thought they were as qualified to be president, if not more so, than Bush— and several of them were actively seeking that job.

In Austin, everyone was in the same building, and he could have a state senator in his office smoking a cigar after a 30-second walk. But for Bush to meet with members of Congress, he had to travel two miles by motorcade, with enough armed guards to attack Cuba. Add that he was responsible for the national defense, and the national economy, and things got truly complex.

Bush was having a so-so presidency up to that point. But on September 11, 2001, terrorists flew airliners full of fuel into the two towers of the World Trade Center in New York, and the Pentagon. Suddenly, everything changed, and Bush quickly became the equivalent of a wartime president.

What would Bullock have thought of Bush's presidency, were he alive to kibitz? Hard to know. Six years into Bush's presidency, some speculated that Bullock wouldn't approve of invading Iraq without an exit strategy; Bradley believed Bullock would have thought of the war equivalent of "cross-fencing," to help ensure success. He would have been skeptical of passing large tax cuts even while running up the biggest national debt in American history. Bush's allowing the Republican U.S. House Majority Leader at the time, Tom DeLay, to engineer partisan congressional redistricting to kill off senior Texas Democrats in favor of freshmen Republicans to pad the GOP's majority might never have happened had Bullock still overseen the Senate.

Historians and Bullock fans, and non-fans, will have to reach their own conclusions. But the fact that Democrats regained control of the House and Senate in the 2006 election was attributed by many observers as due largely to the unpopularity of Bush and the Iraq war.

There were those observers, such as Clay Robison of the *Houston Chronicle*, who bemoaned the fact that Texas's leadership had slid to the point that it couldn't, or wouldn't, raise the money necessary to take care of the state's needs. Robison wrote that, almost seven years after his death, Texas missed Bullock's strong leadership to whip the business lobby into supporting rather than opposing a revenue measure. The headline says it all: "Bullock-like leadership needed to get tax reform done."[3]

Austin American-Statesman outdoor writer Mike Leggett wrote in 2006 that in 1989, while Bullock was still comptroller, he had talked his way out of being mentioned in a story Leggett was writing about people on the Texas Parks and Wildlife Department's lists of those who had various types of game or fish stocked on their land. Bullock was among those listed as requesting and getting the state to stock largemouth bass in a lake in South Texas—for free.

Leggett said Bullock telephoned him.

"Mike, it's Bob Bullock," he said. "Mike, I understand my name turned up on one of those [expletive] lists.

"Mike, I didn't have anything to do with that," Bullock continued. "I had been on that lease the year before those bass were delivered, and I may have told somebody to call Parks and Wildlife, but I don't know how I got tangled up in this." He said he didn't even like to fish.

Leggett believed him, appreciated his candor, and left Bullock out of the story. Half a dozen years after Bullock's death, he cited the telephone call to a group of Parks and Wildlife employees as a model for how public officials come out better if they are direct and frank with reporters instead of trying to hide.

"One of the guys had a strange look on his face, and as the group broke up, asked if he could speak to me," Leggett wrote. They found a deserted corridor.

"That was an interesting story you were telling about Bullock," he said.

"Yeah, he was a smart guy," Leggett said.

"Real smart," the worker replied. "Especially since I still have the cap with the Comptroller of the State of Texas logo on it that he gave me when I delivered those fish down there."[4]

NOTES

INTRODUCTION

1. Ralph Wayne, interview by Patrick Beach, November 1998.
2. Jack Loftis, oral history.
3. David Sibley, interview by Patrick Beach, November 1998.
4. George Christian, interview by Dave McNeely, May 14, 1993.
5. Preston Smith, oral history, Baylor University.
6. Jack Loftis, oral history.

CHAPTER 1

1. Robert Dohoney, oral history, Baylor University.
2. Tom Bullock, interview by Dave McNeely, Oct. 17, 2003, Brenham.
3. Patrick Beach, "The King of Texas; As Lieutenant Governor Passes Gavel, An Era Ends," *Austin American-Statesman*, Dec. 6, 1998.
4. Betty Dohoney, interview by Jim Henderson.
5. Frasier Blount, interview by Jim Henderson.
6. Cecil Stubblefield and Frank Blount, oral history, Baylor University.
7. Cecil Stubblefield, oral history, Baylor University.
8. Robert Dohoney, oral history, Baylor University.
9. Robert Dohoney, oral history, Baylor University.

CHAPTER 2

1. Robert Dohoney, interview by Jim Henderson, 2004.
2. Frasier Blount, oral history, Baylor University.
3. Robert Dohoney, interview by Jim Henderson, 2004.
4. Bob Bullock, interview by Dave McNeely, July 20, 1994.
5. Molly Ivins, "No Bull Bullock," *Texas Observer*, Feb. 3, 1972.
6. George Norris Green, *The Establishment in Texas Politics—The Primitive Years, 1939–1957* (Westport, CT: Greenwood Press, 1979).

7.   Chandler Davidson, *Race and Class in Texas Politics* (Princeton, NJ: Princeton University Press, 1990), p. 224.
8.   Green, *The Establishment in Texas Politics*, p. 189.
9.   Political advertisement, *Hillsboro Evening Mirror*, July 24, 1956.
10.   Robert Dohoney, interview by Jim Henderson.

CHAPTER 3

1.   Richard M. Morehead, "Legislators Considering Racial Laws," *Dallas Morning News*, Jan. 8, 1957.
2.   A. R. "Babe" Schwartz, interview by Jim Henderson and Dave McNeely, Feb. 3, 2005, Austin.
3.   "Bob Johnson Running for Legislature," *Dallas Morning News*, June 27, 1956.
4.   Richard M. Morehead, "Three Bills Offered for Closing Schools," *Dallas Morning News*, Nov. 14, 1957.
5.   Ibid.
6.   Dawson Duncan, "3 Segregation Bills Signed by Governor," *Dallas Morning News*, Dec. 12, 1957.
7.   Sam Collins, interview by Jim Henderson.
8.   Donald Eastland, interview by Jim Henderson.
9.   "Meeting Held on Tunnell's Speaker Race," *Dallas Morning News*, Oct. 22, 1959.
10.   "Rep. Tunnell Drops Out of Speaker's Race," *Dallas Morning News*, June 25, 1960.

CHAPTER 4

1.   Jerry Hall, unpublished biography of Ben Barnes, p. 40.
2.   Ibid., p. 41.
3.   Ben Barnes with Lisa Dickey, *Barn Burning, Barn Building: Tales of a Political Life, From LBJ to George W. Bush and Beyond* (Albany, TX: Bright Sky Press, 2006), p. 31.
4.   Jerry Hall, unpublished biography of Ben Barnes, p. 50.
5.   Ann Fears Crawford and Jack Keever, *John B. Connally: Portrait in Power* (Austin, TX: Jenkins Publishing Co., 1973), p. 98.
6.   Dawson Duncan, "Connally Pitches Campaign on Unity, State Development," *Dallas Morning News*, Jan. 20, 1962.
7.   Crawford and Keever, *John B. Connally*, p. 187.
8.   Ibid., p. 89.
9.   Jerry Hall, unpublished biography of Ben Barnes, p. 59.
10.   Robert Dohoney, oral history, Baylor University, p. 8.
11.   Molly Ivins, "No Bull Bullock," *Texas Observer*, Mar. 3, 1972.
12.   Crawford and Keever, *John B. Connally*, p. 185.
13.   Ben Barnes, interview by Jim Henderson and Dave McNeely, Feb. 4, 2005.

CHAPTER 5

1. Molly Ivins, "No Bull Bullock," *Texas Observer*, Mar. 3, 1972.
2. Ibid.
3. Ibid.
4. Ann Fears Crawford and Jack Keever, *John B. Connally: Portrait in Power* (Austin, TX: Jenkins Publishing Co., 1973), p. 197.
5. Ibid., p. 122.
6. Jerry Douglas Conn, *Preston Smith: The Making of a Governor* (Austin and New York: Jenkins Publishing Co., The Pemberton Press, 1972), pp. 113–114.
7. Preston Smith, oral history, Baylor University.
8. Ibid.
9. Ibid.
10. Ibid.
11. Ibid.
12. Bill Collier, *Inquiry*, Feb. 4, 1980.
13. Jerry Hall, unpublished biography of Ben Barnes, p. 100.

CHAPTER 6

1. Buck Wood, oral history, p. 3.
2. Ibid.
3. Ibid., pp. 10–12.
4. Preston Smith, oral history.
5. Ibid.
6. Buck Wood, interview by Jim Henderson, July 15, 2004.
7. Buck Wood, oral history, p. 12.
8. Cash donations were not outlawed until 1973.
9. Buck Wood, oral history, p. 39.
10. Dick Cory, interview by Dave McNeely, Aug. 4, 2005, Austin.
11. Carlton Carl, interview by Dave McNeely, Nov. 1, 2005, Austin.
12. Buck Wood, oral history, p. 13.
13. Ibid., pp. 13–15.

CHAPTER 7

1. Mickey Herskowitz, *Sharpstown Revisited: Frank Sharp and a Tale of Dirty Politics in Texas* (Austin, TX: Eakin Press, 1994), p. 1.
2. Preston Smith, oral history.
3. Sam Kinch, Jr., in *Points of Entry: Cross-Currents in Storytelling*, 2004.
4. Bo Byers, "Aides' Departure Indicates Smith Won't Run Again," *Houston Chronicle*, Sept. 2, 1971.
5. Austin Bureau, "Bullock Gets Dies' State Post," *Dallas Times Herald*, Sept. 1, 1971.
6. Jon Ford, "Bullock Appointment Expected to Meet Senate Opposition," *Corpus Christi Caller-Times*, Sept. 2, 1971.

7. Buck Wood, oral history, Apr. 2, 2001, p. 20.

8. Ibid., pp. 23–25.

9. Ibid., pp. 25–29.

10. Carlton Carl, interview by Dave McNeely, Nov. 1, 2005.

CHAPTER 8

1. Jon Ford, "Bullock Studying Orr's Eligibility," *Corpus Christi Caller-Times*, Jan. 19, 1972.

2. Ibid.

3. Roland Lindsey, UPI, "Fundraising Is Still Bullock's Primary Duty," *Houston Post*, Nov. 21, 1971.

4. Glen Castlebury, "GOP Leaders Ask Bullock Removal," *Austin American*, Nov. 23, 1971.

5. Art Wiese, "Bullock Promises He Won't Succumb to Republican Demand for Resignation," *Houston Post*, Nov. 23, 1971.

6. Roland Lindsey, UPI, "Bob Bullock: Gov. Smith's Hatchet Man," *Houston Chronicle*, Nov. 21, 1971.

7. Capitol Staff, "Bullock Loan Adds to GOP Complaint," *Austin American*, Jan. 5, 1972.

8. Capitol Staff, "Briscoe Joins Race, Jabs Barnes," *Austin American*, Sept. 30, 1971.

9. The other two senators were Ralph Hall of Rockwall and Joe Christie of El Paso.

10. H. C. Pittman, *Inside the Third House: A Veteran Lobbyist Takes a 50-Year Frolic Through Texas Politics* (Austin, TX: Eakins Press, 1992), p. 43.

11. Molly Ivins, "No Bull Bullock," *Texas Observer*, Mar. 3, 1972.

12. Buck Wood, oral history, p. 38.

13. Ibid., p. 32.

14. Buck Wood, oral history, p. 38.

15. Jerry Conn, interview by Dave McNeely, Apr. 26, 2006, Austin.

16. Austin Bureau, "The War That Wasn't," *Dallas Times Herald*, July 9, 1972.

17. Capitol Staff, "Bullock Confirmed by Texas Senate," *Austin American*, July 7, 1972.

CHAPTER 9

1. State Capitol Bureau, "Bob Bullock May 'Ramrod' McGovern Texas Fund Push," *Houston Post*, Aug. 27, 1972.

2. Associated Press, "Bullock Undergoes Surgery," *Houston Post*, July 22, 1972.

3. Capitol Bureau, "Bullock Named: Insurance Board Choice," *San Antonio Express-News*, Sept. 19, 1972.

4. Bill Collier, "Insurance Head Bullock Aims for Lowest Rates," *Houston Chronicle*, Sept. 19, 1972.

5. Texas Consumer Association, press release, Sept. 19, 1972.

6. Bill Collier, "Brooks Reports Insurance Lobby Fighting Bullock," *Houston Chronicle*, Sept. 21, 1972.

7. Ibid.

8. Stewart Davis, "Fight Rages on Bullock," *Dallas Morning News*, Sept. 26, 1972.

9. Bob Bain, "Barnes Will Oppose Bullock Despite OK," *Fort Worth Star-Telegram*, Sept. 23, 1972.

10. Ibid.

11. Bill Collier, "Bob Bullock Is Man in the Middle of Special Session's Hottest Infighting," *Houston Chronicle*, Sept. 23, 1972.

12. Buck Wood, oral history, p. 62.

13. George Kuempel, "The Bullock Donnybrook; Political Infighting So Bitter One Senator Threw Up," *Houston Chronicle*, Oct. 1, 1972.

14. Ibid.

15. Rick Fish, "Senate Votes Bullock Down," *Austin American*, Sept. 27, 1972.

16. Buck Wood, oral history, pp. 64–65.

CHAPTER 10

1. Austin Bureau, "Battling Bob Bullock to Head Democratic Unity Day in Texas," *Houston Chronicle*, Oct. 3, 1972.

2. Robert Schwab, "Bullock May Cast Eye on District Judge Post," *Austin American*, Oct. 12, 1972.

3. Buck Wood, oral history, p. 67.

4. Ibid., p. 40.

5. Ibid., pp. 39–40.

6. Art Wiese, "Race for Comptroller Marked by Harsh Charges (Calvert Opposed by Former Aide James L. 'Jim' Wilson)," *Houston Post*, May 29, 1972.

7. Buck Wood, oral history, pp. 43–44.

8. Associated Press, "Bullock Announces Resignation," *San Antonio Express-News*, Dec. 20, 1972.

9. Rick Fish, "Bullock Plans Law Practice (Resigning from Secretary of State)," *Austin American*, Dec. 20, 1972.

10. Art Wiese, "Race for Comptroller Marked by Harsh Charges (Calvert Opposed by Former Aide James L. 'Jim' Wilson)," *Houston Post*, May 29, 1972.

11. Buck Wood, oral history, p 74.

12. Darrell Hancock, "Bob Bullock Says He'll Seek Calvert's Comptroller Job," *Houston Post*, June 22, 1973.

13. Art Wiese, "Wild Race Due When Calvert, Bullock Clash," *The Austin Citizen*, July 17, 1973.

14. Ken Wendler, interview by Dave McNeely, Apr. 15, 2005.

15. Garry Mauro, interview by Dave McNeely, Aug. 3, 2005.

16. Ken Wendler, interview by Dave McNeely, Apr. 15, 2005.

17. Ron Calhoun, "Bullock Admits Errors, Stresses Candor in Race," *Dallas Times Herald*, Oct. 23, 1974.

CHAPTER 11

1. Bob Bullock, interview by Dave McNeely, Sept. 6, 1995.
2. Buck Wood, oral history, p. 131.
3. Bill Collier, *Inquiry*, Feb. 4, 1980.
4. Buck Wood, oral history, pp. 131–156.
5. Tom Curtis, "Hatchet Man Turns Reformer," *Washington Post* report reprinted in *Marble Falls Highlander*, Sept. 18, 1975.
6. Buck Wood, interview by Dave McNeely and Jim Henderson, Oct. 30, 2004.

CHAPTER 12

1. Elbert Hubbard, *A Message to Garcia*, originally published in the *Philistine*, March 1899. Reprinted by Thomas Y. Crowell Co., NY, 1924.
2. Jon Ford, *Austin American-Statesman*, Apr. 27, 1975.
3. Ibid.
4. Bo Byers, "Bob Bullock Relishes His Gadfly Status," *Houston Chronicle*, May 16, 1976.
5. Capitol Staff, "Connally Given Holiday 'Roasting,'" *Austin American-Statesman*, Nov. 25, 1976.
6. Austin Bureau, "Complaints of Bias Against Comptroller Are Settled," *Houston Chronicle*, May 31, 1975.
7. Carolyn Barta, "Comptroller Is Spelled B-U-L-L-O-C-K Nowadays," *Dallas Morning News*, Sept. 19, 1975.
8. Dave McNeely, "True Tales Told as Texas Legend Is Laid to Rest," *Austin American-Statesman*, June 19, 1999.
9. "Comptroller Sued by Campfire Girls," *Austin American-Statesman*, Mar. 11, 1975.
10. Buck Wood, interview by Dave McNeely and Jim Henderson, Oct. 30, 2004.
11. Bill Collier, *Inquiry*, Feb. 4, 1980.
12. Ibid.
13. Ibid.
14. Sam Kinch, Jr., in *Points of Entry: Cross-Currents in Storytelling*, 2004.
15. Ibid.

CHAPTER 13

1. Buck Wood, interview by Dave McNeely and Jim Henderson, Oct. 30, 2004.
2. Buck Wood, oral history, pp. 109–114.
3. Ibid., pp. 107–108.
4. Bill Collier, *Inquiry*, Feb. 4, 1980.

5. Carol Fowler and Janie Paleschic, "Bullock Spends Freely on Luxury," *Austin Citizen*, Apr. 21, 1976.

6. Carol Fowler and Janie Paleschic, "*Citizen* Opens Bullock Probe," *Austin Citizen*, Apr. 19, 1976.

7. Thomas M. Reay, executive editor, "Bullock: *Citizen* 'Pathetic Rag,'" *Austin Citizen*, May 13, 1976.

8. Nick Kralj, interview by Dave McNeely and Jim Henderson, Feb. 4, 2005.

9. Bruce Gibson, interview by Dave McNeely, Mar. 8, 2006.

10. Buck Wood, oral history, pp. 197–198.

CHAPTER 14

1. Carlton Carl, interview by Dave McNeely, Nov. 1, 2005.

2. Buck Wood, oral history, pp. 102–105.

3. Monica Reeves, "Comptroller Tells of Desire to Seek Governorship in '82," *Houston Post*, July 22, 1977.

4. Jon Ford, "Bullock Says Hill Stalls Tax Action," *Austin American-Statesman*, July 26, 1977.

5. "Bullock Names Hill Turkey Award Winner," *Austin American-Statesman*, Nov. 24, 1977.

6. Carolyn Barta, "Bullock Had a Purpose in Supporting Briscoe," *Dallas Morning News*, May 25, 1978.

7. Ibid.

8. Bill Collier, *Inquiry*, Feb. 4, 1980.

9. Ralph Wayne, interview by Dave McNeely, June 10, 2002.

10. Bill Collier, *Inquiry*, Feb. 4, 1980.

11. Ibid.

12. Buck Wood, interview by Dave McNeely and Jim Henderson, Oct. 30, 2004.

13. Ronald Powell and Jim Berry, "Bullock Arrested, Charged with DWI," *Austin American-Statesman*, July 12, 1978.

14. Ibid.

15. "Bullock Pleads Guilty, Gets One-Year Probation," *Austin American-Statesman*, July 21, 1978.

16. Buck Wood, interview by Dave McNeely and Jim Henderson, Oct. 30, 2004.

17. Bill Collier, *Inquiry*, Feb. 4, 1980.

18. Clements actually won with a plurality of 49.96 percent, since a Libertarian and a Socialist candidate got enough to deny him a majority.

19. Richard Fish, "Typewriter Seized by Travis DA as Evidence in Comptroller Probe," *Houston Chronicle*, Oct. 14, 1978.

CHAPTER 15

1. Larry Jolidon, "Bullock Says Charges a Shock, Denies Them," *Austin American-Statesman*, Oct. 10, 1978.

2. Felton West, "Bullock Claims Ruling on Grand Jury Report Victory for 'Fair Play,'" *Houston Post*, Aug. 1, 1980.

3. Lucius Lomax, "Breaking the Bob Bullock FBI File," *Quorum Report*, Oct. 6, 2004.

4. Lucius Lomax, "Bullock Is Involved in Auto Accident," *Austin American-Statesman*, Mar. 28, 1979.

5. Anne Marie Kilday, "An Advisory from the Seat of Power," *Fort Worth Star-Telegram*, Apr. 15, 1979.

6. Stewart Davis, "Bob Bullock Apparently Suffers Heart Attack," *Dallas Morning News*, Oct. 12, 1979.

7. Lee Jones, AP, "In 5 Years as Comptroller, Job Has Taken Toll on Bullock," *Houston Post*, Mar. 30, 1980.

8. Dave Montgomery, "Bullock Splits with Clements, Vows to Fight Re-election Bid," *Dallas Times Herald*, Mar. 8, 1980.

9. Ibid.

10. Steve Peters, "Bullock Admits Drinking, Dating; Denies 'Misusing' Power," *El Paso Times*, Mar. 18, 1980.

11. Ibid.

12. Jim Baker, "Bullock, Earle Rattle Sabers," *Austin American-Statesman*, July 9, 1980.

13. Patrick Beach, "The King of Texas; As Lieutenant Governor Passes Gavel, An Era Ends," *Austin American-Statesman*, Dec. 6, 1998.

14. Associated Press, "Two Papers Recipients of Cow Manure Gifts," *Houston Post*, Aug. 30, 1981.

15. Bill Kidd, "Bullock's 'Surprise Packages' Not Complete Surprise," *Midland Reporter-Telegram*, Sept. 4, 1981.

16. Richard Morehead, "Despite Problems, Bullock an Interesting Character," *Dallas Morning News*, Sept. 23, 1981.

17. Ann Arnold, "Bullock Fighting Alcohol Problem," *Fort Worth Star-Telegram*, Sept. 15, 1981.

18. Patrick Beach, "The King of Texas; As Lieutenant Governor Passes Gavel, An Era Ends," *Austin American-Statesman*, Dec. 6, 1998.

19. Carlton Carl, interview by Dave McNeely, Nov. 1, 2005, Austin.

20. Ibid.

21. Buck Wood, oral history, p. 185.

22. Ibid.

23. Mike Cox and Bill Cryer, "Police Stop Bullock After Hostage Report," *Austin American-Statesman*, Sept. 10, 1981.

24. Patrick Beach, "The King of Texas; As Lieutenant Governor Passes Gavel, An Era Ends," *Austin American-Statesman*, Dec. 6, 1998.

25. Ibid.

CHAPTER 16

1. Lee Jones, AP, "In 5 Years as Comptroller, Job Has Taken Toll on Bullock," *Houston Post*, Mar. 30, 1980.

2. *Texas Monthly*, July 2003, p. 148.

3. Bill Collier, *Inquiry*, Feb. 4, 1980.
4. *Texas Monthly*, July 2003, p. 148.
5. Ben Barnes, interview by Dave McNeely and Jim Henderson, Feb. 4, 2005.
6. Nick Kralj, interview by Dave McNeely and Jim Henderson, Feb. 4, 2005.
7. Clay Robison, "'I Am an Alcoholic,' Says Bullock, Back from Clinic," *San Antonio Light*, Oct. 26, 1981.
8. Bo Byers, "'I've Had Too Much'—Bullock Says Treatment Has Put Drinking Days Behind Him," *Houston Chronicle*, Oct. 26, 1981.
9. Patrick Beach, "The King of Texas; As Lieutenant Governor Passes Gavel, An Era Ends," *Austin American-Statesman*, Dec. 6, 1998.
10. It was originally called MasterCharge, but was changed to MasterCard in 1979.
11. Dave McNeely, "Aides Say Bullock, Brimming with Ideas, Is Back on Line," *Austin American-Statesman*, Dec. 27, 1981.
12. *Texas Monthly*, July 2003, p. 147.
13. WFAA-TV broadcast, captured on videotape by Capitol Bureau reporter Carole Kneeland and photographer Paula McCarter.
14. Jack Martin comment to Dave McNeely, sometime in the 1980s.
15. Bruce Hight, "Bullock Gets Early Start on 1986 Race; Comptroller Sets His Sights on Following White into Governor's Mansion," *Austin American-Statesman*, Jan. 8, 1983.
16. Richard S. Dunham, "Bullock Already Gunning for White," *Dallas Times Herald*, Mar. 6, 1983.
17. "Bullock to Undergo Spinal Disk Surgery," *Austin American-Statesman*, Jan. 16, 1983.

CHAPTER 17

1. Ken Herman, "White's Banker Holds a Good Job for a Man Who Would Be Governor," *Houston Post*, Apr. 18, 1983.
2. Billy Hamilton, oral history, Oct. 13, 2003, pp. 24–25.
3. Richard Dunham, "Bullock Already Gunning for White," *Dallas Times Herald*, Mar. 6, 1983.
4. Ibid.
5. Ibid.
6. Ibid.
7. Billy Hamilton, oral history, Oct. 13, 2003, p. 20.
8. Jackie Calmes, "Ubiquitous Bullock Aide Raises Eyebrows, Hackles in Austin," *Dallas Morning News*, Oct. 2, 1983.
9. *Texas Monthly*, collection of Bullock stories from individuals, July 2003.
10. Jerry White, "Bullock Ticketed for Driving 106," *Austin American-Statesman*, Apr. 1, 1983.
11. Patti Kilday, "Aide Denies Bullock Drinking When Ticketed for Speeding," *Dallas Times Herald*, Apr. 2, 1983.

12. Saralee Tiede, "Bullock: The Man of the 11th Hour," *Fort Worth Star-Telegram*, May 28, 1983.

13. Ibid.

14. Buck Wood, oral history, Apr. 9, 2001, p. 116.

15. Bruce Hight, "Comptroller Accuses White of Shirking State Business," *Austin American-Statesman*, Oct. 7, 1983.

16. "Bullock Claims White Wants to Be Next Veep," *Abilene Reporter News*, Oct. 8, 1983.

17. Dave McNeely, "Teacher Pay Session Doubted by Bullock," *Austin American-Statesman*, Dec. 7, 1983.

CHAPTER 18

1. Dave McNeely, "White Out on Limb with Special Session," *Austin American-Statesman*, June 10, 1984.

2. Dave McNeely, "White's Goals Backed as Tax Session Opens," *Austin American-Statesman*, June 5, 1984.

3. Ibid.

4. Linda Ponce, "Bullock Backs State Raises," *Fort Worth Star-Telegram*, June 5, 1984.

5. Bob Bullock, speech to Texas Legislature, June 5, 1984.

6. Saralee Tiede, "Political Bell Tolls for Change in School Funding," *Fort Worth Star-Telegram*, May 20, 1984.

7. Mark White, interview by Dave McNeely, June 11, 1984.

8. Dave McNeely, "White Courts State Lobbyists on Tax Plans," *Austin American-Statesman*, June 12, 1984.

9. Saralee Tiede, "Leadership, Timing Credited in Austin," *Fort Worth Star-Telegram*, July 4, 1984.

10. G. Robert Hillman, "Senate Tentatively Approves School Reforms; Lewis Laid Down the Law in Passing School Reforms," *Dallas Morning News*, June 23, 1984.

11. Dave McNeely, "Hobby Assails Teacher Group After Feud over School Plan," *Austin American-Statesman*, June 29, 1984.

12. Ann Marie Kilday and Glenn Smith, "House Unanimously Rejects Senate Tax Bill," *Houston Chronicle*, July 3, 1984.

13. Patti Kilday and Richard S. Dunham, "Series of Melodramas Preceded Tax Bill Compromise," *Dallas Times Herald*, July 4, 1984.

14. G. Robert Hillman, "Legislature Passes Tax Package," *Dallas Morning News*, July 4, 1984.

15. Saralee Tiede, "Leadership, Timing Credited in Austin," *Fort Worth Star-Telegram*, July 4, 1984.

16. G. Robert Hillman, "Legislature Passes Tax Package," *Dallas Morning News*, July 4, 1984.

17. Saralee Tiede, "Leadership, Timing Credited in Austin," *Fort Worth Star-Telegram*, July 4, 1984.

18. Ibid.

19. Mike Hailey, "Bullock Gives Up Race for Governor; Democratic Comptroller Expresses Doubt of Ability to Beat White in 1986," *Austin American-Statesman*, July 24, 1984.

20. Jack Keever, AP, "Bullock Quietly Walked Away from Dream of Governorship," *Dallas Morning News*, Aug. 5, 1984.

21. Raul Reyes, "Someone Failed to Tell Bullock About the No-nos," *Houston Chronicle*, July 29, 1984.

CHAPTER 19

1. Dave McNeely, "Darkening Clouds on Revenue Promise Stormy Days in Capitol," *Austin American-Statesman*, Jan. 6, 1985.

2. Henry Bryan, "Texas Income Tax Predicted by '94," *Dallas Times Herald*, July 10, 1984.

3. Dave McNeely, "Bullock Urges Agencies to Follow Comptroller's Office in Layoffs," *Austin American-Statesman*, Jan. 30, 1985.

4. Interview with *Quorum Report*, Mar. 1, 1985.

5. Associated Press, "Lewis Sees No Tax Hikes," *Fort Worth Star-Telegram*, Mar. 23, 1985.

6. "Bullock on New York Honeymoon," *Austin American-Statesman*, Apr. 19, 1985.

7. Joy Anderson, interview by Dave McNeely, Apr. 24, 2005.

8. Ibid.

9. Dave McNeely, "Governor Is Given High Ratings by 46 Percent in Texas Poll," *Austin American-Statesman*, June 6, 1985.

10. Terrence Stutz, "Approval of White Falls Sharply in Poll," *Dallas Morning News*, Dec. 24, 1985.

11. Lee Jones, "Bullock to Seek 4th Term," *Fort Worth Star-Telegram*, Oct. 15, 1985.

12. Saralee Tiede, "Bullock Says State Cash Poor," *Fort Worth Star-Telegram*, Nov. 1, 1985.

13. Associated Press, "White Rejects Bullock Income Tax Idea," *Houston Post*, Nov. 2, 1985.

14. G. Robert Hillman and Sam Attlesey, "Insults Fly in Race for Governor; Both Campaigns Charge Name-calling," *Dallas Morning News*, Nov. 1, 1986.

15. G. Robert Hillman, "Clements' Aide Reports Illegal 'Bug'; Official Stops Short of Accusing Opposition," *Dallas Morning News*, Oct. 7, 1986.

16. David Hanners and George Kuempel, "Bug Finder Refuses to Take Polygraph," *Dallas Morning News*, Oct. 24, 1986.

17. David Hanners, "Campaigns Virtually Cleared in 'Bug' Case; FBI Says Focus of Inquiry Is Elsewhere," *Dallas Morning News*, Oct. 28, 1986.

CHAPTER 20

1. Dave McNeely, "The Numbers Man," *Austin American-Statesman*, Feb. 1, 1987.
2. Ibid.
3. Comptroller news release, Feb. 4, 1987.
4. Editorial, "Bullock Breaks Income-tax Ice," *San Antonio Express-News*, Feb. 13, 1987.
5. Dave McNeely, "Hobby Sees Opportunity to Run for Governorship in 1990," *Austin American-Statesman*, Jan. 2, 1987.
6. Carolyn Barta, "Is 1990 Race Starting Now?," *Dallas Morning News*, Feb. 2, 1987.
7. Ibid.
8. Dave McNeely, "Mattox Dealing His First Cards Before Hobby Bids on 1990 Governor's Race," *Austin American-Statesman*, May 28, 1987.
9. Wayne Slater, "'New' Bullock Touts Tax Plan; Bad-boy Days Behind Him, but Comptroller Still Driven," *Dallas Morning News*, Apr. 20, 1987.
10. Dale Rice and Raul Reyes, "Bullock Gives Governor Bad Budget News; State Revenue Lower Than Expected, Clements Says," *Dallas Times Herald*, June 12, 1987.
11. Bob Bullock, speech to joint legislative session, June 22, 1987.
12. Sam Attlesey, "Clements to Be Focus of Inquiry; 2 Lawmakers Talk of Impeachment," *Dallas Morning News*, June 23, 1987.
13. Bill Hobby, interview by Dave McNeely, Aug. 1, 2006.
14. Dave McNeely, "Attorney General Dishes It Out About Hobby's Gold Spoon," *Austin American-Statesman*, July 1, 1987.
15. Dave McNeely, "Hobby Responds in Kind with Campaign Barbs Against Mattox," *Austin American-Statesman*, July 9, 1987.
16. Virginia Ellis, "Hobby's Decision to Quit Stuns Texas' Power Brokers," *Dallas Times Herald*, July 28, 1987.
17. Kenneth F. Bunting, "Hobby Shocks Capital, Saying He Won't Run," *Fort Worth Star-Telegram*, July 28, 1987.
18. Ibid.
19. G. Robert Hillman, "Bullock Makes Bid for Lieutenant Governor," *Dallas Morning News*, Sept. 11, 1987.

CHAPTER 21

1. *Andrews County News*, Sept. 17, 1987.
2. *Canadian Record*—"Bullock for Lt. Governor," Sept. 24, 1987.
3. "Credit Mr. Bullock," *Diboll Free Press*, Sept. 18, 1987.
4. "We Salute Bullock," *The Victoria Advocate*, Sept. 13, 1987.
5. *Childress Index*, Sept. 15, 1987.
6. Harry Bradley, interview by Dave McNeely, Mar. 8, 2006.

7. *Quorum Report*, Oct. 1, 1987, p. 2.
8. Ibid., p. 1.
9. Associated Press, "Hopefuls Say Bullock Campaigning Too Early," *San Antonio Express-News*, Jan. 3, 1988.
10. Ron Calhoun, "Edwards Plans to Challenge Bullock—Intimidation or Not," *Dallas Times Herald*, June 13, 1988.
11. Ibid.
12. Dave McNeely, "Edwards Says He's Eager to Take on Bullock in Statewide Race," *Austin American-Statesman*, June 26, 1988.
13. Anne Marie Kilday, "Campaign Turns Testy; Edwards, Bullock Trade Barbs," *Dallas Morning News*, Nov. 17, 1989.
14. Anne Marie Kilday, "A Raucous Race; Lieutenant Governor Contest Matches Veteran Bullock, Underdog Edwards," *Dallas Morning News*, Nov. 29, 1989.
15. Mark McKinnon, interview by Dave McNeely, Mar. 1, 2005.
16. Sam Attlesey, "Bullock Well-liked by Voters, Poll Says; Advantage for Hobby's Job 'Enormous,'" *Dallas Morning News*, Aug. 22, 1989.
17. Dave McNeely, "From Day 1, Democrats Knew Campaign Would Be Negative," *Austin American-Statesman*, Apr. 10, 1990.
18. George Christian, interview by Dave McNeely, Jan. 11, 2002.
19. Greg Hartman, interview by Dave McNeely, July 12, 2006.
20. Anne Marie Kilday, "Bullock, Mosbacher Ads Analyzed," *Dallas Morning News*, Oct. 25, 1990.
21. Associated Press, "Senators Threaten Power Play; Mosbacher Win Might Spark Effort to Cut His Authority," *Dallas Morning News*, Oct. 12, 1990.
22. Cindy Rugeley, "Mosbacher Assails Bullock on State Income Tax Stance," *Houston Chronicle*, Oct. 9, 1990.
23. Anne Marie Kilday, "Bullock TV Ads Link Mosbacher to Spills in Gulf, Red Ink at State Welfare Agency," *Dallas Morning News*, Oct. 16, 1990.
24. Dave McNeely, "Richards Gets the Upper Hand in Handshake Skirmish," *Austin American-Statesman*, Oct. 16, 1990.
25. Lieutenant Governor-Elect Bob Bullock, news release, Dec. 17, 1990.

CHAPTER 22
1. Paul Hobby, interview by Dave McNeely, Aug. 19, 2005.
2. Patricia Kilday Hart, *Texas Monthly*, collection of Bullock stories from individuals, July 2003, p. 144.
3. Bob Bullock, inaugural address, Jan. 15, 1991.
4. Jane Ely, "Watching for a Bullock Blowup," *Houston Chronicle*, Jan. 27, 1991.
5. Kim Ross, interview by Dave McNeely and Jim Henderson, Feb. 2, 2005.
6. Bob Bullock, Jackson Day speech to Dallas County Democrats, Dallas, Feb. 29, 1992.
7. Bill Ratliff, interview by Dave McNeely and Jim Henderson, Feb. 3, 2005.
8. Bill Haley, interview by Dave McNeely, May 10, 2006.

9. Dave McNeely, "Heavy-handed Tactics May Diminish Bullock's Success," *Austin American-Statesman*, Apr. 23, 1991.

10. Paul Hobby, oral history, Sept. 2, 2004, p. 16.

11. Andy Sansom, interview by Dave McNeely, Dec. 17, 2005.

12. Patricia Kilday Hart, *Texas Monthly*, collection of Bullock stories from individuals, July 2003, p. 122.

13. Paul Hobby, interview by Dave McNeely, Aug. 19, 2005.

CHAPTER 23

1. Gib Lewis, interview by Dave McNeely and Jim Henderson, Mar. 21, 2005.

2. Mary Beth Rogers, interview by Dave McNeely and Jim Henderson, Apr. 14, 2005.

3. Paul Hobby, oral history, p. 11.

4. Ibid., pp. 11–12.

5. Bob Bullock, "State Income Tax Could Help Ease Budget Crisis," *Amarillo Daily News*, Mar. 21, 1991.

6. Ibid.

7. Kaye Northcott, "Bullock's Forceful Style Shows in Tax Proposal; Some Say the New Lieutenant Governor's Stance on a State Income Tax Is a Political Gamble. But He's Convinced of the Need and Confident About His Future," *Fort Worth Star-Telegram*, Mar. 10, 1991.

8. Wayne Slater and Anne Marie Kilday, "Bullock to Push for State Income Tax; Richards, Lewis See Little Support for Idea," *Dallas Morning News*, Mar. 7, 1991.

9. Paul Hobby, oral history, p. 7.

10. Herbert A. Sample, "Senators Reluctantly OK Bill; Critics Pin Hopes on Follow-up Measure," *Dallas Times Herald*, July 31, 1991.

11. Bruce Gibson, interview by Dave McNeely, Mar. 11, 2005.

12. Terrence Stutz, "State Environment Superagency OK'd; But Senators Lament Bill's Flaws," *Dallas Morning News*, July 31, 1991.

13. Ken Armbrister, interview by Dave McNeely, May 9, 2006.

14. *Texas Monthly*, Oct. 1991, p. 147.

15. Paul Burka, Patricia Kilday Hart, and Ellen Williams, "Ten Best, Ten Worst," *Texas Monthly*, Oct. 1991, p. 146.

16. Paul Hobby, oral history, p. 13.

17. Ibid., p. 15.

18. Bruce Gibson, interview by Dave McNeely, Mar. 8, 2006.

CHAPTER 24

1. *Texas Monthly*, July 1993, p. 103.

2. Gary Scharrer, "Bullock Tells Senator That Short Skirts Will Help Her Work," *El Paso Times*, Jan. 22, 1993.

3. Stefanie Scott, "Richards Stands by Bullock After He Makes 'Sexist' Joke," *San Antonio Express-News*, Jan. 23, 1993.

4. David Elliott, "Bullock Draws Fire for Making 'Skirt' Joke," *Austin American-Statesman*, Jan. 22, 1993.

5. Stefanie Scott, "'Sexist' Joke Has Bullock in Hot Water; Zaffirini Says Remark Did Not Trouble Her," *San Antonio Express-News*, Jan. 22, 1993.

6. Andy Sansom, interview by Dave McNeely, Dec. 17, 2005.

7. Gov. Ann Richards, Lt. Gov. Bullock, and House Speaker Gib Lewis, joint statement just before a special session convened on Nov. 10, 1992.

8. Bill Ratliff, interview by Dave McNeely and Jim Henderson, Feb. 3, 2005.

9. Buck Wood, oral history, pp. 118–120.

10. Andy Sansom, interview by Dave McNeely, Dec. 17, 2005.

11. John Montford, interview by Dave McNeely, June 7, 2006.

CHAPTER 25

1. W. Gardner Selby, "Bullock's Obsession Pushed Museum," *San Antonio Express-News*, Apr. 21, 2001.

2. Buck Wood, oral history, p. 117.

3. Christy Hoppe, "Plotting a Return: Bullock Leads Drive to Restore Texas Notables' Last Resting Place," *Dallas Morning News*, June 19, 1994.

4. Andy Sansom, interview by Dave McNeely, Dec. 17, 2005.

5. Harry Bradley, interview by Dave McNeely, Mar. 8, 2006.

6. Paul Hobby, interview by Dave McNeely, Aug. 19, 2005.

7. Andy Sansom, interview by Dave McNeely, Dec. 17, 2005.

8. Harry Bradley, interview by Dave McNeely, Mar. 8, 2006.

9. Paul Hobby, oral history, Dec. 17, 2004, p. 26.

10. Dan Van Cleve, interview by Dave McNeely, Dec. 9, 2003.

11. Mary Lenz, "Only Question About Bullock Is His Health," *Houston Post*, Sept. 19, 1994.

12. Dave McNeely, "No Ill Will to Bullock, But What If He Dies?," *Austin American-Statesman*, Sept. 18, 1994.

13. Bob Bullock, interview by Dave McNeely, Sept. 6, 1995.

CHAPTER 26

1. Mark McKinnon, interview by Dave McNeely, Mar. 1, 2005.

2. *Texas Monthly*, collection of Bullock stories from individuals, July 2003.

3. Terrence Stutz, "Lezar Targets Clinton in Race Against Bullock," *Dallas Morning News*, Mar. 30, 1994.

4. Carolyn Barta, "What's in a Name? Ask Tex," *Dallas Morning News*, May 23, 1994.

5. Dave McNeely, "FCC Backs Lezar's Right to Run Anti-Clinton Ads," *Austin American-Statesman*, Aug. 9, 1994.

6. Max Sherman, interview by Dave McNeely, May 11, 2006.

7. Dave McNeely, "Bullock U: Lieutenant Governor's Influence Extends Through Legions of Ex-employees Toughened Under His Tenure," *Austin American-Statesman*, Sept. 17, 1995.

8. Andy Sansom, interview by Dave McNeely, Dec. 17, 2005.

9. Ronnie Earle, interview by Dave McNeely, Sept. 4, 2004.

10. R. G. Ratcliffe, "GOP Senators Opt to Attend Bullock Bash," *Houston Chronicle*, Sept. 13, 1994.

11. Terrence Stutz, "GOP Senators Told to Skip Bullock Event; But Some Call Democrat's Fete Good for Relations," *Dallas Morning News*, Sept. 12, 1994.

12. R. G. Ratcliffe, "GOP Senators Opt to Attend Bullock Bash," *Houston Chronicle*, Sept. 13, 1994.

13. Terrence Stutz, "GOP Senators Told to Skip Bullock Event; But Some Call Democrat's Fete Good for Relations," *Dallas Morning News*, Sept. 12, 1994.

14. Mary Alice Robbins, "Lezar Requests Leniency for Bullock Fraternizers," *Amarillo Daily News*, Sept. 23, 1994.

15. Mary Alice Robbins, "GOP Leaders Stop Short of Censure," *Amarillo Daily News*, Sept. 25, 1994.

16. Mary Lenz, "Enraged Bullock Vows to Ignore Foe for Making Health an Issue," *Houston Post*, Oct. 7, 1994.

17. Scripps Howard and the Office of Survey Research at the University of Texas. Conducted annually since 1994 for Harte-Hanks Communications.

18. George W. Bush and Karen Hughes, *A Charge to Keep* (New York: William Morrow & Co., 1999), p. 112.

19. Chuck Bailey, interview by Dave McNeely, July 26, 2005.

20. Cliff Johnson, interview by Dave McNeely, Nov. 11, 2003.

21. Paul Hobby, interview by Dave McNeely, Aug. 19, 2005.

CHAPTER 27

1. George W. Bush and Karen Hughes, *A Charge to Keep* (New York: William Morrow & Co., 1999), p. 112.

2. Dave McNeely, "A Bond 'True and Deep,'" *Austin American-Statesman*, Apr. 27, 2001.

3. Bush and Hughes, *A Charge to Keep*, p. 113.

4. Rodney Ellis, interview by Jim Henderson, Feb. 3, 2006.

5. Paul Hobby, interview by Dave McNeely, Aug. 19, 2005.

6. Ken Armbrister, interview by Dave McNeely, May 9, 2006.

7. Pete Laney, interview by Dave McNeely, May 9, 2006.

8. Dave McNeely, "Bush's Personal Approach Scores Political Points," *Austin American-Statesman*, Apr. 4, 1995.

9. Bush and Hughes, *A Charge to Keep*, p. 113.

10. Carlton Carl, interview by Dave McNeely, Nov. 1, 2005.

11. Dave McNeely, "A Bond 'True and Deep,'" *Austin American-Statesman*, Apr. 27, 2001.

12. Dave McNeely, "Missing Bullock's Unvarnished Advice," *Austin American-Statesman*, Sept. 9, 1999. Another, more G-rated version of the story, after Bush became president, was that Bullock had said, "The honeymoon's

over." After kissing Bullock, Bush then said, "If the honeymoon's over, I want to get the last kiss."

13. Jack Loftis, oral history, pp. 7–8.
14. Terrence Stutz and George Kuempel, "Bullock Criticizes Way Casino Bill Managed," *Dallas Morning News*, Mar. 23, 1995.
15. Stuart Eskenazi, "Casino Lobbyist Stands by Criticism of Bullock," *Austin American-Statesman*, Mar. 23, 1995.
16. Rob Johnson, interview by Dave McNeely, July 12, 2005.
17. Gordon Johnson, interview by Dave McNeely, Feb. 6, 2006.
18. Kent Caperton, interview by Dave McNeely, May 2, 2006.
19. Gordon Johnson, interview by Dave McNeely, Feb. 6, 2006.
20. Dave McNeely, "Senate's 'Big Daddy' Leaves Void Hard to Fill," *Austin American-Statesman*, Mar. 28, 1995.
21. Paul Burka and Patricia Kilday Hart, "Ten Best and Ten Worst," *Texas Monthly*, July 1995, pp. 102–115.

CHAPTER 28

1. Mike Ward, "Bullock vs. the Boar: No Clear Winner," *Austin American-Statesman*, Jan. 19, 1996.
2. Paul Hobby, oral history, Dec. 17, 2004, p. 32.
3. W. Gardner Selby, "Bullock's Obsession Pushed Museum," *San Antonio Express-News*, Apr. 29, 2001.
4. John Montford, interview by Dave McNeely, June 7, 2006, San Antonio.
5. Kent Caperton, interview by Dave McNeely, May 2, 2006.
6. Bruce Gibson, interview by Dave McNeely, Mar. 8, 2006.
7. Cliff Johnson, interview by Dave McNeely, Nov. 11, 2003.
8. Bill Ratliff, interview with Dave McNeely via e-mail, June 26, 2006.
9. *Texas Monthly*, July 1997, p. 90.
10. Ibid., p. 93.
11. Paul Hobby, oral history, Dec. 17, 2004, pp. 29–30.
12. Terrence Stutz and George Kuempel, "Bullock Says He Won't Seek Re-election," *Dallas Morning News*, June 6, 1997.
13. John Moritz, "Bullock Says This Will Be His Last Term," *Fort Worth Star-Telegram*, June 6, 1997.
14. Patrick Beach, "The King of Texas; As Lieutenant Governor Passes Gavel, An Era Ends," *Austin American-Statesman*, Dec. 6, 1998.
15. George Kuempel, interview by Dave McNeely, June 20, 2006.
16. Ben Barnes, interview by Dave McNeely and Jim Henderson, Feb. 4, 2005.
17. W. Gardner Selby, "Bullock's Obsession Pushed Museum," *San Antonio Express-News*, Apr. 29, 2001.
18. Paul Hobby, oral history, p. 32.
19. Harry Bradley, interview by Dave McNeely, Mar. 8, 2006.

EPILOGUE

1. Jan Bullock, speech to 2000 Republican National Convention, Philadelphia, Aug. 3, 2000.

2. Peggy Fikac and Timothy Inklebarger, "President Lauds Civility at New Bullock Museum; But a Civil Tone Is Sometimes Lacking as Protesters Boo Bush," *San Antonio Express-News*, Apr. 28, 2001.

3. Clay Robison, "Bullock-like Leadership Needed to Get Tax Reform Done; Clay Robison Observes That Bob Bullock's Iron Fist May Be Missing but His Influence Still Lingers over Texas Tax Policy," *Houston Chronicle*, Apr. 2, 2006.

4. Mike Leggett, "When Contemplating Government Trouble, Bullock's Smarts Ring True," *Austin American-Statesman*, Feb. 12, 2006.

INDEX